Also by Chris Patten

East and West

COUSINS AND STRANGERS

COUSINS

AND

STRANGERS

AMERICA, BRITAIN, AND EUROPE
IN A NEW CENTURY

CHRIS PATTEN

TIMES BOOKS

HENRY HOLT AND COMPANY | NEW YORK

Times Books
Henry Holt and Company, LLC
Publishers since 1866
175 Fifth Avenue
New York, New York 10010
www.henryholt.com

Henry Holt® is a registered trademark
of Henry Holt and Company, LLC.
Copyright © 2006 by Christopher Patten
All rights reserved.
Distributed in Canada by H. B. Fenn and Company Ltd.
Originally published in the United Kingdom in 2005 under
the title *Not Quite the Diplomat* by Penguin, London.

Library of Congress Cataloging-in-Publication Data
Patten, Chris, date.
    Cousins and strangers : America, Britain, and Europe in a new century /
Chris Patten.—1st American ed.
        p. cm.
    Rev. ed. of : Not quite the diplomat. 2005.
    Includes index.
    ISBN-13: 978-0-8050-7788-9
    ISBN-10: 0-8050-7788-X
    1. World politics—21st century. 2. International relations—History—21st century.
3. Europe—Foreign relations—United States. 4. United States—Foreign relations—
Europe. 5. Great Britain—Foreign relations—United States. 6. United States—Foreign
relations—Great Britain.   I. Patten, Chris, date. Not quite the diplomat.   II. Title.
D863.3.P37 2006   2005053825
327.1'7'09182109051—dc22

Henry Holt books are available for special promotions
and premiums. For details contact: Director, Special Markets.

First American Edition 2006
Designed by Victoria Hartman
Printed in the United States of America
1   3   5   7   9   10   8   6   4   2

For my growing family

CONTENTS

1

HAPPY FAMILIES

Forget Europe wholly, your veins throb with blood.
To which the dull current in hers is but mud . . .
O my friends, thank your God, if you have one, that he
Twixt the old world and you set the gulf of a sea.

—James Russell Lowell

It is, I suppose, what Donald Rumsfeld might call a known known: even while we are pelting one another with genetically modified tomatoes, we know really that there is more that unites North America and Europe than divides us. The speech that asserts this proposition, so regularly delivered and sometimes even heeded, comes easily: the young American Republic formed from the human, cultural, and political stock of old Europe; the shared transatlantic attachment to enlightenment values; the embrace of participative democratic government under the rule of law; the common sacrifices in war; the joint postwar commitment to new global forms of economic and political governance; the struggle to repel Communism's advance; the vision of a world, prosperous, democratic, and free; hands stretched across the ocean to bind a "special relationship"; "Westward, look, the land is bright"; to "the indispensable nation" add "the indispensable partnership." And so on. Both sides of the ocean can do this stuff in their sleep.

Like many known knowns, it is broadly true, but it is not of course the whole story. Moreover a known *un*known is that we cannot be entirely sure what is going to happen to this notionally indispensable partnership in the coming years. Old clichés of international governance and alliance—the Atlantic partnership, European integration, shared Western values—have given way in the blink of an eye to another set of clichés—shifting tectonic plates, the new continental union that hit the buffers, the republic that became an empire. To raise this question, to suggest that change may be in the air, to strip away some of the myths that obfuscate the story of the alliance—both those that assert that it has always been plain sailing and those that suggest that it has only been in recent times, since the arrival on the scene of George W. Bush, that it has hit rough-ish water—is to court disapproval. For as Shakespeare noted in *Henry IV, Part 2*:

> Yet the first bringer of unwelcome news
> Hath but a losing office.

It is time we faced unwelcome news. Unless America, Britain, and Europe discuss these issues free of cloying cliché and political prejudice, we will find it tough to manage the changing nature of the transatlantic relationship to our mutual benefit and to that of the rest of the world. We will also set back the prospect of having the values that we in America and Europe publicly esteem, and sometimes uphold, gaining sway in other continents as the century advances.

At the beginning of the 1890s, America might have been described as a free rider in a world made pretty safe by Britain's imperial reach and naval might. The British navy had eleven bases and thirty-three coaling stations in the seas around America, which—while claiming by then the status of the world's greatest industrial power—possessed no battleship and had only 25,000 men under arms. America had successfully pursued for years its revolutionary foreign policy, offering friendship to all but concluding alliances with none. In a world of empires, America the Republic had chosen another path. That all changed with the Spanish-American War of 1898. America annexed Hawaii, Guam, Wake Island, and the Philippines; in the Philippines alone 200,000 civilians died between 1898 and 1902. The Republic's innocence was lost, but not its aspiration to avoid foreign entanglements, wherever possible. Though persuaded reluctantly to come to the aid of Britain and France late in the First World War, America was not keen to be enmeshed in the problems of war, peace, and economic depression with which others wrestled unsuccessfully in the 1920s and 1930s. Neville Chamberlain, Britain's prewar prime minister, was not alone in thinking that "it is always best and safest to count on nothing from the Americans but words."

That could not have been said after the Second World War and its aftermath. Now America, the planet's mightiest military and economic power, faced a world in which the oldest empires were disintegrating; only the new Soviet empire in Europe remained, threatening the rest of the continent with subjugation to tyranny. America embraced, with becoming reluctance, the new role of global leader, in command of a virtual empire of commercial and cultural predominance and of more or less willing dependent feudatories. "We have got to understand," said Dean Acheson, "that all our lives the danger, the uncertainty, the need for alertness, for effort, for discipline, will be upon us. This is new to us. It will be hard for us." And so it was, though the task was handled with extraordinary dexterity and commendable commitment.

Even for a great power, diplomacy is not easy, and America has had to cope regularly with the assumption that it is throwing its weight around, even when it has been doing no such thing. It also has had to deal with three other problems. First, there was the resentment of those who had been saved, militarily and economically. In the *Analects*, Confucius noted the colleague who was cross with him, even though, as Confucius pointed out, he had done him no favors. Second, there was condescension masquerading as sophistication. Third, there was resistance to what was seen as the Americanization of indigenous cultures and ways of life: we dressed like Americans, listened to their music, watched their films, and drank their carbonated drinks, even while we rejected some of what they seemed to stand for, particularly in the miserable years of the McCarthyite inquisition and during the failed efforts to bring what Senator J. William Fulbright called "little pissant" Vietnam to heel.

It is plain wrong to see anti-Americanism as a phenomenon of recent years, the reaction to an assertive, nationalist president, whom we in Europe do not understand and with whom we assuredly fail to empathize. In the most creative, generous-spirited, and comradely years of American leadership there were still those in Europe who carped and bitched. Sometimes there was at least a shred of justification for the resentment— at America entering World War II so late, and at the ill-disguised relish with which Americans read the last rites over the British empire. But more frequently the European antagonism was reprehensible. Unsure whether it should take greater exception to the help it was offered, or to the prospect that it might not receive all the assistance it wanted, France took the lead, displaying what the historian Robert Gildea describes as "a kind of petulant ingratitude." *Le Monde*, founded in 1944 after the liberation, supported an armed and neutral Europe standing between the United States and the Soviet Union. The arrival of the new NATO commander in Europe in 1952 was greeted by French riots. Those political fatheads, Simone de Beauvoir and Jean-Paul Sartre, were in the thick of the troublemaking. As early as 1946, de Beauvoir was complaining that America's attitude to Europe and France was one of "arrogant condescension." The American soldiers who had once been "our liberty" were now "our dependence and a mortal threat." Later she was to opine that "*our* victory had been stolen from us," though her use of the first-person plural possessive in this sentence begged a few questions. But as the early victories in the battle to keep Coca-Cola out of France were reversed by the French courts, it became clear that no corner of France was safe from the incoming American tide.

The British had their own special brand of patronizing contempt, which was not anti-American, old boy. It is just that Europeans, said Harold Nicolson to an American acquaintance, were "frightened that the destinies of the world should be in the hands of a giant with the limbs of an undergraduate, the emotions of a spinster, and the brain of a peahen." You find the finest literary flowering of these sentiments in the novels of Graham Greene, particularly *The Quiet American.* Greene was prescient about what was to become the bloody quagmire of Vietnam, but even so the depths of his hostility to America are pretty shocking. Again and again, he puts the boot in. The young American idealist Alden Pyle "was determined to do good, not to any individual person but to a country, a continent, a world. . . . He was in his element now with the whole universe to improve." Most famously Greene notes, and he is clearly talking about all Americans, not just Pyle, "I never knew a man

seen used in the last war. Fortunately, President Eisenhower pulled the plug on this crazy Middle Eastern adventure before it went too far, partly because of his proper concern about its impact on opinion in the Arab world. Prime Minister Anthony Eden retired to the Caribbean, and then a manor house in Wiltshire; Foreign Secretary Harold Macmillan ("first in, first out") succeeded him at Downing Street; I went back to cricket and Conan Doyle.

Our house was not very bookish. There were book club editions of Nevil Shute and L. P. Hartley, Thor Heyerdahl's *Kon-Tiki* adventures, books on the heroes and heroics of the Second World War—escapes, dam-busting, navigating cruel seas. Above all there was Damon Runyon and S. J. Perelman, a mark I think of how comfortably and naturally we accommodated ourselves to America's cultural *imperium*. My father's job probably made this inevitable. Before skiffle and the Mersey sound, most of the popular music he published was from the other side of the Atlantic—the hit tunes of Johnny Ray, Frankie Lane, Guy Mitchell. One of his first big successes was the latter's "She Wears Red Feathers (And a Hula-Hula Skirt)." My parents' taste was rather better than this. Our 78s featured Frank Sinatra, Ella Fitzgerald, big band jazz—the music of a country that we instinctively admired and respected, glamorous, generous, gee-whiz. We were Americaphiles. How could we be anything else? All that seemed savviest and sassiest, wittiest and wisest, came from across the Atlantic. Weekly cinema visits confirmed our instincts. From one suburban film palace to another—"Don't be disappointed if we can't get in," my father would say on each of our weekly visits—we followed the cultural trail blazed by Hollywood. (It was a nice surprise to discover when I went to Oxford that other countries had been making films, too.) I was an unabashed recipient of what is charmingly called America's soft power.

Yet today, European assumptions that America is much like us, only bigger, faster, and richer, are constantly upended. For Britons, who share their native tongue with most Americans, this is a pretty regular experience. Shared language creates a presumption of similarity. I remember the shock on my first visit to America when I realized that I felt more at home in Athens, Greece, with just a few English speakers, than I did in Athens, Ohio. This sense of cultural alienation varies from one part of

who had better motives for all the trouble he caused," and in the frontispiece to the novel (published in 1955) he quotes Byron:

> This is the patentage of new inventions
> For killing bodies, and for saving souls
> All propagated with the best intentions.

So it was not only the boulevard Bolsheviks, the frequently traduced French intellectuals, who seethed and scorned. Within a few years of American-led military victory, the foundation of the United Nations and the launch of Marshall aid, here was old Europe showing its appreciation. As Randy Newman once sang:

> We give them money—but are they grateful?
> No, they're spiteful and they're hateful. . . .

There was never a golden age in transatlantic relations, when all Europeans doffed their hats to the superpower that defended our freedom. We Europeans were always a bit tiresome, and sometimes—as I have said—there was a good reason for it.

For all the talk about family, we are at once cousins and strangers. We are more different than we like to admit, and are surprisingly ignorant about one another. Europeans note with surprise how many Americans have never traveled outside their own country and how some politicians even make a virtue out of not possessing a passport. Even more tellingly, Studs Terkel notes how in his home city of Chicago the taxi drivers, who come from every part of the world, regularly express to him their astonishment at how little their American passengers know about their countries of origin. Casual disregard of the world outside has much to do with being a superpower. Some days you can scour in vain to find a story about Europe in even quality American newspapers. But this reflects, in part, where most of the significant political action is. In any newspaper in any other part of the world, there is page after page of news about America—its politics, its business, its popular culture. The rest of us are hungry consumers.

I have lived my life as a pretty enthusiastic citizen of America's undeclared empire, which chose deliberately not to impose an emperor on its denizens: a touch, that, of political genius. I was born the month before the D-Day landings brought American boots and blood to French soil for the second time in less than thirty years. My father was not one of that military host. He was serving in Palestine with the Royal Air Force, leaving behind his pregnant wife and my older sister. My mother had made her wartime home in her parents' cathedral city, Exeter, until much of it was flattened in an air raid.

My wife's father was less lucky than mine. A Cambridge athlete from the generation after the young men remembered in *Chariots of Fire*, he hurdled in the 1936 Berlin Olympics, briefly made a career with Britain's biggest chemical company and then joined the Seaforth Highlanders at the outbreak of war. He fought through North Africa and Sicily, went to Normandy in time for the fight across the *bocage* and was killed just after the Allied breakout at Falaise, shortly before my wife's birth. The list of the war dead at his university college—as at many other Oxford and Cambridge colleges—contains German names as well as British, Dominion, and American. We brought young men together at our eminent universities to learn about the values of Western civilization, and then they returned to their homes and were required in due course to kill one another—from Newman's "umbrageous groves" to trenches and tanks and the war graves of Europe, like the one near Caen where Major John Thornton, the Seaforth Highlander, lies.

The American boys who came from high corn and bluegrass, from tenement block and front porch, to help save Europe once again from the bloody results of rampant nationalism were led by men who believed that the young of their nation should not be required a third time to cross the Atlantic to rescue the Old World. Europe's cemeteries contained too many of their own young heroes already. So it was scarcely surprising that American leaders, policymakers, and diplomats were such eager supporters of the efforts to prevent another European civil war through a unique pooling of sovereignty between France, Germany, and four other countries, initially achieved by bringing together the industries that fed modern conflict, coal and steel. European integration was an American geostrategic objective from the very start, and for Washington it was desirable that Britain should be part of the enterprise. Our

American friends did not share our own opinion that Britain c[ould] benignly, patronizingly, apart from the construction of a new Eu[rope] the cherished friend and valued partner of the superpower, the le[ader of] its own worldwide empire turned commonwealth, the sagaciou[s] wisher to our continental neighbors in their quaint endeavors. W[ith] the gallantry of our recent history, whatever the majesty of Chu[rchill's] prose, Britain was no longer a top dog, even though we could [still] claim to invitations to the top table.

I grew up during the years when Churchill still growled abo[ut past] glories, but then his wartime lieutenants, Anthony Eden and [Harold] Macmillan, were confronted in their different ways with the re[ality of] Britain's decline. Discharged from the Royal Air Force, my fath[er had] gone to London, building on the prewar contacts he had made a[s a pro]fessional musician to become a popular music publisher, working i[n "Tin] Pan Alley." We lived in semidetached suburban West Lond[on, an] environment about which I have a passingly Proustian sensitivi[ty. The] suburban front-garden smell, to which Michael Frayn alludes [at the] beginning of his novel *Spies*, I was able to identify immediately—[for] I spring from that world of privet hedges, mock Tudor, cherry bl[ossom] and well-polished family cars embalmed between London's arteria[l roads] and its Underground lines. My parents were not very political; in[deed I] suspect that my mother would have thought it vaguely indece[nt—and] certainly uncomfortable to get involved in a deep—let alone ro[wdy—] discussion of either politics or their Catholic religion.

The first international event I recall, courtesy of the *Daily E[xpress,]* was the gallantry of the "Glorious Gloucesters" in the Korean W[ar. Of] much greater consequence was the Suez debacle in 1956. My fath[er had] only recently taken me aside, with much embarrassment all arou[nd, to] give me a little booklet explaining, improbably, how I might in the [future] play my part in reproducing the species. He told me for a secon[d time] that he wanted to say a word to me privately. I was not to tell my m[other] or sister; what he had to say would only worry them. Events i[n the] Middle East looked very dangerous. The British and French invas[ion of] Egypt, to stop President Nasser from nationalizing the canal [owned by] private European hands, could trigger another, much larger war[. The] weapons now available in the world were more terrible than any h[umanity]

the country to another. I recall a long visit of speaking engagements on the West Coast in the mid-1990s, when I was still governor of Hong Kong, that began in Orange County, California. It might as well have been the moon. I dined off that legendary rubber chicken, with a limp salad, iced water, and weak coffee and then tried to answer questions from an audience that clearly regarded me as a quaint, even exotic, creature with curious views well off any recognizable political map. I moved north to Los Angeles and then on to San Francisco and Seattle (one of my favorite cities anywhere in the world). As I struck north, I felt increasingly comfortable, though San Francisco is sometimes politically a little piquant even for my own tastes. But Seattle felt like home, a lovely city whose inhabitants, I suspect, fib about the climate in order to keep outsiders away.

The surprising realization that you are very foreign in many parts of the United States comes hand in hand with the shock of discovering how difficult it is to generalize about the country as a whole. That, in a way, is what makes me question the endlessly parroted observation that we are all, Europeans and Americans, much the same, and share basically the same values. Which Americans are we talking about? Do we mean those who are more obese than any people I have seen anywhere in the world, or those who live a life governed by ascetic fitness regimes with carefully controlled diets of vitamin supplements and steamed broccoli? Do we compare ourselves to evangelical Christians, who wait expectantly for Armageddon and a rather dramatic end to the Middle East peace process, or to those whose religion is an intolerant gospel of political correctness that puts many of the values of the Age of Enlightenment to the sword, seeking, for example, to hound from office the president of one of the world's greatest universities for speculating aloud about the sources of gender differences? Do we identify with those who profess the infallibility of rugged, individual capitalism, scattering its riches widely to the benefit of all, or those who appear to stack the cards in favor of those who have plenty and who ignore those who have little or nothing? Which America shares European values?

Insofar as these things bother George W. Bush (after all, he was elected for a second term, and without the judicial intervention of the Supreme Court), the president's problem with much European opinion is that he stands at the heart of several of these puzzling questions about how much we Europeans really *do* have in common with our American partners. The European identity itself is admittedly complex. What does an Andalusian peasant have in common with a Swedish lumberjack, a Catholic priest in Trieste with a Lutheran pastor in Tallinn? There are certainly differences in Europe. But taking the issues of religion, patriotism, political conservatism, and inequality, Europeans are clearly more like one another than they are like Americans—a lot more, and all these issues have become increasingly important to the way America is seen and behaves around the world.

Alexis de Tocqueville wrote, "People always bear some mark of their origin." We should not therefore be too surprised that America today asserts its religiosity with such selective and self-centered force. The Puritan founding father John Winthrop argued that the early colonists were creating "a City upon a Hill, the eyes of all people are upon us." The colonists were doing the Almighty's work. "Thus stands the case between God and us," said Winthrop, for "we are entered into Covenants with Him for this work." From the very beginning, then, Americans saw themselves in Herman Melville's words as "the peculiar, chosen people— the Israel of our time, we bear the mark of the Liberties of the world. . . . God has given to us, for a future inheritance, the broad domain of the political pagans, that shall yet come and lie down under the shade of our ark, without bloody hands being lifted. God has predestinated, mankind expects, great things from our race, and great things we feel in our souls." Some of those who lay down "under the shade of our ark" needed some persuasion. True, America is predominantly the home of old Europeans who fled west to escape political persecution or economic hardship, or who simply emigrated out of the hope of a better life. Most of them found one, not least the relations of my Irish forebears—nine out of my stepfather's ten western Ireland uncles emigrated to North America—who followed the "tenement trail" from slums to suburbs. But there were others who had the choice made for them—the native Americans (W. H. Auden's "cudgeled people") and the African victims of the slave trade.

The concept of "a chosen people" can be attractive when its leaders summon their fellow citizens to a generous and wholehearted commit-

who had better motives for all the trouble he caused," and in the frontispiece to the novel (published in 1955) he quotes Byron:

This is the patentage of new inventions
For killing bodies, and for saving souls
All propagated with the best intentions.

So it was not only the boulevard Bolsheviks, the frequently traduced French intellectuals, who seethed and scorned. Within a few years of American-led military victory, the foundation of the United Nations and the launch of Marshall aid, here was old Europe showing its appreciation. As Randy Newman once sang:

We give them money—but are they grateful?
No, they're spiteful and they're hateful. . . .

There was never a golden age in transatlantic relations, when all Europeans doffed their hats to the superpower that defended our freedom. We Europeans were always a bit tiresome, and sometimes—as I have said—there was a good reason for it.

For all the talk about family, we are at once cousins and strangers. We are more different than we like to admit, and are surprisingly ignorant about one another. Europeans note with surprise how many Americans have never traveled outside their own country and how some politicians even make a virtue out of not possessing a passport. Even more tellingly, Studs Terkel notes how in his home city of Chicago the taxi drivers, who come from every part of the world, regularly express to him their astonishment at how little their American passengers know about their countries of origin. Casual disregard of the world outside has much to do with being a superpower. Some days you can scour in vain to find a story about Europe in even quality American newspapers. But this reflects, in part, where most of the significant political action is. In any newspaper in any other part of the world, there is page after page of news about America—its politics, its business, its popular culture. The rest of us are hungry consumers.

I have lived my life as a pretty enthusiastic citizen of America's undeclared empire, which chose deliberately not to impose an emperor on its denizens: a touch, that, of political genius. I was born the month before the D-Day landings brought American boots and blood to French soil for the second time in less than thirty years. My father was not one of that military host. He was serving in Palestine with the Royal Air Force, leaving behind his pregnant wife and my older sister. My mother had made her wartime home in her parents' cathedral city, Exeter, until much of it was flattened in an air raid.

My wife's father was less lucky than mine. A Cambridge athlete from the generation after the young men remembered in *Chariots of Fire*, he hurdled in the 1936 Berlin Olympics, briefly made a career with Britain's biggest chemical company and then joined the Seaforth Highlanders at the outbreak of war. He fought through North Africa and Sicily, went to Normandy in time for the fight across the *bocage* and was killed just after the Allied breakout at Falaise, shortly before my wife's birth. The list of the war dead at his university college—as at many other Oxford and Cambridge colleges—contains German names as well as British, Dominion, and American. We brought young men together at our eminent universities to learn about the values of Western civilization, and then they returned to their homes and were required in due course to kill one another—from Newman's "umbrageous groves" to trenches and tanks and the war graves of Europe, like the one near Caen where Major John Thornton, the Seaforth Highlander, lies.

The American boys who came from high corn and bluegrass, from tenement block and front porch, to help save Europe once again from the bloody results of rampant nationalism were led by men who believed that the young of their nation should not be required a third time to cross the Atlantic to rescue the Old World. Europe's cemeteries contained too many of their own young heroes already. So it was scarcely surprising that American leaders, policymakers, and diplomats were such eager supporters of the efforts to prevent another European civil war through a unique pooling of sovereignty between France, Germany, and four other countries, initially achieved by bringing together the industries that fed modern conflict, coal and steel. European integration was an American geostrategic objective from the very start, and for Washington it was desirable that Britain should be part of the enterprise. Our

American friends did not share our own opinion that Britain could sit benignly, patronizingly, apart from the construction of a new Europe—the cherished friend and valued partner of the superpower, the leader of its own worldwide empire turned commonwealth, the sagacious well-wisher to our continental neighbors in their quaint endeavors. Whatever the gallantry of our recent history, whatever the majesty of Churchill's prose, Britain was no longer a top dog, even though we could still lay claim to invitations to the top table.

I grew up during the years when Churchill still growled about past glories, but then his wartime lieutenants, Anthony Eden and Harold Macmillan, were confronted in their different ways with the reality of Britain's decline. Discharged from the Royal Air Force, my father had gone to London, building on the prewar contacts he had made as a professional musician to become a popular music publisher, working in "Tin Pan Alley." We lived in semidetached suburban West London, an environment about which I have a passingly Proustian sensitivity. The suburban front-garden smell, to which Michael Frayn alludes at the beginning of his novel *Spies*, I was able to identify immediately—privet! I spring from that world of privet hedges, mock Tudor, cherry blossom, and well-polished family cars embalmed between London's arterial roads and its Underground lines. My parents were not very political; indeed, I suspect that my mother would have thought it vaguely indecent and certainly uncomfortable to get involved in a deep—let alone rowdy—discussion of either politics or their Catholic religion.

The first international event I recall, courtesy of the *Daily Express*, was the gallantry of the "Glorious Gloucesters" in the Korean War; of much greater consequence was the Suez debacle in 1956. My father had only recently taken me aside, with much embarrassment all around, to give me a little booklet explaining, improbably, how I might in the future play my part in reproducing the species. He told me for a second time that he wanted to say a word to me privately. I was not to tell my mother or sister; what he had to say would only worry them. Events in the Middle East looked very dangerous. The British and French invasion of Egypt, to stop President Nasser from nationalizing the canal out of private European hands, could trigger another, much larger war. The weapons now available in the world were more terrible than any he had seen used in the last war. Fortunately, President Eisenhower pulled the plug on this crazy Middle Eastern adventure before it went too far, partly because of his proper concern about its impact on opinion in the Arab world. Prime Minister Anthony Eden retired to the Caribbean, and then a manor house in Wiltshire; Foreign Secretary Harold Macmillan ("first in, first out") succeeded him at Downing Street; I went back to cricket and Conan Doyle.

Our house was not very bookish. There were book club editions of Nevil Shute and L. P. Hartley, Thor Heyerdahl's *Kon-Tiki* adventures, books on the heroes and heroics of the Second World War—escapes, dam-busting, navigating cruel seas. Above all there was Damon Runyon and S. J. Perelman, a mark I think of how comfortably and naturally we accommodated ourselves to America's cultural *imperium*. My father's job probably made this inevitable. Before skiffle and the Mersey sound, most of the popular music he published was from the other side of the Atlantic—the hit tunes of Johnny Ray, Frankie Lane, Guy Mitchell. One of his first big successes was the latter's "She Wears Red Feathers (And a Hula-Hula Skirt)." My parents' taste was rather better than this. Our 78s featured Frank Sinatra, Ella Fitzgerald, big band jazz—the music of a country that we instinctively admired and respected, glamorous, generous, gee-whiz. We were Americaphiles. How could we be anything else? All that seemed savviest and sassiest, wittiest and wisest, came from across the Atlantic. Weekly cinema visits confirmed our instincts. From one suburban film palace to another—"Don't be disappointed if we can't get in," my father would say on each of our weekly visits—we followed the cultural trail blazed by Hollywood. (It was a nice surprise to discover when I went to Oxford that other countries had been making films, too.) I was an unabashed recipient of what is charmingly called America's soft power.

Yet today, European assumptions that America is much like us, only bigger, faster, and richer, are constantly upended. For Britons, who share their native tongue with most Americans, this is a pretty regular experience. Shared language creates a presumption of similarity. I remember the shock on my first visit to America when I realized that I felt more at home in Athens, Greece, with just a few English speakers, than I did in Athens, Ohio. This sense of cultural alienation varies from one part of the country to another. I recall a long visit of speaking engagements on the West Coast in the mid-1990s, when I was still governor of Hong Kong, that began in Orange County, California. It might as well have been the moon. I dined off that legendary rubber chicken, with a limp salad, iced water, and weak coffee and then tried to answer questions from an audience that clearly regarded me as a quaint, even exotic, creature with curious views well off any recognizable political map. I moved north to Los Angeles and then on to San Francisco and Seattle (one of my favorite cities anywhere in the world). As I struck north, I felt increasingly comfortable, though San Francisco is sometimes politically a little piquant even for my own tastes. But Seattle felt like home, a lovely city whose inhabitants, I suspect, fib about the climate in order to keep outsiders away.

The surprising realization that you are very foreign in many parts of the United States comes hand in hand with the shock of discovering how difficult it is to generalize about the country as a whole. That, in a way, is what makes me question the endlessly parroted observation that we are all, Europeans and Americans, much the same, and share basically the same values. Which Americans are we talking about? Do we mean those who are more obese than any people I have seen anywhere in the world, or those who live a life governed by ascetic fitness regimes with carefully controlled diets of vitamin supplements and steamed broccoli? Do we compare ourselves to evangelical Christians, who wait expectantly for Armageddon and a rather dramatic end to the Middle East peace process, or to those whose religion is an intolerant gospel of political correctness that puts many of the values of the Age of Enlightenment to the sword, seeking, for example, to hound from office the president of one of the world's greatest universities for speculating aloud about the sources of gender differences? Do we identify with those who profess the infallibility of rugged, individual capitalism, scattering its riches widely to the benefit of all, or those who appear to stack the cards in favor of those who have plenty and who ignore those who have little or nothing? Which America shares European values?

Insofar as these things bother George W. Bush (after all, he was elected for a second term, and without the judicial intervention of the Supreme Court), the president's problem with much European opinion is that he stands at the heart of several of these puzzling questions about how much we Europeans really *do* have in common with our American partners. The European identity itself is admittedly complex. What does an Andalusian peasant have in common with a Swedish lumberjack, a Catholic priest in Trieste with a Lutheran pastor in Tallinn? There are certainly differences in Europe. But taking the issues of religion, patriotism, political conservatism, and inequality, Europeans are clearly more like one another than they are like Americans—a lot more, and all these issues have become increasingly important to the way America is seen and behaves around the world.

Alexis de Tocqueville wrote, "People always bear some mark of their origin." We should not therefore be too surprised that America today asserts its religiosity with such selective and self-centered force. The Puritan founding father John Winthrop argued that the early colonists were creating "a City upon a Hill, the eyes of all people are upon us." The colonists were doing the Almighty's work. "Thus stands the case between God and us," said Winthrop, for "we are entered into Covenants with Him for this work." From the very beginning, then, Americans saw themselves in Herman Melville's words as "the peculiar, chosen people— the Israel of our time, we bear the mark of the Liberties of the world. . . . God has given to us, for a future inheritance, the broad domain of the political pagans, that shall yet come and lie down under the shade of our ark, without bloody hands being lifted. God has predestinated, mankind expects, great things from our race, and great things we feel in our souls." Some of those who lay down "under the shade of our ark" needed some persuasion. True, America is predominantly the home of old Europeans who fled west to escape political persecution or economic hardship, or who simply emigrated out of the hope of a better life. Most of them found one, not least the relations of my Irish forebears—nine out of my stepfather's ten western Ireland uncles emigrated to North America—who followed the "tenement trail" from slums to suburbs. But there were others who had the choice made for them—the native Americans (W. H. Auden's "cudgeled people") and the African victims of the slave trade.

The concept of "a chosen people" can be attractive when its leaders summon their fellow citizens to a generous and wholehearted commitment to the ideals of a religion that boasts charity (in the case of Christianity) as the greatest of its three theological virtues. Martin Luther King Jr.'s crusade for justice for black Americans, couched in biblical language, gave many non-Americans the vision of a city *being built* on a hill. It was work in progress. When black Americans were "free at last," we sensed that there was a chance for more people in other countries to be free as well. The example was catching. Yet too often the chosen people seem to have assumed possession of a golden share in God. They are unique among His creatures, like many of Queen Victoria's subjects, practicing and aspiring to standards that no one else can attain; because of their uniqueness they are able to impose their own way of doing things on all the lesser people of God's largely unfavored earth. Might is clothed in holy orders—and the "orders" embrace both meanings of the word. A former Archbishop of Canterbury, Robert Runcie, setting out the limits of Christian patriotism in an admirable sermon at the religious service held after the successful conclusion of the Falklands campaign in 1982, argued, "Those who interpret God's will must never claim him as an asset for one nation or group rather than another." It was true of Britain then, and it should be true of America now. The American theologian Reinhold Niebuhr went much further, exploring the irony of a country full of committed Christians tempted in the postwar years to play God with the world, helped by nuclear weapons and the CIA. Today President Bush's rhetoric is packed with references to the concordance between God's will and America's mission. "The liberty we prize," the president says modestly, "is not America's gift to the world, it is God's gift to humanity." But America—God not being immediately available to do the job Himself—defines both the liberty and the best way to secure it. Indeed, when the president was deemed to have misspoken, because of unfortunate medieval parallels, of launching a "crusade" against Islamic terrorism, he was enunciating a profound truth. In the view of many of his supporters, Bush plays a quasi-sacerdotal role: God's instrument to accomplish His will on earth and, by direct identification, the will of His chosen people.

The prominence of religiosity in American political language, electoral rhetoric, and policy making belies the experts who predicted, not long ago, that religion would play a declining role in international politics. Our late Polish pope helped to redraw the boundaries of freedom in Europe, though he does not seem to have had much impact on the family behavior of Europeans. Islamism grows in intensity—and, in some of its manifestations, toxicity. So how influential (and benign) is American religion? Clearly the importance of evangelical Christians has been strengthened by their alliance with right-wing Catholics on issues such as abortion, stem cell research, sex education, and gay marriage; and with right-wing Jews around the Middle East peace process (although if I were Jewish I would think twice about throwing in my lot with those Christians who foretell an imminent last battle between Good and Evil in the Holy Land and the conversion of the Jewish race to Christianity). Many Europeans, including those like me who are practicing Christians, are uncomfortable with the messages, behavior, and beliefs of America's fundamentalist Christians, just as we are with fundamentalism elsewhere. We have suffered from fundamentalism in Europe ourselves. I used to muse, when we were condemning the Taliban's desecration of Buddhist carved figures in Afghanistan, about those troops of Oliver Cromwell riding from one English cathedral to another to smash the heads off the Christian statuary. We are still not entirely free from religious fundamentalist bigotry; Northern Ireland comes to mind. But on the whole, this is part of our history, and the Christian message is usually today conveyed in moderate tones that do not deny past crimes done in God's name nor the existence of the modern world.

One reason why "Come to Jesus" oratory may grate is that while Europeans have not wholly turned their backs on religion it seems to matter less to us than to Americans. According to the Pew Research Center, 59 percent of Americans say that religion is very important to them, but only 27 percent of Italians, 21 percent of Germans, and 11 percent of the French say the same. America remains, in G. K. Chesterton's phrase, a nation "with the soul of a church," a church moreover with some surprisingly traditionalist views, for reasons that may not be wholly dissimilar from the reasons for Islamic fundamentalism. In its seeming destruction of familiar landmarks and signposts, globalization perhaps encourages a reversion to what we take to be simple ancient truths and customs. The church, mosque, or temple provides an oasis of certainty, order, and beauty from the assault of alien ideas and temptations. In his book *The European Dream*, Jeremy Rifkin sets out some of the statistical evidence of religious belief in America, where 46 percent of the population describe themselves as born-again Christians, in what has been called the fourth great religious revival to sweep America in the last three centuries. Over two-thirds of Americans believe in the devil (the figure is the same for college graduates and for those without a college degree). One-third of all Americans believe that every word in the Bible is God's and one-quarter think that the teaching of creationism should be mandatory in publicly funded schools. A Gallup poll in 2004 showed that almost half of Americans believe in creationism and just over a quarter in evolution. Four out of ten Americans believe that the world will end with an Armageddon battle between Jesus and the Antichrist, and 47 percent think that the Antichrist is on earth already. (There are no figures for those who believe he is camped out on New York's UN Plaza.)

Does all this actually matter? Rifkin notes that according to the World Values Survey, most Europeans, Canadians, and Japanese reckon that there can never be absolutely clear guidelines about what is good and evil; circumstance plays a part in determining the distinction. Most Americans, on the other hand, believe that the guidelines about what is good and evil are clear and apply to everyone, regardless of circumstances. If you are trying to form a common transatlantic view of what sort of world we want to live in and how we can achieve it, it is hard to believe that these differences are of little consequence. Perhaps they will matter most in those areas likely to have the greatest impact on the human condition, where science provides the evidence and the goad for international policy: for example concerning the environment. Does Jesus have a view on gas-guzzling sports utility vehicles? I do not spurn religion's role in public debate, but recall Einstein's observation, "Science without religion is lame, religion without science is blind."

As one might expect, the chosen people are more nationalistic than those all too aware of their own imperfections. The visitor to the United States is struck by the public evidence of this. Drive through American suburbs and you see so many flagpoles with the Stars and Stripes fluttering over the front lawns. In Britain, it takes an international football tournament, or the very occasional commemoration of a wartime victory, or a rite of passage in the House of Windsor to get the British to fly the flag, often led by a regiment of patriotic taxi drivers. For a party to celebrate the fifth year after my departure from Hong Kong, I hung the old governor's Union Flag from a first-floor window of my home. My neighbors thought I had gone mad. One also gets the impression that American visitors to Washington's tourist sights are doing more than spending a jolly family holiday in the capital. They are like Catholics visiting Rome, solemnly trooping around the shrines of a religion. In a National Opinion Research Center poll, the United States ranked first among twenty-three countries in its citizens' sense of national pride. Seventy-two percent of Americans said they were very proud of their country. Less than half the sample in the main Western democracies— including Britain, Denmark, France, Italy, and the Netherlands—said the same. It may surprise Americans to learn that the Pew Research Center found that only one out of every three Frenchmen believed that their culture was superior to others; the figure for Americans was about twice as big. What on earth has got into France's cheese-eating brigade—has "defeatism" joined "surrenderism"? While generally kind and welcoming to visitors, Americans have long resented—even more than most others—any criticism of their country. Tocqueville called this "irritable patriotism"; it is not new, but it can be unsettling.

As a British, indeed as a European, conservative, I believe among other things in markets, individual enterprise, limiting government's role, participative pluralism, personal responsibility, the importance of the family, and the rule of law. I am a Catholic and a patriot. So far, I suppose, I am describing someone who could be part of the fast-growing American Right. Dig a little deeper and the comparison starts to look a bit tattered. Capitalism does not for me supersede democracy, nor guarantee it. Nor is it synonymous with the very rich bosses of large corporations making ever more out of a system rigged to their benefit. Those who play casino capitalism should not be what Tom Wolfe described as "Masters of the Universe"; they should be subject to the same laws and ethical values as the rest of us. Capitalism should operate within the law, not the law within capitalism. Capitalism is not a form of religion. It is offensive that senior figures in political life find it so easy to confuse making their own private fortune with the public good; the names of Vice President Dick Cheney and Halliburton come to mind without much intellectual strain. The world joins America in showering rewards on those who promote the most gimcrack schemes to make themselves rich, at least for a while. The geniuses who invented the pyramid of derivatives at Long-Term Capital Management were awarded the Nobel Prize for their cleverness, not long before the whole edifice came crashing down with the financial community digging deep into its pockets to prevent too much collateral damage. To every excess, there comes a reaction. Failure to insist on high corporate standards, and on a sense of responsibility to something broader and more important than maximizing the reward to senior executives, strips away part of the essential protection of and justification for what remains the best system for maximizing the prosperity of a community.

It is curious that the apologists for the most rampant and uncontrolled forms of capitalism are invariably the greatest critics of government, even though they usually seek to suborn government and the public purse for their purposes. They seek handouts and tax breaks, government contracts and commercial sponsorship. The lobbyists of corporate America crowd around the policymakers and legislators of Washington, helping to make its environs one of the wealthiest parts of the country. Government spending, not least at the Pentagon, helps promote industrial development and the fabulously endowed research programs on university campuses. The first telegraph line was built by the federal authorities; so too the technology that lies at the heart of what used to be called the New Economy. "Both the basic science and the technology of the Internet," writes Godfrey Hodgson in *More Equal Than Others*, "were largely the product of research and development done under the impetus of the Cold War." What sense can it make to believe that wealthy corporations should be able to lean on government but that everyone else should stand on their own feet?

For most members of the Left and Right in Europe, the debate about the role of the state comes down to a matter of degree. As a European conservative, I believe strongly that the state should not do too much. I would like to see the state doing rather less and individuals doing rather more for themselves. I do not think it makes sense for conservatives to trade promises with the Left about greater public spending on state services. Conservatives should offer lower taxes, better management of the public sector, and the use of market instruments for enhancing the quality of public provision and the resources available to it. I think there is room for greater private provision in health care, education, and pensions. I am happy to define a center-right domestic agenda in these terms, and to be attacked and to be described as an expenditure cutter as a result. I know of no sensible definition of *conservatism* that includes the belief in a big state and writes its manifestos on blank checks for public services.

But I *do* believe in good public services for those who require them. Slash-and-burn is not a conservative approach to government. Government is not inherently suspect, to be treated as an enemy of a conservative society. As an intellectually and politically committed conservative I believe in stability and order under the rule of law; I want government that is responsive, respected, and properly endowed to carry out its many functions.

I am also sufficiently conservative to believe in balancing the government's budget. I do not like deficits—either when they are run up by governments or by households. As a conservative in America, I would be appalled at the size of the structural budget deficit and the trade deficit (both now standing at 5 percent or more of GDP) and at the debts carried by ordinary families. Are these things signs of a vigorous, family-oriented conservative society? America has to attract more than two billion dollars a day—weekends included—just to finance its current account deficit. More than four dollars out of every ten of Treasury bonds, bills, and notes are presently held by foreigners. In 2004, America attracted 80 percent of global savings. In this mad world, the savings of poor Chinese peasants purchase American Treasury securities to help keep interest rates in the United States lower and the financing of the deficit more secure. The trade-off for the Chinese and other Asians for investing in this mountain of paper is that it eases the pressures on them over the exchange rate of their own currencies and over the size of their surpluses with America. They fund U.S. debt so that Americans will continue to buy their products. But how would I view this as a conservative with European values living in America? I would surely be unhappy about my country borrowing so much from the rest of the world in order to purchase whatever the rest of the world is making. What an old-fashioned conservative I have clearly become!

I would also be uncomfortable at the scale of household borrowing. Is this a sign of sustainable prosperity or is it a bubble? Americans now save less than 2 percent of their disposable income. The savings rate in the euro area is about 12 percent. Total household debt in the United States represents 84 percent of GDP compared to 50 percent in the euro area. More shocking, American debt represents 120 percent of personal disposable income. (The euro area figure is 80 percent.) Real increases in wealth come from technological progress or productivity increases, not from asset inflation.

Indebtedness does not feature in my own list of family values, nor do I like the idea of the state abandoning families financially while condoning interference in their private lives. When we talk about the European social model, we are often referring to policies that vary a good deal from country to country, that do not always work particularly well anymore, and that certainly require reform. But these policies have one underlying characteristic: we do not believe that extremes of inequality make for social stability, a proposition that used to find favor in America. Indeed, Tocqueville begins *Democracy in America* by intoning, "Amongst the novel objects that attracted my attention during my stay in the United States, nothing struck me more forcibly than the general equality of condition among the people." He could not write the same sentence today. Inequality of wages in America is growing, with corporate chief executive officers earning 107 times as much as average workers, double the ratio in 1989 and five times the figure of forty years ago. There are similar figures for income and wealth: the incomes of the richest grew three times as fast as those of the average family in the 1990s, and during the same period the very rich also increased their share of national wealth. Republican firebrand Theodore Roosevelt argued that "this country will not be a permanently good place for any of us to live in unless we make it a reasonably good place for all of us to live in." Presumably growing inequality is regarded by most voters as an acceptable condition since the issue does not overturn administrations in the way that it would anywhere in Europe (in parts of which inequality has also been growing, though with much less extreme results).

Europeans use the state and public funding to support families in a way that would presumably appall an American conservative, who would believe that most social ills can be alleviated by economic trickle-down (from the bank accounts of the rich to the small wage packets of the poor) or by voluntary action by charitable organizations, for example, church groups. In Europe, more or less free health care and education stand at the heart of family policy. Partly as a result, we live longer than Americans and have a much lower infant mortality rate. The health statistics of urban Washington, D.C., contain little to distinguish them from those of a developing country. America spends more than anyone else on health care but ranks thirty-seventh in quality of service. Standards of literacy and numeracy among American schoolchildren are poor in comparison with their European and Asian peer groups. (In contrast, American higher education remains the best in the world, partly because of government research funding but more so because of the generous support of alumni much encouraged by the American tax system.) Failing social improvement, there is always policing and the penitentiary. In Europe there are 87 prisoners per 100,000 people, in America 685.

For many Europeans the greatest difference in values comes in attitudes toward human life. It would be dishonest to pretend that Europeans are uniformly opposed to capital punishment; they are not, even if their governments are. But there is far more public opposition to the state taking life than exists in America, and I do not believe that any European country, despite the long-term and continuing threat of terrorist violence, would today restore capital sentences for the most wicked crimes. The greatest difference in attitudes lies elsewhere. In April 2005, when the newspapers were full of reports of the case of Terri Schiavo, the brain-damaged Florida woman for whom the U.S. Congress, the president, and the Republican Party's supporters on the religious Right rallied in unprecedented clamor, the news also reported that yet another teenage boy had opened fire on his schoolmates and family, killing nine people. What chance of Congress passing laws to restrict gun sales and gun ownership to prevent any more of these sadly frequent childhood slaughters? There is occasionally evil and insanity, even among children, everywhere. But what sort of family values turns a blind eye to the access that minors have to weapons in America? Worse still, what family code raises its voice against doing anything serious and effective to prevent further teenage atrocities? What would we be told by the right-to-lifers, who worked through the night to "save" Terri Schiavo, about the incontinent use of firearms? The usual argument is that it is not the guns that are the problem, it is the people who use them. Extend the argument. It is not the crack cocaine that is the problem, it is the people who use it. It is not the missiles that are the problem, it is the North Koreans who may fire them. Sometimes you extend an argument to absurd lengths to demonstrate its inherent weakness and folly. But this argument begins stupid and ends in small coffins. As it happens, I have always voted in favor of more legal restrictions on abortion and against capital punishment, and I think there is some consistency between the positions. But I deplore excessive political interference in right-to-life issues, especially when it is so hypocritical.

Let me reprise my positions as a conservative European. I am a fiscally conservative, family supporting, free-market internationalist, who as a Catholic thinks that my church has gone too far in what it preaches on the family and sexuality. Reading the study of American conservatism by John Micklethwait and Adrian Wooldridge (*The Right Nation*, 2004), I thought I had found an American conservative with whom I could sympathize. He supported civil rights, a higher minimum wage, and larger immigration quotas. He favored higher taxes when necessary to pay for education and for the nation's science and defense funding. He was "a member of Planned Parenthood and a friend of Estelle Griswold, the woman whose legal challenge to [Connecticut's] ban on contraception later persuaded the Supreme Court to enshrine the right of sexual privacy" in American law. As a senator, he co-sponsored the legislation that established the Peace Corps. He hated McCarthyites and scorned partisanship. According to the authors, "his hostility to the radical right was as much aesthetic as intellectual." His name was Prescott Bush, the present president's grandfather.

Micklethwait and Wooldridge argue that Prescott Bush's brand of conservatism is now only for students of history. The new Right, they argue, is the new establishment, whose rise, to paraphrase Tocqueville, has been "so inevitable, and yet so completely unforeseen." Perhaps they are correct. But while a country's center of gravity shifts from time to time, I am more persuaded by those who argue that George W. Bush was reelected as a war president than by those who contend that he succeeded principally because he articulates the new conservative values of a growing majority. Yet certainly for the moment, it looks as though the divisions in attitude between Europe and America may grow, or that, at the very least, they will not dissolve, and that previous assumptions of unity across the Atlantic may come to appear as the unnatural consequences of the Cold War.

One of the main criticisms of this thesis of a swelling conservative majority in America comes from those who argue that because of immigration, the country will become more Hispanic and Asian over the coming years. But this should not bring too much comfort to Europeans looking for evidence of shared values. The main source of immigration to America in the past has been Europe. Even as late as the 1950s, more than two-thirds of those admitted for settlement to America came from Europe and Canada. By the 1990s, fewer than one in five new immigrants to America set out from Europe; almost half were from Latin America and one in five from Asia. It has been estimated that by the middle of the century half the total American population will be Hispanic. Who can tell what the consequences will be for American attitudes and values?

That America is in many respects so different from Europe is a proposition more likely to be opposed than the statement that the country is a mighty superpower economically, culturally, and militarily. As an economic powerhouse, America is little bigger than Europe—each economy represents about 30 percent of world GDP, with Europe exporting rather more. What is striking is that whatever the cultural and attitudinal differences, the economic ties between the two regions are intimate and growing and appear to survive unscathed despite occasional political turbulence. The figures assembled by Dan Hamilton and Joseph Quinlan, in their paper "Partners in Prosperity" for the Center for Transatlantic Relations at John Hopkins University, are compelling. Despite NAFTA, the rise of Asia, and emerging markets elsewhere, the United States and Europe remain by a long way each other's most important commercial partners. The transatlantic economy generates roughly $2.5 trillion in total commercial sales each year. Most American and European investments flow to each other rather than to lower-wage developing nations. Despite all the rows over Iraq in 2003, corporate America invested nearly $87 billion in Europe in that year, with $7 billion in Germany, and $2.3 billion in France, a 10 percent increase on the previous year. (This was the year of the American bumper stickers proclaiming, "Iraq Now, France Next.") American investments in the Netherlands in that year were almost as great as in the whole of Asia. Over the past decade, U.S. firms have put ten times as much capital into the Netherlands as into China, and twice as much as into Mexico. Total European investment in the United States exceeds $1 trillion; this accounts for nearly three-quarters of all accumulated foreign investment in America. American companies make half their annual foreign profits in Europe, and many European multinationals regard America as their most important market. It would take an awful lot of uneaten French fries and boycotted bottles of Evian to equal the value of the growth each year in European sales to the American market.

There are, periodically, suggestions that we should try to stimulate further transatlantic economic integration by working to create a free trade area around our ocean. This would be a vast political undertaking, and I have doubts about how much it would accomplish and how long it would take to achieve results. Most of the barriers to even greater trade and investment flows across the Atlantic are not old-fashioned tariffs, but complex issues of harmonizing our financial and other regulations. Negotiating improvements here would be a marathon, with twenty-five countries on one side and America's quasi-independent regulatory agencies on the other, buffeted as they are by protectionist industrial lobbying. It will, for example, take a painfully long time to negotiate an open skies agreement between America and Europe that would bring so many benefits to air passengers. Security concerns add a troublesome dimension. As a European commissioner I shared responsibility with my Dutch colleague, Fritz Bolkestein, for negotiating with the Americans on their right to have access to the details of passengers traveling to the United States. American concerns were wholly understandable; the way they went about expressing them was rather less so. With Bolkestein I had a wretchedly complicated job trying to squeeze concessions from impossible conditions out of the Americans, and then sell the same concessions to the European Parliament. The Americans thought the two of us were unreasonable; the Parliament thought we were Washington's patsies. American officials have a tendency to declare their policy and negotiate about it afterward, creating all sorts of problems for their partner, in this case over European data protection legislation. Perhaps this is the sort of behavior that you expect from a superpower. But is it imperial? Are we all dealing today, like it or lump it, with the new Rome to whom, as outlying feudatories, we must pay homage and our dues?

America's military might, and the way it is deployed, provide the evidence that some seek in order to make this charge. America spends more on defense than Europe, Russia, and China combined—indeed, probably as much as the rest of the world put together. Through the last decade, defense spending has amounted to about 4 percent of America's GDP. America could knock over any government in the world if it wanted to do so. It has the technology to destroy with greater precision than a military machine has ever had before, though the precision is far from perfect, as many Iraqi and Afghan casualties testify. It can spy on us all, friend or foe, its satellites reporting back what we say and photographing everything we do, though there is a second caveat here. As both former Secretary of State Colin Powell and the UN Security Council retrospectively discovered after the Iraq war, the interpretation of evidence can sometimes mislead. Like a Shakespearean monarch giving orders to his baronial followers—Essex to Warwick, Pembroke to Carlisle—an American president can say "go" and his tanks and guns will be embarked on carriers or deployed from airplanes and helicopters to whatever land he wishes, however inhospitable the terrain. America's military might is truly awesome and its field commanders—the commanders in chief responsible for all this coiled and sometimes deployed power—travel the world like the proconsuls of old. With their own planes, diplomatic advisers, technology, telecommunications, and legions, they are more potent by far than any ambassador or assistant secretary from the State Department.

So this may look like an empire—if an "unofficial" empire—but is it a *real* empire? The existence of so much military power on its own does not make it so. In any event, as Professor Joseph Nye has observed, the

U.S. defense burden in the 1990s was lighter than it had been in the 1950s. While the American economy has grown, military spending has declined steeply in relative terms from an average of 10 percent of GDP in that earlier period to 4 percent today. Moreover, past empires spent much higher proportions of their wealth on military power than does the United States today. Nor is there much sign of an imperial impulse to take up "The White Man's Burden," to use the racist title of Rudyard Kipling's poem, written in 1899. In his excellent biography of Kipling (*The Long Recessional*), David Gilmour notes that Kipling meant to address the poem to the American people, exhorting them to annex the Philippines. "The message to the Americans," writes Gilmour, "was close to the justification Kipling habitually gave for British rule in India. After the rulers have taken possession, they remain to toil and to serve, to prevent famine and to cure sickness, to dedicate their lives and even to die for the sake of the 'new-caught, sullen peoples.' It is literally a thankless task: no pomp, no material reward, 'no tawdry rule of kings'—just the blame and hate of the people 'ye better.'"

This was, indeed, the best justification for nineteenth-century imperialism, but to their credit it never had much appeal for Americans in the twentieth century, and I cannot imagine many Americans choosing this path of duty, sacrifice, and dominion today. American universities do not train an imperial caste; Americans do not on the whole seek territory—though they are concerned about military bases and secure oil supplies. They import people rather than export them—most Americans resident abroad are in rich countries making or saving money, not settling and seeking to govern or exploit the poor. The historian Niall Ferguson, who would rather like the Americans to take on the role of a liberal empire, notes that even American officials would prefer to stay at home rather than go off somewhere abroad to learn Arabic. He quotes one CIA case officer, "Operations that include diarrhea as a way of life don't happen." There are too few Alden Pyles to run a real empire, something I have heard bemoaned by a few—admittedly, a very few—right-wing Europeans. I recall sitting one glorious July evening in the open air at a dinner at Stanford in Northern California, listening to the once very left-wing now very right-wing British polemicist Paul Johnson lecturing the assembled rather conservative throng on the burdens of empire. It was as though, drawing on Kipling's words, he was calling on Americans to

> Go bind your sons to exile
> To serve your captives' needs,
> To wait in heavy harness,
> On fluttered folk and wild . . .

Generously, he offered that Britain would be there alongside; the implication was that we would, once again in Kipling's words, "commit ourselves to searching [our] manhood / Through all the thankless years." The Americans, polite if puzzled, heard him out, got into their Cadillacs and Mercedes, and drove back to their homes in Palo Alto to prepare for another busy and profitable day at the office. Americans are not by nature imperialists: hallelujah.

There have, as I noted earlier, been lapses. The Spanish-American War was one such. "The taste of Empire is in the mouth of the people," wrote the *Washington Post*, "even as the taste of blood in the jungle." Albert Beveridge, soon to be senator of Indiana, proclaimed the Americans "a conquering race. . . . We must obey our blood and occupy new markets and if necessary new lands," taking them from "debased civilizations and decaying races." He poured scorn on anti-imperialist arguments: "Cuba not contiguous? Puerto Rico not contiguous? The Philippines not contiguous? [We shall] *make* them contiguous and American speed, American guns, American heart and brain and nerve will keep them contiguous forever!" Mark Twain was called a traitor for opposing this grabbing. "Shall we go on," he asked "conferring our Civilization upon the peoples that sit in darkness, or shall we give those poor things a rest? Shall we bang right ahead in our old-time, loud, pious way, and commit the new century to the game; or shall we sober up and sit down and think it over first?"

For much of the twentieth century, America seemed to heed Mark Twain. Its greatness was measured not in territorial acquisition or in military or political domination, but in its exemplification of the benefits of liberal democracy, human rights, individual freedom, and material progress. But is that how things are still seen around the world today?

Even if American attitudes have not changed fundamentally, even if America has not explicitly set its sights on donning the imperial mantle, has the longevity of American predominance and the way it is today expressed—symbolically, diplomatically, politically, and militarily—shifted sentiment decisively against American leadership?

I noted earlier that transatlantic rows are not new. There were disagreements over America's growing commitment in Vietnam in the 1960s and the associated radicalization of a generation that detested American militarism. There was the removal of NATO from France and of France from NATO. Then came Henry Kissinger's "Year of Europe" in 1974, when both sides of the Atlantic were reeling from the after-effects of the oil shock and looking for a better way to understand each other's decisions. So concerned were Europe's foreign ministers that they held an emergency informal meeting at a German castle called Gymnich which has since given its name to the now regular, twice-a-year informal summits that these ministers still hold. Five years later, Helmut Schmidt set off years of demonstrations with his brave decision to allow the United States to station a new generation of nuclear weapons—medium-range Cruise and Pershing missiles—on German soil. When President Ronald Reagan spoke to the Bundestag in 1982, 400,000 protesters took to the streets. Has anything really changed? Or have we merely witnessed a spasm of rage before, during, and since the Iraq war—in Europe and beyond—much like the occasional brouhahas of the past decades?

I am not sure that it is as simple as that. Even before the Iraq campaign, surveys of international opinion—for example, those carried out by the excellent Pew Research Center—showed growing disenchantment with America. Its image is on the skids, even in countries whose populations previously held extremely favorable views of the United States, such as Britain, Poland, and Turkey. As the *Financial Times* reported in discussing a 2003 Pew Survey, "Views of America are becoming more contradictory and ambivalent: some remain positive but . . . uneasiness or outright hostility to America's position as sole superpower and global hegemon is creating more negative perceptions." The newspaper went on to argue that these political attitudes were rubbing onto the market attractions of some of the most popular American consumer brands. Maybe the professional skills of President Bush's former spokesperson,

Karen Hughes, who has been drafted into the State Department to overhaul and improve its public diplomacy, will transform attitudes to and impressions of America.

The problem is in part the cumulative aggregation of images. Even as a senior foreign official dealing with the U.S. administration, you are aware of your role as a tributary: however courteous your hosts, you come as a subordinate bearing goodwill and hoping to depart with a blessing on your endeavors. Some of this may be the result of security, to some extent understandable, though it is a pity that these necessary controls (not only in the United States) seem so frequently to be in the hands of men and women who have suffered a charm and initiative bypass. In the interests of that humble leadership to which President Bush rightly aspires, it would be useful for some of his aides to try to get into their own offices for a meeting with themselves sometime! Attending any conference abroad, American cabinet officers arrive with the sort of entourage that would have done Darius proud. It is as though military preeminence insists on being reflected in political ostentation. Hotels are commandeered; cities are brought to a halt; innocent bystanders are barged into corners by thick-necked men with bits of plastic hanging out of their ears. It is not a spectacle that wins hearts and minds. The avoidance of calamity cannot surely demand such public relations fiascoes. The *Newsweek* columnist Fareed Zakaria noted, shortly after the war on Iraq, that "having traveled around the world and met with senior government officials in dozens of countries over the past year, I can report that with the exception of Britain and Israel, every country the administration has dealt with feels humiliated by us." Ms. Hughes—more power to her elbow—might spare a moment or two to look at what the impact of American hegemony feels like close-up.

How much has President Bush himself been the problem? It is true that his is a brand that does not travel well. From Dayton to Delhi, President Clinton could make himself loved with behavior, words, and body language, so accurately described by Joe Klein in his book on the Clinton presidency, *The Natural*. No one could say that Bill Clinton's appeal outside America was because he did not seem American. He is a man of his place and his times, more gifted than anyone I have met in politics at moving a conversation seamlessly from interesting anecdote to principle to policy wonkery. First he would tell you a story about a village he had visited in India where someone had just acquired a computer; then he would muse on the extent to which technological progress could easily increase the divide between rich countries and poor; finally, there would be some credible scheme for bridging this divide. He talked and talked until he felt he could do no more to make himself loved by everyone in the room. His charm lasered in on everyone in his company. Until he thought that he had won you over, or could do nothing else to accomplish this objective, a meeting with him would run on and on. He was a scheduler's nightmare. I have met some people in politics whose choice of career has surprised me: they clearly do not like people very much. But there was no questioning why Bill Clinton was a politician: he loved us all to bits, all God's children. Big, beefy, brainy—he could not get enough of people.

Whatever may be the personal skills with which President Clinton woos and wows non-Americans, it is plainly the case that his successor has much more difficulty charming Europeans and others. In some ways this is not very fair. In person, he comes across as a likable man, friendly, courteous, direct. The head slightly on one side, he draws you with a smile and a kind word into his circle, for a moment or two, deploying the magnetic force that comes with being the world's Number One. The last time I met him, in Ireland in the summer of 2004, he greeted me with a cheery, "Dad says to say 'Hi.'" Oh yes? And the effort was more natural than calculating. The president's walk is the most curious thing about him, the arms swing loose from the shoulder, the wrists face forward. Is this the way my physiotherapist wants me to rearrange my shoulder-slumping posture?

It may not be the man himself who rubs Europeans the wrong way, but the reputation with which he arrived in office and the policies he has pursued there. President Bush came in with the reputation of a dim cowboy, at best intellectually lazy, given to tripping over even the simplest words in the language that he spoke in his odd jerky drawl. Much of this was patronizing and wrong. It was not as if, when he came to Sweden for his first summit with Europe's leaders in 2001, he was sitting down at the table with a group of philosopher kings, though one or two of them clearly saw themselves as such in his company. When we had our first restricted session with him—half a dozen on each side—he seemed well briefed, articulate, amusing, and comfortable delegating issues to his colleagues. He had no need to show that he was "the boss"—he obviously was. At subsequent meetings, I never found myself disliking the man however much I disagreed with what he was saying. (It is usually easier in politics if you dislike the person as well as his ideas, which leaves me feeling more comfortable in the presence of Vice President Cheney.) My great surprise at observing Bush was in realizing how little he could be described as a chip off the old block. His father was more East Coast, more low-key, even as president somehow less noticeable. I remember a reception at Buckingham Palace in 1991, when Britain was chairing the Group of Seven meetings of industrialized nations. We were milling about, sipping warm champagne, when I heard a tall gentleman with an American accent behind me responding to the pleas from the lady next to him about the state of the National Health Service. "I'm so sorry, ma'am, but I can't help you. My name is George Bush, I'm president of the United States." No one would have made that sort of mistake with his Texan son. But perhaps, anyway, the father and the son were distanced by the younger president's experiences, from hell-raising, money-losing, and booze to born-again Christianity. When Bob Woodward asked President Bush the younger whether he consulted his father on the Iraq war, he replied, "He is the wrong father to appeal to in terms of strength. There is a higher power I appeal to." Such an appeal cannot help but unsettle a European. British prime minister Tony Blair's media rottweiler Alastair Campbell once said, "We don't do God," when a journalist tried to push the question. But the fact that Europeans "don't do God" is not a reason for heaping ridicule on a politician who does.

On the other hand, style is not at all the issue with Bush's vice president. Indeed, it can be said that Dick Cheney does not do style; he is what and who he is, and sees no reason to disguise it or pretend to be anything else. If Cheney were not averse to even the most distant reflections of transparency, this "I don't give a damn what you all think of me" attitude might command a certain reluctant admiration. As it is, he is an implacable presence—conservative if not reactionary; a champion of low taxes for the very rich and of the "make as much of it as you can" philosophy of capitalism; aggressively nationalist; conspiratorial; the leader of the Washington branch of the Likud Party. I too am a conservative, but there's little question that Cheney's conservatism is built from timber grown in a very different part of the forest.

Behind all these matters of touch, feel, impression, and image lies a far more substantive question. Henry Kissinger drew attention to America's awesome power in his book *Does America Need a Foreign Policy?*, published in 2001. He wrote, "At the dawn of the new millennium, the United States is enjoying a preeminence unrivaled by even the greatest empires of the past. From weaponry to entrepreneurship, from science to technology, from higher education to popular culture, America exercises an unparalleled ascendancy around the globe." But that, he concedes, is not enough. It does indeed create its own set of problems. You can be almost too powerful, or be seen to be too powerful, for your own good. His sentiment was foreshadowed by Edmund Burke who, near the height of Britain's imperial pomp, commented: "I dread our own power and our own ambition; I dread our being too much dreaded. . . . We may say that we shall not abuse this astonishing and hitherto unheard of power. But every other nation will think we shall abuse it. It is impossible but that, sooner or later, this state of things must produce a combination against us which may end in our ruin." Kissinger the historian knows this as well as anyone, and indeed in the dying sentences of his book he notes that the challenge facing the United States is "to transform power into consensus so that the international order is based on agreement rather than reluctant acquiescence."

It is not an impossible trick to do. For so long the world's verdict was that America stood for very, very much that was good. It had given the rest of us the postwar international order. It was plainly a land of opportunity and individual freedom. The real source of its greatness was not its unrivaled power but the fact that the world bought into its dream, recognized its intellectual and scientific supremacy, and acknowledged the strength of its economic and political model. How on earth can America regain that global image? How can it rebuild international order based on agreement, and how can Europe help?

2

NOW WE ARE SIXTY

I cannot deny my past to which myself is wed;
The woven figure cannot undo its thread.

—Louis MacNeice, "Valediction"

A few months before starting to write this book, I celebrated my sixtieth birthday. Along with all the sympathetic cards, I received information through the post about my entitlement to a winter fuel allowance and an application form for a "free travel" bus and train pass. These are just a couple of prized examples of the famed European social model, cradle to (almost) grave, the need for whose comprehensive overhaul is an urgent consequence of Europe's long-term demographic changes and of its inadequate efforts to reinvigorate its economy. Social solidarity requires growth to pay for it, and growth requires workers to create it.

European assumptions about welfare need to be reviewed; so do European opinions about the way our world works and is made both prosperous and secure. Nothing in politics is forever—except it seems Britain's existential hunt for its own identity: to lose ourselves in Europe or to discover our post-imperial role as America's spear carrier, or at least its interpreter and apologist to the world's wimps. Meanwhile, the great if perennially crisis-wracked European project to create a union of free-trading democracies strikes out in directions unimagined by those who first created it around Franco-German reconciliation. And Washington's leaders of the "free world" (as we used to call our alliance against Soviet tyranny and Communist advance) seem keen to close the chapter, which they above all others have written, that described, regulated, and sustained so much of the life of our planet for half a century. If the western front has fundamentally changed, or been broken by events and cultural disjuncture, what international configuration will emerge during the short interval of years before the rise of China and India itself reshapes the world's power politics?

Growing up in London in the 1940s and '50s, I belonged to a family that loved America and most things American, though none of us had ever been there. It was in part a natural consequence of my father's job as a conduit for American popular music but also reflected the way in which much of the postwar generation took America's leadership for granted. It might rile us from time to time, yet on the whole it was a comfortably accepted and benign given in our lives. That said, my parents were also—despite reading Lord Beaverbrook's anti-European popular daily newspaper—more than comfortable with our continental neighbors. My own mother, unlike most of my friends', used garlic when she cooked and shopped sometimes at an Italian delicatessen in Soho, demonstrating that it was possible to purchase olive oil without going to a chemist's shop. We went to restaurants whose exotic connections with the Mediterranean were advertised by the wicker-covered Chianti bottles that served as lamps. We sometimes drank wine at meals. My sister—five years older than I—left her convent for the French lycée, and went for her first job to Strasbourg to work for the Council of Europe, and for her second to Rome with the United Nations. We sometimes took vacations abroad, forsaking beach cricket in Devon for beach cricket (to the surprise of the natives) in Brittany. On our first foreign holiday we drove France's *pavé* roads to Luxembourg in my father's "Lanchester." Visiting Paris on the way home I locked myself in the lavatory at the Weppler Hotel, an event that left me timorous about the locks in hotel bathrooms throughout my childhood.

These holidays and my father's occasional business trips to Radio Luxembourg—the pirate radio station that brought pop music and the soccer betting-pool forecasts of Keynsham's infamous Horace Batchelor to the crystal sets of Britain's youth—instilled in him a huge admiration for the recuperative skills of the French and the Germans. He tended to judge the economic ascent of France almost entirely in terms of the smoothness of the motoring, as the infrastructure of *l'hexagon* benefited from postwar recovery. His admiration for Germany's revival was boundless. By nature a generous and kind man, I heard him speak more frequently of the spectacular rise of Germany from its wartime legacy of starvation and rubble than of the years he had lost, and the friends too, fighting it. Like Foreign Secretary and later Prime Minister Harold Macmillan, though he would not have known it, he regarded Germany's triumphant economic progress as a knock-down argument for joining it and others in what was then called the Common Market.

I first heard the case for this put with stunning eloquence when I went up to Balliol College, Oxford. It was the college of Macmillan, who resigned from the premiership in 1963 at the beginning of my second academic year, but came in the following calendar year to address his fellow college members as the university's chancellor. It was the best speech I have ever heard, and I was pleased to hear variants of it, complete with the same thespian gestures and pauses, on several occasions during the following twenty years. The Edwardian drawl, the hooded eyes, the magnificent studied put-downs, the mixture of plump archaism with demotic metaphor—all that was the complement to a simple argument I have always found totally convincing, though today there is a great deal more that can be added to it. Macmillan began by evoking the long hot summer of 1914, described the talented friends who had left Oxford with him that year for the Golgotha of Picardy, recounted their experiences as (in Sassoon's words) "citizens of death's grey land," counted off those who had never returned, recalled the memorials from the Menin Gate to the great arch at Thiepval that were forgotten as we drifted into another terrible war, pointed to the historic decisions taken at Messina and in Rome to prevent the slaughter of a third generation on our continent, and said that one day we too must be part of this adventure, whatever the present whim of an old general to whom we had in the past given so much. Know-all young cynics choked back tears and then stood to cheer, recognizing perhaps that to speak like this of the fire, you have first to pass through it.

In my first year at Oxford, President John F. Kennedy skillfully defused the Cuban Missile Crisis, while my left-wing friends marched to the Martyr's Memorial to denounce Yankee imperialism. In my second year, the president was shot. There is famously a handful of public events in all our lives, imprinted forever on our memories. Those of us who are old enough all know where we were when we first heard of Kennedy's assassination, as we remember the circumstances on September 11, 2001, when we learned about or watched on television the atrocities in New York and Washington. During the evening of November 22, 1963, I was at a party given in college by one of my history dons when two or three hard-left students burst into the room to tell us gleefully what had happened in Dallas. For them it was almost a cause of celebration that such a popular American president should be cut down to make way for a man who could not possibly charm the world in the same way. It was the moment of my university years when I felt most outraged and most political.

Politics did not then feature much in my life. At college, I acted, wrote revues, played rugby and cricket, and allowed myself to be stretched intellectually rather less than the elastic would actually have permitted. Insofar as I had any political views, they were pretty much bang in the middle. I liked and admired moderate, reform-minded conservatives such as Macmillan, Iain Macleod, and Rab Butler, and thus thought Alec Douglas-Home's selection as Tory leader by the party elite was absurd. With Douglas-Home nestled in the premiership, I was attracted by Harold Wilson's look of modernity—until he and the Labour Party got into office and I saw him in depressing action. My parents had been gentle, undemonstrative Conservatives, who voted the party line at every election but otherwise seemed largely untouched by political sentiment. That is probably as far as I would have traveled politically myself had it not been for the good fortune of winning my first-ever visit to America.

An old member of my college, William Coolidge—a wealthy Boston Brahmin—had established as one of his many philanthropic benefactions a fund at Balliol to enable a group of those who had just taken their final examinations to cross the Atlantic and travel around the United States each year. I guess that part of his intention was not simply to broaden our horizons but to invest in the creation of future Americaphiles. In most cases, including mine, that was certainly the result. The scholarship in those days was gold-plated. We crossed to New York on the *France*, drinking cocktails, watching films, and failing to pick up American beauties who all seemed to dance like Cyd Charisse. Then we flew up to spend a few days with Mr. Coolidge—Bill, as we were encouraged to call him—on his Massachusetts estate, where the paintings were even finer than the wine. We were kitted out at the Harvard Co-Op—lightweight suits and slacks, burgundy loafers, Oxford cotton shirts with button-down collars; given a Hertz credit card and a thousand dollars in traveler's checks; presented with a list of Coolidge's friends and old Balliol men who had agreed to put us up as we traveled the country; and then set off in pairs to cross and recross America, taking either the northern or southern route.

I drove off in a Dodge Dart for Ohio, Illinois, and all points westward with my friend Edward Mortimer (who was to become a distinguished foreign correspondent, commentator and author, and director of communications at the United Nations). It was my happy experience then and on many subsequent visits to be received everywhere with kindness and generosity. As Charles Dickens said, after his second visit to the United States, "Wherever I have been, in the smallest places equally with the largest, I have been received with unsurpassable politeness, delicacy, sweet temper, hospitality, and consideration." Americans are exquisite hosts. Thank you for visiting with us, they would say, as we were fêted from Chicago to Billings, Montana, from Salt Lake City to San Francisco and Los Angeles. We were in Southern California at the time of the Watts riots and drove (probably foolishly) through this grim Los Angeles neighborhood a day or two after most of the violence had subsided. Traveling back east through Las Vegas (where we watched a historically questionable nude showgirl tableau of the French Revolution), the Grand Canyon, Santa Fe, and New Orleans, we had another brush with contemporary history in Alabama. We were driving a rental car with a Pennsylvania number plate and were mistaken for civil rights workers in a small town where brave young campaigners from northern campuses had recently been murdered. Our host on that part of the trip, a courtly newspaper editor, came to our rescue explaining that we were English—"They're just like us over there," he said.

Back in New York, with some weeks of the scholarship still to run if we wished, Edward chose to return to Oxford and I was searching for something to do. Bill Coolidge had a bright idea. A rich friend of his was helping to raise money for the New York City mayoral campaign of the Republican congressman from the silk stocking district, John Lindsay. It was suggested that I should stay in his friend's Fifth Avenue apartment and help on the campaign, headquartered at the Roosevelt Hotel. I turned up for duty and was assigned to be an assistant to a Yale- and Balliol-educated young lawyer from Texas who was responsible for the campaign's research, particularly regarding the records of Lindsay's opponents. Sherwin Goldman was witty, civilized, generous, and smart as a whip. He took me in hand, giving me a crash course in New York, its politics, and its cultural delights. Thanks to Sherwin, who now runs the New York City Opera Company, I got to the Met and attended several Balanchine ballets. I was also introduced to the (for me) mostly static mysteries of American football and had my first pastrami on rye at the Carnegie Deli on Seventh Avenue.

It was America, and Sherwin, more than anything or anyone else, that infected me with politics, a virus that I have never subsequently managed to remove from my bloodstream. I was given a lot of freedom to follow my barely formed political instincts and allowed to focus in particular on the past and present pronouncements of the Conservative Party candidate in the campaign, William F. Buckley, Jr. Conservative in America, as compared to my homeland, translated well to the right of the Republican, a quite moderate Lindsay. Buckley was a sort of cult conservative, mannered, funny, well read. He liked to tease and shock, raping and pillaging the political and social consensus of the day in fluently written books and articles. He had worked hard to earn Gore Vidal's sobriquet, "Hitler, but without the charm." It was a joy to mine his obiter dicta for nonsense and contradiction, though I doubt whether much of my material was ever used. Buckley was not a serious candidate in any real sense, commenting memorably when asked what would be the first thing he would do were he to win the mayoralty of that difficult city, "Demand a recount." His main danger to Lindsay was that he might siphon off the right-wing Republican votes needed to beat the uncharismatic, diminutive Democratic opponent, Abraham Beame, who had been tarnished as a crony of the outgoing mayor. Nevertheless, I was made to feel a crucial cog in the campaign, was given plenty of access to Lindsay himself, and became a sort of mascot—a young novelty Englishman, complete with nice manners, a funny accent, and an odd vocabulary. A smoker in those days, I recall the first time, like the character in a Bateman cartoon, that I asked for a fag.

Lindsay was a great candidate—"supercalifragelisticexpialidocious," as the advertisement on Times Square put it. Tall, handsome, and stylish, he spoke well, looked a dream on television, and appeared to enjoy the vulgarities of political campaigning, glad-handing, eating pizzas, and hugging New York. I suspect he was a better candidate than he was a mayor, though there cannot have been many tougher jobs in those days than running that big, dangerous, glamorous, bankrupt city. He did win, sweeping the Democrats from City Hall, and thus ended for me a glorious fall in New York—golden days, exciting times. In mid-November, I embarked on the old *Queen Elizabeth* and spent four days throwing up as we crossed the stormy Atlantic.

Since that first visit to the United States I have returned again and again, as a tourist and holidaymaker, as a lecturer, as a young member of Parliament, as a cabinet minister, as a colonial governor, as a European commissioner, and nowadays as a university chancellor. During a tribute to Roy Jenkins, who was my predecessor as Oxford's chancellor, Arthur M. Schlesinger, Jr., noted that "few British politicians in the nineteenth and early twentieth centuries . . . showed much interest in the United States, or knew much about American history or institutions." It was only after the Second World War, with the advent of easier travel by jet, that British politicians like Jenkins started to go to America in force to find out what it was really like. For my political generation in the United Kingdom it would have been inconceivable not to be a regular visitor: there was so much in America that one needed to understand, and in due course, there was so much business to do.

As a British minister and public servant, my contacts with America, with its political classes and policymakers, have centered on two issues, about which I shall have more to say later in this book. My first ministerial job was as a parliamentary secretary in the Northern Ireland Office under two Conservative secretaries of state with whom I closely identified myself politically, Jim Prior and Douglas Hurd. Since then my career has been intermittently entangled with the affairs of the province and the attempts to promote political reconciliation on our archipelago, most recently in my role as the chairman of the Independent Commission on Policing in Northern Ireland, set up under the Belfast Agreement of 1998. As a moderate and as an English Catholic, I was often dispatched to America to take part in conferences on the divided politics of the north and to lobby about security issues. In the first category of events, I would find myself aligned with moderate spokesmen for Dublin's position, including Peter Sutherland and Mary Robinson, as we shared platforms with nationalist, republican, and unionist leaders from the north. I used to think it educational for audiences from Boston to Los Angeles to observe the Northern Ireland politicians telling audiences how culturally different they were from their political foes as they appeared with every passing row more and more similar. Peter, Mary, and I would occasionally get in a word ourselves, speaking for different governments but sounding remarkably similar.

Talking to American audiences in those days, and particularly lobbying on Capitol Hill, was to receive a crash course in American exceptionalism. This reflects the central role that America has played as an actor rather than a disinterested observer in so many of the dramas of the Irish story—the famine, the plague ships, the formation of the Fenians, the gunrunning in the cause of liberation and anticolonialism. The attitude of many Americans is more naive than hypocritical; they fail to realize how subjective is the neat division of the world into evil terrorists and noble freedom fighters. For me to use the word *terrorism* in the context of Northern Ireland during those visits was to risk a rumpus. Friends of mine had been killed by the IRA. I had no sympathy for the use of violence for political ends. I thought it wicked. I was pleased to have the chance to argue from time to time that it was (to put it at its mildest) unhelpful that the IRA could raise money pretty openly in American cities, where they would also spend it on acquiring weapons. For those fighting Irish terrorism, America was in this sense arguably a much bigger problem than, say, Libya. If terrorism simply divided "us" from "them," then in this case America was with "them."

I never got anywhere with my arguments. I conceded, of course, many of the grievances of Irish history: I was, after all, a British citizen because of the greatest of them. I argued against Unionist intransigence, which has again and again searched for ways of extracting defeat from the jaws of victory, ensuring that each time the Unionist leaders are driven by reality to negotiate, they have to do so from a weaker position than the last time they were at the table. I accepted that to accomplish our security objectives there would have to be a political settlement, though this stuck in the gullet of all who thought terrorist slaughter evil. In other contexts than Irish politics this sort of political realism would have been called by my American interlocutors "rewarding violence." But nothing changed. The collecting tins continued to be passed around; the weapons were purchased; and Irish Republican leaders who had killed and maimed were regularly welcomed to the White House, from which had rung out in recent years so many absolutist sermons about the wickedness of terrorism. This only seemed to change after four feisty sisters, the Macartneys, demanded legal justice for the murder of their brother in a Belfast pub by IRA–Sinn Fein members. Their evidence, which they bravely took all the way to Washington, D.C., drew attention to the disagreeable tendency in parts of the Irish Republican movement to cover up the difference between politics and violence. We can only hope that the latest renunciation of violence lasts.

I made several visits to the United States while I was chairing the policing commission. My team and I received much help on technical issues from American police chiefs, many of whom were part of the Irish diaspora. We discovered how much tougher were the rules of engagement for Northern Ireland's police officers, when faced with public order violence, than for most American forces. We were comprehensively grilled by American civil liberties organizations and by politicians about past policing practices and the steps we intended to take to make sure that the reformed and reorganized police service in Northern Ireland gave a proper and transparent priority to human rights. I regarded interrogation on these issues as wholly reasonable, and considered our ability to satisfy these American experts' concerns as one of the benchmarks of our success. For me, this experience has cast an interesting light on the American pushback on Abu Ghraib, Guantánamo, and related matters.

A second issue, concerning human rights in Hong Kong, also brought me sharply into contact with American attitudes and policies. In my book *East and West*, I have written of my efforts as the last governor of

Hong Kong to deliver on at least some of the promises made to its citizens about democracy, the rule of law, and civil liberties. The support that I got in these endeavors was at best mixed. The British government was supportive enough, though you did not need a high degree in reading body language to recognize that there were parts of the bureaucracy at Whitehall that believed I was several sandwiches short of a picnic. The British business community was at best nervously polite about me but mostly pretty hostile. The media, on the other hand, were friendly. European opinion was curious about the whole fuss, by and large taking the view that this was a bit of last-minute British grandstanding. France, in particular, was not going to let anything interfere with the aims of its commercial diplomacy in China. For the most consistent, intelligent, and outspoken support, I could look only to the United States. President Clinton, the State Department, and politicians from both parties were regularly and openly helpful. American nongovernmental organizations, lawyers' groups, and human rights lobbyists batted for us; the media, too. Above all, the local American business community was intelligently forthright about the importance of respecting and retaining the protection of Hong Kong's liberties through the rule of law, strong institutions, and our first limited essays at democratic accountability. Again and again, they made the connection between economic liberty and political liberty, between Hong Kong's economic success and its way of life as a free society. It was good to have some friends who believed so uninhibitedly in the same things that I did and were prepared to say so.

In the early stages of my political life, I was little involved in European affairs. Of course, the issue of Britain's membership in the Common Market—or European Community, as we came to describe it—squatted in the middle of national politics, seeping poison into the main parties. The Labour Party was turned inside out by the issue in the 1980s and Conservatives endured a similar fate in the following decade. Only the third-party Liberals remained ever-faithful to the European project, periodically benefiting from the support of electors who regarded their votes as a way of registering a protest against the other parties rather than as an endorsement of the whims and fancies of Liberalism's high command.

Others with whom I worked in the Conservative Party had long been involved in various pro-European organizations, arguing the case for Britain's European destiny in language often as extreme as that of their opponents. But the opposition was definitely in the minority, usually regarded as slightly cranky as well as "unhelpful," a dreadful thing to be in mainstream Tory circles. The Conservative Party usually liked to follow its leader and it liked to be liked. The leadership was pro-European, so the loyal thing to be was pro-Europe. Moreover, bright young party members, touched by the sort of ambitions that help drive our political system and government, would naturally wish to mimic the attitudes and vision of their elders. Were you more likely to be chosen for a plum parliamentary constituency by declaring your belief in Britain's membership in a club it could aspire to lead (while, naturally, preserving the "special relationship" with America) or by doubting the geostrategic wisdom of party leaders such as Macmillan, Douglas-Home, Edward Heath, and all the rest? It was no contest. You also had the comfort of knowing that most newspapers would applaud your pro-European views and excoriate any heresy. Several newspapers, which were then more uncritically pro-European than I have ever been, have in the intervening years totally changed their tunes, perhaps—as they claim—because Europe has been transformed into a different enterprise or perhaps because their proprietors and editors have switched.

There will be time later to examine just how much the European project has altered, and to consider whether there is any truth in the argument that we were sold a pup, signing up to one thing while getting quite another. What the proponents of this argument usually mean is that we agreed to enter into a free-trade area but have found ourselves trapped in a federalist union well on the way to becoming a superstate. This argument rewrites history. When Britain initially declined to join the European Common Market, as it was then called, one of the reasons was its explicit commitment to political integration. We decided that the United Kingdom would move instead to create a free-trade area outside the Common Market comprising our main European trading partners who had also kept their distance from Brussels. But this organization—the European Free Trade Area (EFTA)—failed to meet the U.K.'s economic and political goals. EFTA eventually blew apart without the anchoring weight of true political ambition, and most of its members are today part of the European Union. So we had tried to build a simple free-trade area and concluded that it was the European Common Market, and later the European Union, that best suited us. As to the whinging about a federalist trap, such vocal calls for a European federation are not usually heard today except in one or two odd corners of Europe's chanceries and parliaments; the European project has far fewer federal ambitions now than it had thirty years ago.

It was in this climate, after the dissolution of the EFTA, that the referendum campaign over the United Kingdom's membership in the European Community played out. It was 1975, shortly after I had become director of the Conservative Party's research department, and Labour leader Harold Wilson had negotiated cosmetic changes in our terms for membership in the hope that the prettying up would be sufficient to allow Britons to confirm our place in the community. As has been the case with Britain's two other European referendum votes, the campaign was the child of government weakness. Wilson wanted to hold together his party, split as it was over Europe. The campaign's success achieved this in the short term, but short meant short. Throughout the early 1980s, Labour tore itself to shreds over the subject, doing more damage to its prospects than the Democrats and their trade union allies did to themselves over NAFTA. The rows over Europe provoked the exit from Labour's ranks of some of its most attractive figures and the establishment of the Social Democratic Party, and ensured that the party would be unelectable for years, until Neil Kinnock and then Tony Blair put it back together again. Labour's turmoil in the 1980s presaged the mess in the Conservative Party a decade later.

The referendum campaign was the first time I had worked closely with Margaret Thatcher, who had only recently been elected leader of the Conservative Party in a surging peasants' revolt against the incumbent, Edward Heath. As the party's leading pro-European, he was brought huffily out of the tent, to which he had retreated to lick his wounds (a process that took many years), to play a prominent part in the all-party "yes" campaign for European membership. Thatcher was for once wisely happy to play second fiddle. But it was not because of any hesitation about the cause. She made some good pro-European speeches, which I helped to draft, and never tried by word or gesture to put any distance between herself and Heath and his co-campaigners.

One of those on the other side of the argument was the uncle of my wife, Lavender, Sir Derek Walker-Smith, who later became a life peer, taking the name of his Hertfordshire constituency, Broxbourne. Derek was a distinguished Conservative parliamentarian and a successful barrister. He had entered the House of Commons after the war, chaired the influential committee of Conservative backbench MPs, and been appointed Minister of Health by Harold Macmillan. He was never happy about the decision to sue for terms to join the European Community. His argument was principled and, as I shall argue later, the core of the question that has to be answered one way or the other, once and for all, if Britain is ever to find its place in Europe. For Derek, the great struggles in British history had been to establish and safeguard the sovereignty of Parliament. The law was made at Westminster, and interpreted and administered by the courts and judges of the land. By signing the Treaty of Rome we were conceding the supremacy of another law-making body—the European Council and Parliament—and accepting that European courts and judges should have overriding authority in the maintenance of the rule of law in Britain. This represented a rupture in British history. It changed fundamentally the way we were governed, the way free men and women chose to run their own affairs—and could they then be as free as they once had been? Were we not surrendering cherished liberties?

Derek Walker-Smith put his case for many years with the skill of a top-class courtroom advocate. The clauses of each sentence were locked in place with a jeweler's skill; the very rotundity of his prose caused gentle amusement. I once heard him declare, "When I hear the words 'economic and monetary union,' I am able without undue strain or difficulty to contain my enthusiasm within the bounds of public decorum." They don't, as my father would have said, make them like that these days. Derek fought the good fight at Westminster and he took it to the European Parliament, where he became in his later years the chairman of its legal affairs committee. He was obsessive about his arguments in the sense that he did not give them up. But he did not allow this passion to subsume all other considerations: the Conservative Party's political prospects; the national interest; the obligation on responsible politicians to eschew mindless populism; and moderation in all things. He did not set out to wreck the Conservative Party with whose leaders he had disagreed, and since the die had been cast he believed that the role he should play was to make the best of what had been decided. This was the national interest, and he served it in the European Parliament and in organizations of European lawyers.

As a minister, my first experience of working with the European Community in Brussels came as a member of the Council of Development Ministers; indeed, I was plunged into chairing it since my promotion to the Overseas Development Administration coincided with the periodic six-month British presidency of the European Community. Our main task and achievement was the reform of Europe's policy of food aid, preventing the dumping of surpluses on poor developing countries in ways that threatened their ability to sustain indigenous agricultural production. I was also caught up in lengthy renegotiation of the Lomé Convention, which brought Europe and most of its former colonies together in a contractual trade and cooperation agreement. I co-chaired with a smart finance minister from Senegal the subcommittee that determined the amount of aid that would lubricate the deal and found myself locked into what has become a familiar position down the years, between the rhetoric of heads of government and the more down-to-earth preoccupations of their finance ministers.

After three years in that job I was moved in 1989 to the British environment department, a lumbering Whitehall giant that covered a range of sensitive issues from planning, housing, urban regeneration, and water privatization to local government, local tax, and national and international environmental protection. Environmental issues had shot up the political agenda, with a surge of support for Green Party candidates in the elections that year for the European Parliament. It was thought that the department needed a friendlier face after the stewardship of my predecessor, Nicholas Ridley, whose many qualities did not include public geniality.

Ridley was close to Thatcher, a strong believer in markets, and a stridently, and in due course fatally, public critic of the European enterprise.

He was by no means a safe politician, so while the prime minister was happy to comfort herself from time to time with his prejudices, she probably recognized that his ability to self-detonate made it necessary to hold him at a safe distance. Like Thatcher's right-wing party chairman Norman Tebbit, he did, however, have a license to snarl. Ridley's predecessor in the position, Michael Heseltine, had taken a particularly active interest in the economic and social renewal of Liverpool after the riots there in 1981, and the heads of the Catholic and Anglican dioceses in the city were particularly grateful for Heseltine's leadership. When Ridley took over, he showed no interest in Liverpool whatsoever, and after some months, the clerical leaders asked for a meeting with him. The encounter was worse than frosty. Heseltine, they noted, had regarded himself as the minister with special responsibility for Liverpool. Did he, Nick Ridley, feel the same? Well, he drawled, he was responsible for protecting the Natterjack toad, for combating pollution, and for the discharge of sewage sludge, so he supposed he could add Liverpool to his list. And that was Ridley's way with his fellow Britons.

Indeed, when I moved into the environment secretary's office, my difficulties in Europe were exacerbated further by Ridley, who had shifted over to run the department of trade and industry. At the time, the European commission, buoyed by enthusiastic support from most of the northern member states, was trying to raise environmental protection standards. The Italian commissioner responsible, Carlo Ripa di Meana, whose wife's testimony concerning his performance in bed earned him a certain notoriety and the tag—for reasons into which I have never indelicately inquired—"the orgasm of Utrecht," was putting Britain under a lot of pressure. It was ironic, given that our readiness to implement whatever was agreed to almost certainly exceeded that of the country from which he hailed. But discussions were complicated since we were in the throes of privatizing the water industry, a policy regarded at the time by most of the public as a crime against nature and quite possibly a sin against the Holy Ghost. A condition of the sale of the water companies was for us to make clear to would-be shareholders and investors what health standards would be expected of them and how much additional investment would be required in order to meet these standards. My attempts to hold the line in Europe on politically defensible positions were constantly undermined by Ridley. We would argue a position in cabinet or a cabinet committee, but just before the meeting in Brussels Ridley would pop up the back stairs in Downing Street to convince Thatcher that we were being too feeble with the wretched Europeans and should harden our line. I would get new, sometimes incoherent, instructions giving me less elbow room to reach a settlement. I remember in particular being cornered during negotiations over the dumping of sewage sludge in the North Sea. This is not the easiest practice to defend, particularly in the face of assault from our marine neighbors, or indeed from indignant British holidaymakers. (I recall the saying, "You cannot swim off Blackpool beach any longer; you can only go through the motions.") Looking back, I think it is fair to say that European membership has driven up our environmental standards, especially in relation to air and water quality.

On environmental issues, Thatcher was not always a back-marker. She was an early convert to the case that our climate was being changed by fossil fuel emissions and the destruction of tropical forests. She understood earlier than most others the arguments about the greenhouse effect, and enthusiastically backed my efforts in Europe and at an international conference in London in 1990 to strengthen the Montreal Protocol's restrictions on the use of ozone-depleting halons and chlorofluorocarbons. Perhaps by that stage in her premiership, it helped that the main pressure for these changes did not come through European directives.

Conventional wisdom holds that Europe brought Margaret Thatcher down, and in this case, I believe the conventional wisdom is correct. Yet what happened was both more subtle and more complicated than that— or at least so it seemed to the minister (that is, me) responsible for implementing the policy that drained away most of Thatcher's public support: the poll tax. Entangled in a Downing Street duel with her Chancellor of the Exchequer Nigel Lawson and her Foreign Secretary Geoffrey Howe over whether "her" pound should shadow the deutschmark or even join the European exchange rate mechanism, the prime minister allowed her attention to be diverted from what she normally did best—ascertaining the impact of any and every policy on Conservative voters: homeowners and taxpayers. The Conservatives had been committed since mid-1974 to reform the local tax system, known as domestic rates. Ministers had run through almost every option without picking a winner before a collection of very clever minds hit upon a woefully foolish scheme. Charity deters me from setting out the roll of honor of the poll tax's authors. Initially this tax had the dubious virtue of simplicity. Everyone would pay an equal contribution to the cost of local services, reflecting not ability to pay (except at extremes of poverty) but the distributed expenditure of local councils. The poll tax, or "Community Charge" as it was never called save by government spokesmen, was railroaded through the cabinet against the heavy resistance of Lawson and the Treasury. To his credit, his political judgment was absolutely correct; to his discredit, he then did everything in his power to ensure that its introduction was disastrous, beginning with a financial settlement for local councils in 1989–90 which was bound to bring far higher bills for local taxpayers.

I had been transferred from the department of overseas development—where I had been happily removed, most of the time, from domestic politics—to the environment department just in time to take responsibility for the first year's operation of the poll tax. This was what in rugby football is called a hospital pass. It did not take long for me to realize just how calamitous the new tax was likely to be. On the whole, the old system of domestic rating had borne proportionately least heavily on middle-income families in mid-price properties in averagely prosperous areas, who in general could be described as swing voters in close-call constituencies. These families were really clobbered by the new tax system, which also doubled at a stroke the number of direct taxpayers in the country. Shortly after I moved to the environment department's bleak slab blocks (now demolished) in Marsham Street, I commissioned a study of what would actually happen to people's bills in a selection of constituencies in the first year of the tax's operation. Predictably, the poll tax homed in like a heat-seeking missile on swing voters in marginal seats. I went to see Thatcher with the figures, and with a complicated, expensive but manageable scheme to cap the losses people would suffer in moving from the old tax to the new. Lawson was furious, dressed me down, and complained to Thatcher—not unreasonably—that my proposal would scupper the alleged merit of the original, which linked umbilically each council's spending plans with the demands placed on taxpayers. Thatcher did not really focus on the political storm that was inevitably going to hit us. She was distracted; her mind was elsewhere, plotting the next move to thwart Lawson and Howe, as well as the European creep of Germany, France, and Italy in the outsized personalities of Helmut Kohl, François Mitterrand, and Giulio Andreotti. Our scheme for partial salvation died the death of a thousand cuts and caveats in cabinet committees. A policy only slightly less unpopular than the Black Death was unleashed on the land, and Conservative members of Parliament muttered darkly about what it would do to them and whether, for their part, they could do anything about it and its authors.

Thatcher's feud with her treasury secretaries, Lawson and Howe, was only settled by their sequential departures from her cabinets, securing in the process the deservedly rapid rise of John Major to prime minister. But with each ministerial resignation came more bad blood, more turbulence in the parliamentary party. It is more than politically incontinent to lose senior figures like this, raging into the night. More troublesome still, Thatcher appeared to cross the line between forceful European diplomacy and obsessive hysteria. The voice went up; the support went down. She left the stage with one last magnificent performance in the House of Commons, shouting defiance into the teeth of the gale.

As party chairman under Major's premiership, I played only a small role in the successful attempts to tear the fangs out of the poll tax and reestablish a more normal relationship with our European partners. I was with the prime minister in Bonn when he memorably pledged that Britain would resume its position at the heart of Europe. Since my days at the research department I had enjoyed a close relationship with members of the German Christian Democratic Union, and admired the party's role in the reconstruction of German democracy, in working out a philosophy that combined market economics and social responsibility, and ultimately in the reunification of Germany. I had also established a good rapport with Chancellor Kohl, in every sense one of the political giants of the last fifty years, and this helped secure an objective born more of political common sense than of philosophical conviction. In these early days of Britain's involvement in the European Community, British Conservatives in the European Parliament formed a group on their own, alongside but outside the main center-right political alliance dominated by Christian Democrats mainly from Germany, Italy, and the Benelux countries, leaving the Conservatives with less influence than they should have had. There were of course differences in national party programs, but these hardly seemed to raise insurmountable obstacles. With the strong approval and support of Prime Minister Major, the foreign secretary, the party's chief whip, and the members of the European Parliament themselves, I set about completing the negotiations for British membership in the larger conservative group, a process that had begun during Thatcher's premiership. It involved some bizarre outings—explaining to obscure Christian Democrat politicians that the Conservative Party had been around for some time, perhaps a couple of centuries longer than their own parties and that it was not a populist rump; there were also some especially taxing encounters with several Italian politicians whom the judicial authorities would shortly and permanently remove from the scene. Eventually we got what we wanted, a modest success, though one that causes apoplexy in the "Euroskeptic" parts of today's Conservative Party, who object even to a loose alliance with politicians who are more enthusiastic about the European Union than they.

Major's principal triumph for European policy at this time was the negotiation of the Maastricht Treaty in 1991, an exemplary combination of party management and European diplomacy. Major handled his cabinet and parliamentary colleagues with great skill, keeping the ministers informed and involved in working out all the bottom lines. The treaty deepened the integration of the European Union—laying the foundations for a common foreign and security policy—though Major cleverly negotiated British opt-outs from those bits of it he disliked, for example, on social policy and the introduction of the euro. So successful politically was the operation that Europe, and Britain's place in it, was hardly mentioned throughout the general election campaign that shortly followed, even by those who were to become virulent critics of the treaty in the next parliament. (This was the election in which the voters of Bath alas chose my competitor, thus securing for all practical purposes my departure from full-time, mainstream British politics.)

Later, after five years as governor of Hong Kong, trying to manage Britain's exit from empire with as much dignity and decency as was possible in the circumstances, I returned home, chaired the policing commission on Northern Ireland, and went to Brussels in 1999 as one of Britain's two European commissioners, with responsibility for external relations, coordinating the main areas of policy where the European Commission came into contact with the rest of the world, from development assistance to political cooperation. Much of this book is infused with my experience in that job, working in the boiler room of the efforts to create a common European foreign and security policy, and in the course of that work dealing with the world's only superpower, the not-so-United States of America.

The preceding autobiographical pages—the nearest I shall ever get to writing my memoirs—will explain, I hope, the way in which I came to hold the opinions I took with me to Brussels, the intellectual baggage that I unpacked in 1999 in my flat overlooking Cinquantenaire Park. I came to the job in the European Commission as someone who loved and admired America and who believed—without a disproportionate sense of romance—that Britain had taken historically the right decision about joining the European Union, but who thought as well that the politics of Britain's membership and the success of Europe itself were in the first case confused and in the second hampered by the gap between rhetoric and reality. I have some sympathy for the Cleopatra's nose view of history. People *do* make a difference in how events play out, so perhaps the (to be polite) pretty uninspiring present generation of European leaders bears some of the responsibility for today's muddle. This is particularly true in the two countries around which the whole sovereignty-sharing enterprise was formed, France and Germany. Each country faces a complex existential question, to which I shall shortly turn. Maybe, given our own psychodrama in Britain, we should show some understanding about the difficulty their leaders have in answering it. What is clear is that so long as France, Germany, and Britain are confused about their own roles in Europe, so long will Europe be mixed up, too.

There have always been two French visions of Europe. General Charles de Gaulle believed in a Europe of nation-states led by France and Germany, with the latter paying for its past by accepting the primacy of the French national interest on matters of major substance. Indeed, Harold Macmillan said of de Gaulle, "He speaks of Europe, but he means France." The tradition lives on. The other French conception of

Europe was Jean Monnet's; his was a Europe in which the nation-state submerged itself in a greater, continent-wide, or at least Western Europe-wide, enterprise. Nation-states were old hat. It is difficult to straddle both positions intellectually and politically without the risk of serious rupture. The French political class were able to do so for so long without too much discomfort because France was running the show, dominating the Brussels bureaucracy, standing guard over some of its most sacrosanct programs, like the Common Agricultural Policy, and providing both the language and the culture of decision making. *Autres temps, autres moeurs.* In some ways I was always surprised that France had made so little fuss (that is, until the treaty referendum campaign in 2005) about the transformation of the European Union in recent years, as it has successfully grown to twenty-five states and been swayed by profound changes in other countries, most notably Germany. So long as France does not really know what sort of Europe it wants, so long as it tries from time to time to turn the clock back almost whimsically to a golden age of French superior distinctiveness, so long as its politicians, led foremost by President Jacques Chirac, remain trapped in an ignorant and impoverishing hostility to the policies required to create jobs and compete successfully in the world, France will punch significantly below its weight and Europe will be all the poorer.

There are occasional manifestations of the French trying to hold a line badly frayed by events, with which I have some sympathy. One concerned me very directly. During the behind-the-arras discussions about the choice of a European Commission president to succeed Romano Prodi (who, after he had stepped down as Italian prime minister, had the job of president of the European Commission from 1999 to 2004), my own name was canvassed with some enthusiasm on both the right and the left of the political spectrum. My most prominent supporter was in fact French, the former president Giscard d'Estaing, who had recently presided over the convention that drafted the proposed European constitution. In the margins of a meeting of European foreign ministers, Pierre de Boisseu came to see me. De Boisseau is France's senior bureaucrat in Brussels, cynical, manipulative, clever. He is the sort of Frenchman we British need so that we can recall occasionally how wonderfully generous we were to sign the entente cordiale, the treaty of friendship with France dating to 1904. "Well," Boissieu said, "I have been to the Elysée and I have a message for you. They think you're very good, but they can't accept you as president." The reasons adduced were clear—Britain was outside the euro zone and outside the so-called Schengen area within which European citizens could travel without a passport. He was very civil about it; the French had been surprised at how comfortable they had often found it to work with me; they thought I was independent minded. But there it was. "Let's be clear," I said. "You can't accept a British president." In response, I got a wintry smile. It is worth recalling that Margaret Thatcher had twice, in 1985 and 1989, accepted a French candidate, Jacques Delors, for the position; and I suspect that in 2004, Prime Minister Blair could probably have been persuaded to support the talented French Socialist trade commissioner Pascal Lamy (now sensibly chosen to run the World Trade Organization).

At the European Council in Edinburgh (the heads of state or government summit that was held under the British presidency) in 1992, my friend Tristan Garel-Jones, then minister for Europe, was discussing Britain's hesitations about committing itself to European monetary union with Germany's Chancellor Kohl. He mentioned worries about a loss of sovereignty. Kohl responded by saying that his own political purpose had always and everywhere been to submerge German sovereignty in a wider and broader European sovereignty. I know myself how strongly he felt that. He had been brought up near the historic borders of France and Germany, land that had been fought over again and again. He had seen the terrible aftermath of the Second World War. He wanted to end division and warfare in Europe. More than that, he believed that the emergence of an economically powerful, reunited Germany would only be tolerable to its neighbors if it subsumed itself in Europe, if Germany's national interest was clearly no more and no less than Europe's interest. To reinforce the point, Germany should be prepared to pay the lion's share for Europe's policies, subsidizing the farmers and the poorer regions throughout the European Union. Germany had to show that it had slayed its demons by paying for the welfare of its neighbors.

Germany no longer has anything to prove. It is a stable, successful democracy. That has been one of the great political stories of the last fifty years. It continues to pay over the odds for the rest of Europe while also footing the continuing huge bill for reunification. The Kohl case for Europe—essentially no more war and limited German power—is still valid, but it cannot possibly have the same resonance for the emerging generation of political leaders. So what sort of European Union does today's Germany want? Does it want to see more sovereignty shared? Hardly. In practice, it fights increasingly against the liberal economic policies coming out of Brussels, which it fears will dismantle the last remnants of economic corporatism that formed the least attractive part of its postwar political settlement. It resists interference with the autonomous prerogatives of its regional states. No one speaks more clearly than Germany about "subsidiarity," Brussels-speak for taking decisions at the lowest appropriate level. Where does Germany stand as Britain and France bicker about how we should handle our relations with America? Its heart is with Paris, and its head (usually) with London.

With France and Germany prominent advocates of the idea, the European Union has expressed the ambition to make more of an effective political contribution on the world stage. It wants its member states to act and speak where possible in concert, the impact of the whole being thought to be greater than what can be achieved by individual countries. Yet this question, and particularly its effect on our relationship with America, our past savior and increasingly confusing partner and friend, is still unanswered.

It is confusing not least because it sometimes seems as though the United States is heading off in a totally different direction to the one it successfully taught us, its transatlantic cousins, to take. After the First World War, President Woodrow Wilson tried to establish a network of international agreements, rules, and institutions that would compromise traditional views of national sovereignty and curtail the brutal excesses of nationalism. Wilson's world order was scuppered by Washington politics and European mistakes. After the Second World War, Wilsonianism was again on parade; and this time America made it stick—the Marshall Plan, NATO, the Treaty of Rome—obliging European nation-states to turn their backs on nineteenth-century assumptions about national governance and international relations. This was the only way we could be saved not only from the menace of Soviet Communism but also from our own worst, most distinctive and destructive instincts. European integration was in a sense the price we had to pay for America's protection. It was America that taught us to share sovereignty, both on our own continent and beyond. We are all Wilsonians now.

But is America? Cut through all the arguments about Iraq, the Middle East, Iran, and Afghanistan; the role of the United Nations; global democracy; proliferation of terrible munitions; terrorism; environmental hazard. Is not the real thing we need to know simply this—does America still believe in the world it created, the world it encouraged and led the rest of us (to our vast benefit) to accept? Has the great republic which ruled our hearts and destinies with such accomplished imperial ease, partly because it eschewed the prerogatives of the emperor, now risked its safety and its standing today by claiming for itself imperial rights? Augustus and the wisest of his successors preserved their inheritance and guarded the boundaries of Rome's empire by exercising restraint; Edward Gibbon's great history tells what happened when later emperors forgot that lesson. So under American tutelage, we in Europe turned our back on the bellicose, nationalist politics of the nineteenth and early twentieth centuries, and through our new modes of cooperation—imperfect, sometimes clumsy, even vainglorious—are bent on coping with the problems of the twenty-first.

Meanwhile, America seems intent on going back to the politics of the century we were previously urged to abandon. Back to the gun-slinging Theodore Roosevelt, but with precision-guided missiles. Is that past to be all our futures, or can we even now, by greater European exertion, help to avoid it and save our great friend from itself? Can we help preserve the Republic's mostly benign empire? Can we convince the United States, in these days when the geostrategic leadership from which we benefited in the age of the Soviet threat has become a subject for the history books, that Europe still counts for something, and is still worth heeding?

Sometimes historical change comes slowly, creeping up imperceptibly until you suddenly realize you are living in a new country or a new age. At times, change arrives with dramatic speed. One moment this world, the next another—cards swept from the table. A friend of mine, William Waldegrave, a minister in the British Foreign Office, was visiting Berlin in early 1989. While he was there the East German border guards behaved badly, breaking all the established conventions, and picked up a young man who had swum—he thought—to safety across a boundary canal, only to be arrested by the guards as he scrambled up the bank on West Berlin's side. Waldegrave protested vehemently and publicly. Local advisers told him he had overstepped the mark; there were ways of handling these matters, customary practices that respected the sensitivities of East Germany. East Berlin and its Communist authorities needed subtler handling. Within months, there were no East Berlin authorities, because there was no wall dividing East from West, no East Berlin, no East Germany. All gone, with no respect for those delicate sensitivities, all swept away into history's voluminous ashcan.

Will the world we have grown up in change as rapidly as that? Do we have time to shape events in a way that satisfies a transatlantic, American and European, consensus before whatever is left of the western front is challenged by the rise of India and China? And what will Britain—still unsure whether it speaks first for America to Europe or for Europe to America—make of all this and contribute to it? Will Britain be caught trying to work out even today just who we are and what we want to be as the world moves on? Will we remain trapped in the past while others make the future? Time to look again at the dreams of the old lion, and to see whether we in Britain, to borrow a thought of Alan Bennett's, can really make a policy out of the last night of the Proms.

3

NOT TUPPENCE FOR THE REST

The nations, not so blest as thee,
Must, in their turns, to tyrants fall:
Whilst thou shalt flourish great and free,
The dread and envy of them all.

—James Thompson, "Rule, Britannia!"

When Tony Blair's press office announced that I was to become the second British member of the European Commission in Brussels—joining Labourite Neil Kinnock there—the *Daily Telegraph*, bidding me a tear-free farewell, opined editorially that I was "turning my back on the British way of life." The writer packed into one curious insult much that explains the long-running psychodrama of Britain's relationship with the continent just off whose northwestern shores our shared islands remain situated, despite efforts to give them a little shove (at least emotionally) toward mid-ocean. We are encouraged to believe by one of Britain's foremost and most obsessive Europhobes, Christopher Booker, that there are only a small number of plots to be used, albeit in various guises, in all storytelling. He could have extended this thesis to the area—the European Union—of his fervent political prejudices. It would certainly be correct to conclude that the geostrategic soap opera in which Britain has been engaged now for over fifty years contains not only the same plots, appearing over and over again, but much the same dialogue and even many of the same characters. This is not a storyline that includes many surprises.

The *Daily Telegraph*'s adieu begs a very large question: What exactly *is* the British way of life? At which point consensus goes up in smoke and we run the risk of provoking a row likely to break through those bounds of public decorum of which Derek Walker-Smith spoke so eloquently. However we approach that question, the way in which it is raised cuts to the heart of the problem of making Britain comfortable with a European role. It touches a raw nerve of xenophobia. We hear the distant wail of air-raid sirens in the night and catch a whiff of the garlic breath of duplicity and cowardice. Those things we hold dear, those icons that help define us—warm pints of beer, pounds of our own bangers, the Queen's head on her realm's coin and paper notes, parliamentary democracy encased in Barry's and Pugin's Westminster gothic—are under attack by an insidious alien foe. All this is happening because the God-fearing taxpayers of Britain have had the wool pulled over their eyes by a self-serving and invariably unelected elite. So, "turning our back" on our own heritage, the high and mighty take the Eurostar to Brussels to sell the nation's birthright for a mess of euros, all in the name of a political enterprise to which the British electorate has never given its approval, having in the past been hoodwinked into signing on for a quite different political journey.

Do Americans have to bother about the intricacies of these internal disputes—populist, political, cultural? I have an American political scientist friend who used to think, more than half seriously, that he should perhaps try to learn the rules and the vocabulary of cricket in order to get his head around the mysteries of British political life. This was not a wholly foolish perception, though cricket is the sort of game that has to be allowed to percolate the consciousness rather than be learned as though it were merely a game for twenty-two players. Similarly, to understand not only Britain's relationship with Europe but also how Americans can best manage Britain's relationship with their own country, it is useful if not indispensable to understand modern Britain's debate with itself about who we are and what we want to be. (Without wanting to sound too pedagogic or prissy there is one pressing issue of nomenclature and fact that sensible Americans should try to get right if they

want to be taken seriously when addressing Britain and the "special relationship" between our two countries. The country that loves to love
America is the United Kingdom of Great Britain and Northern Ireland;
you can call it Britain for short, though you might annoy Irish Republicans in Northern Ireland when you do so. Britain is not England or
Scotland or Wales—it is all of them. We are not wholly consistent about
these issues ourselves, but as in other countries, we are more likely to
forgive our own mistakes in talking about ourselves than we are to forgive mistakes of others. It is a cobble of identities, not unlike that of
Americans'.) The best of American diplomats, from Dean Acheson to
Ray Seitz, have had no difficulty comprehending why Britain lived in a
state of argumentative ambivalence that made us sometimes infuriatingly
slow in pursuing what our friends could clearly see was in our very best
interest.

Some self-styled British Euroskeptics will protest that presenting the
argument about national identity and attitudes to Europe in the Techni-
color terms I used earlier caricatures what can often be a perfectly sensible
and moderate critique of the way the European Union operates and the
direction it has taken. There is some truth in this. The problem is that
the term "Euroskeptic" covers all manner of positions; it is stretched
elastically from those who criticize aspects of policy or of EU management, while remaining more or less enthusiastic supporters of membership, to those who hate the whole enterprise and want to get out. Some
Euroskeptics want the EU to make course corrections that could be both
practical and acceptable to many other countries, for example they
(sensibly) wish to see a radical overhaul of the Common Agricultural
Policy, which subsidizes farming production and food exports. Others
agree with most of what the Union does but dislike a particular policy
and do not wish to be part of it. For example, I think it is perfectly
possible to be an enthusiastic supporter of a positive British role in
Europe, while opposing our membership in the euro zone. There may
be, in the medium and long term, an economic and political price to be
paid for self-exclusion, but there is also what the former British diplomat
Sir Percy Craddock might have called a "colorable" case for this attitude.
Moreover, even those who in the last few years would have supported
British membership in the eurozone would be hard-pressed to find a

good word for the domestic policies pursued within it by the governments of its three largest economies, Germany, France, and Italy.

There are supporters of Britain's EU membership who define themselves as skeptics, partly because they doubt the wisdom of mindless
boosterism around any human organization and partly because they
refuse to suspend their rational faculties regarding the limits of the particular organization based in Brussels. These Euroskeptics will have
found much in the 2005 referendum results in France and the Netherlands to convince them that their lack of gung-ho enthusiasm has been
justified. Yes, they might recognize the EU's achievements, from the
single market to enlargement to the construction of a model of regional
cooperation that provides an example to the world about how to coordi-
nate a common response to common threats and common opportunities.
Yes, they might also note that the EU was not a superstate in the making
but a conglomeration of nation-states, sometimes banging uneasily against
one another, whose greatest federal threat was the bombastic intona-
tions of its champions. They might even think that the crisis discerned
by the departing limousine-load of European politicians, led by Jacques
Chirac and Gerhard Schröder, was in fact a heaven-sent—or more accurately electorate-sent—opportunity to slow down the process, review old
assumptions, redefine purposes, and trim ambitions without seeking to
wreck the whole enterprise.

There are three other groups of Euroskeptics, whose views ascend
the scales from wishful thinking to amnesia to hostility bordering on
xenophobia. First, there are those who advocate an approach to Europe
in which Britain picks and chooses which policies it wants to embrace,
negotiates acceptable exits from the ones it dislikes, and in the process
shows to the other member states the sort of Europe to which they would
really like to belong, if only they could come to appreciate that *Britain*
knows what is best for them. The assumption behind this approach is
that other European countries need us far more than we need them, and
that if only we spoke firmly enough to them they would fall obediently
into line. This is pretty much the position that the Conservatives have
embraced since they became the opposition party. Charity suggests,
however, that this is a naive position, since the Conservative Party could
never deliver on this thunder, even if they regained power.

The resounding "No" votes in the referendums embolden some of these Conservative critics to claim a victory for their own approach. Was it not now clear that British Euroskepticism was on the march right across Europe? Were we not witnessing European voters, stumbling like the prisoners' chorus in *Fidelio* into the light, recognizing—not to have understood, the fools, that we had known what they wanted all along— that the European project had gone too far, that Europe should become something quite different. Quite different, though quite what exactly is rarely spelled out. These Euroskeptics could take comfort at least from one thing: the votes showed that the nation-state lives and flourishes. For all the horror stories about the creation of a country called Europe, here were two countries within Europe voting the same way for different reasons.

There is a second group of Euroskeptics that includes a fair sprinkling of those who used to be passionate supporters of the United Kingdom's membership in the European Union. They consider themselves the dis- illusioned. They argue, for instance, that recent developments in the EU involve the wholly unacceptable subordination of our own parliament to European institutions. But since Britain joined Europe thirty years ago, we have had to heed European legislation as our own. Edward Heath had made the point explicitly, for example, in a parliamentary debate in the 1960s after Prime Minister Wilson had announced his review of the case for British membership:

> Those who say that the British people must realize what is involved in this are absolutely right. There is a pooling of sovereignty. Member countries of the Community have deliberately undertaken this to achieve their objectives, and, because they believe that the objectives are worth that degree of surrender of sovereignty, they have done it quite deliberately. . . . When we surrender some sovereignty, we shall have a share in the sovereignty of the Community as a whole, and of other members of it. It is not just, as is sometimes thought, an aban- donment of sovereignty to other countries; it is a sharing of other people's sovereignty as well as a pooling of our own.

Moreover, the issue was at the heart of the 1975 referendum cam- paign publicity against joining the European Community. The rejected constitutional treaty, negotiated in 2003–04 but rejected by the French and Dutch in 2005, would have made no fundamental change to the role of the British Parliament and courts that had not been hard fact since 1973.

Finally, there are the people who claim to be Euroskeptics but are really Europhobic. They do not want to adjust Britain's relationship with Europe, but to change it so fundamentally as to destroy the European Union in any shape acceptable to its existing members, for example, by scrapping all application of European laws in the United Kingdom. Failing such adaptations, they want complete withdrawal—indeed they usually want this with or without any debate about change.

While there are, as I have said, different shadings between these various, allegedly skeptical positions, the portmanteau expression usually incorporates policies and attitudes that would be unsustainable as a set of policies and attitudes for responsibly and self-interestedly managing Britain's relations with Europe. Critics of Euroskepticism are entitled to assume the worst rather than the best about this anti-EU movement for a clear reason: its growing popularity is largely associated with the success among the EU's most hostile opponents in boiling the debate down to a perceived European threat to national identities.

No wonder that there is bemusement and confusion among Britons. Flying back from Tokyo to Brussels a few years ago, I was confronted head-on by the fundamental question that continues to curdle Britain's relationship with our European partners. My visit to Japan had itself been revealing. I had gone there just after the eruption of a media controversy at home about whether Britain's absence from the eurozone would have any damaging impact on the enthusiasm of Asians to invest in our country. Most of the British press had pooh-poohed the idea. At my first meeting with the Japanese prime minister, Jonichiro Koizumi, in his democratically shabby office, I embarked on a long overview of the satisfactory state of Europe's relations with Japan. As I finished my remarks, Koizumi, barely containing his impatience, came directly to the point. "When," he asked, "is Britain going to enter the eurozone?" And so it continued, at meeting after meeting, from the finance minister to the foreign minister to the trade minister to the members of the Keidanren, Japan's industrial federation. If Japanese investors had been unfazed by our determination to sit out the first years of economic and monetary union, their political representatives showed a curious way of expressing this insouciance. Reflecting on this in my British Airways lounger at 40,000 feet, I was interrupted by a charming flight attendant who set about laying my table for breakfast. "Do you mind, Mr. Patten, if I ask you a personal question?" Wondering what was coming next, I nervously welcomed the inquiry. "Do you think," she said, "that Britain will ever actually join Europe?"

We could forget all the high-minded and low-minded politics of decades, throw the dust sheets over the conference tables, pack the visionary waffle back in the lexicons. Would we ever *actually* (a word redolent with aspiration harbored but ambition thwarted) join Europe? Who indeed could tell, because the question reminds us that it is a subject for therapists as well as political scientists? It has divided parties, consumed the most promising political careers in flames, enfeebled and even destroyed governments, helped to vulgarize and demean parts of our media, distorted the debate about Britain's world role and purpose, and corroded our ability to pursue our national interest. It is as though a higher destiny had ordained that the United Kingdom can only have a relationship with Europe that inevitably becomes fractious and irritating, a relationship that before long has otherwise perfectly serious politicians going through a pantomime of foot-stamping, finger-wagging, and name-calling. However much history we shared with them—look, for example, at the genealogy of our own royal family, Saxe-Coburg before Windsor—we had recently found ourselves dragged into continental wars, had helped to save them by our own exertions, and then, damn it, they had lacked the grace to let us take the political and economic lead in Europe, a lead we had earned with our own blood. Two terrible wars and a long peace marked the last century. We in Britain ended it as we began it, troubled, confused, and divided about our relationship with our neighbors.

Britons are still shaped, all of us, by our history, imprisoned even though we may know little of it. It is a rather narrow and limited historical memory of Britain's "finest hour" in the Second World War: one great dramatic moment of sustained courage, so uplifting that, horrendous though some of its aspects were, we were swept along by it, our morale raised so that fewer of us than before or since took our own lives.

We gave up our lives when we did for king and for country. The one thing we do all remember from our history is this: we won the war.

In 1999, the German culture minister, Michael Naumann, caused a furious row when he remarked, "England is obsessed with the war. It is the only nation in the world that has decided to make the Second World War a sort of spiritual core of its national self, understanding, and pride." Exaggerated though this may be—certainly it is not so prevalent an attitude as the right-wing press would like it to be—it does contain a few nuggets of truth. There was an enormous amount to be proud of in the way we stood alone for two long years. Yet in recent years we have done much to be proud of as well. We shut down our empire with, on the whole, exemplary skill and more honor than might have been anticipated. We established a welfare democracy that worked quite well for decades. We created the best public broadcasting service in the world. We fought Irish Republican terrorism without trampling too heavily on civil liberties. We did not entirely forget the public virtues celebrated by Michael Oakeshott: civility, courage, clubbability. And we managed a decline in our geopolitical stature without violence or too much self-pity. From one of the big three at war's end, the United Kingdom slipped to what many might call a top-rank, second-division country. Though as the *Times* of London pointed out as long ago as 1963, in the context of the European debate, there was no divine right by which Britain could stay at the head of the second division.

Other European countries found it a little easier, perhaps more convenient, and occasionally necessary to forget the past, or at least to reinvent it. But as Jean Monnet noted in his memoirs, "Britain had not been conquered . . . she felt no need to exorcise the past." We had not only been invincible; for those two years we had stood alone against most of the rest of our own continent. Some even took comfort from our isolation. King George VI told his mother how much happier he was "now that we have no allies to be polite to and pamper." This was a little like whistling past the cemetery. The years 1940 and 1941 were hard and worrying. John Colville, Churchill's private secretary, records in his diary in September 1940, that "the P.M. seems rather more apprehensive than I had realized about the possibility of invasion in the immediate future and he keeps on ringing up the Admiralty and asking about the weather in the Channel." The Home Guard waited on the white cliff tops; the Spitfires cut trails of vapor in the sky above Kent and Sussex; Mother Russia stirred in the east—and we survived by the skin of our teeth.

The bare essentials of the story are true; Britain did stand on its own, fortified by not much more than courage, protected by not much more than brave fighter pilots in their teens (or barely out of them) and the English Channel. But there was plenty of room for myth to round off the jagged edges of the tableau. Would we all have fought on the beaches, and then contested every inch of chalk from the North Foreland to Dungeness as the German forces landed on "Blighty's" shore? Arguments in the British war cabinet in May 1940 about the possibility of negotiating an end to hostilities with Germany remind us that even in the cordite atmosphere of warfare there were those arguing for compromise with evil. Since Churchill not only made our history but also wrote it, no hint of another side of the British character clouds the glorious picture. More important was the Left's rewriting of the history of the 1930s and their part in it. For the old-time, rabble-rousing leader of the Labour Left, Michael Foot, and others on his side of politics, the war and its early catastrophes were the result of the treason of our ruling classes, appeasers who refused to arm our threatened nation, treacherous toffs: Wodehousian in their manners and Nazi in their sympathies. The Londonderry House set was indeed pretty ghastly; many of its members were anti-Semitic. They feared that their own patrician interests were threatened by democracy and the lower orders, and could be best protected by a bit of no-nonsense, jackbooted discipline. Yet the Left's view of history ignores the fact that one reason why appeasement flourished in the 1930s is because it was popular, and indeed their own policy; the national government's foreign policy was supported by about 70 percent of the public until Munich, and could still command a majority in opinion polls thereafter. As for Foot's Labour Party, even after it had abandoned pacifism with the election of Clement Attlee as leader in 1935, it still voted against rearmament on ten different occasions between then and the outbreak of war. The leaders of the working class were every bit as much to blame for Britain's lack of preparation, and for the shameful encouragement of German aggression, as were the country-house appeasers.

Others perpetrate their own national myths, sometimes from

ignorance, sometimes from political convenience, sometimes from necessary design. I lose count of the number of times I have heard American presidents date the beginning of the Second World War from the attack on Pearl Harbor. Forget, for example, about the Poles who had already died by the tens of thousands. America-centric history is more excusable than the French rewriting of the past that has been utilized to create "a certain idea of France," to adapt General de Gaulle's phrase. The concept of *la France résistante*, of a nation united in brave underground opposition to German occupation, is (even if one stretches Francophilia to the breaking point) more than exaggeration. The fiftieth anniversary of D-Day brought with it a poll in *Le Figaro* that showed that 90 percent of French people thought that the Free French forces had played a major part in the liberation of 1944–45; another poll in *Le Monde* indicated that half the country thought the Resistance had done quite as much as the Allies to win the war. A remarkable number of postwar French politicians rather rapidly acquired glamorous war records or shed all evidence of more questionable ones. Thus is national history made everywhere. The real stuff of history, appearing occasionally through the mists of convenient fiction, rankles and hurts. "I may be cynical," Harold Macmillan wrote in his diary, "but I fear it's true—if Hitler had danced in London we'd have had no trouble with de Gaulle."

At war's end, Germany and much of the rest of Europe was flattened. The British publisher Victor Gollancz's *In Darkest Germany* describes a country on the edge of starvation, at the heart of a continent roamed by ragged throngs of displaced people searching for a home. Britain, though exhausted by war, began the years of peace in incomparably better shape than its defeated or liberated neighbors. In 1947 Britain exported as much as France, Germany, Italy, the Benelux countries, Norway, and Denmark combined. In the 1940s the franc was a pretty worthless currency, and the year after the end of hostilities France's national income was only one-half of what it had been in 1938. Germany and Italy were in even worse shape. If not "to the victor—the spoils," at least victorious Britain had a big start on its neighbors as they settled to the task of postwar reconstruction. What was this world to be like, and how were its alliances and partnerships to be configured?

Just as Winston Churchill has left his indelible print on the defining moment of Britain's recollected history, and therefore on our sense of national identity, so too his words even more than his actions provide the prism through which we have sought to argue and define our role in the modern world. It should be regarded as absurd to debate where the United Kingdom should be and where we should go at the outset of the twenty-first century through battling forensic analyses of the writing and speeches of a politician born in 1874. Churchill is fought over by pro- and anti-Europeans, each side seeking to enlist his testimony in history's dock. Truth to tell, as a witness he does not really suit anyone's arguments, though the fact that such efforts are made to shoehorn him into today's political debate is an important reminder of why that argument is so sterile and debilitating.

"Dear Winston," as Margaret Thatcher used to call him with proprietary devotion, must reach near the top of the very short list of authentic British national heroes. An unsurpassed wartime leader, he was in many ways larger than life. The story that he painted over a mouse on a Rubens (which hangs at the top of the stairs at Chequers) because he judged it too small for the composition, is classic Churchill chutzpah: audacious, theatrical, supremely confident in his own judgment and ability—and splendidly unreasonable. He deserves recognition not only as statesman, leader, and historian, but as a political visionary. He was not always right. He got India badly wrong and opposed votes for women long after he should have seen the inevitability of this change, even if he could not accept the case for it. But for all that, he had great swoops of intuition about the future and they were often right. He often saw in events more than others could discern. He was never afraid to think big: looking abroad to discover what the future might hold, and then mobilizing intellectual and political support to meet the challenge. He was a voice in the wilderness in the 1930s, foreseeing the coming war with Hitler. In Fulton, Missouri, in 1946, by contrast, he was heeded. He described how an "iron curtain" had descended across the continent— and his phrase defined an era. That speech was entitled not "The Iron Curtain," but "The Sinews of Peace." Churchill was not a Cassandra, predicting the worst, but a statesman striving for the best, confident that a new war could be prevented if the free world banded together to deter aggression.

As a half-American internationalist, it is not surprising that Churchill recognized the importance of the transatlantic alliance, working tirelessly and brilliantly to bring America into the war until the Japanese did the job for him. Yet he was always clear-sighted. He accepted that American aims would not always coincide with Britain's. This became plain after the war—with America's determination to hasten the end of the British empire, with the wrestlings over the Suez Canal, and with Britain's decision to develop its own nuclear weapons.

One might have expected Churchill's American affections. It is more surprising that he took such a long view of Europe. He wrote as early as 1930 about a "United States of Europe," and his call for partnership between France and Germany in his speech in Zurich in September 1946 was remarkable. But he remained ambiguous about Britain's own role. We were "*with* Europe, but not *of* it . . . linked but not comprised . . . interested and associated, but not absorbed." He advocated federalism. But he saw it as something for the continent, proceeding with Britain's benign support. Britain, for its part, played in a different, bigger league. Churchill imagined three interlocking circles or rings: of Empire (the British Commonwealth), Europe, and Britain's transatlantic affinities. It is hardly surprising that Churchill failed to see how quickly Britain's power would diminish after the war; how rapidly the empire would fade to a memory; and what a small political role the commonwealth would come to assume. What *is* remarkable, given Churchill's reputation as a patriot—indeed his magnificent life and character came close to defining patriotism—is that he saw the case for sharing sovereignty many years before that idea entered the political mainstream, a point that I will develop in the next chapter.

Churchill's enthusiasm for creating new political structures in Europe exceeded that of most of his British contemporaries, and he was certainly more positive than they about the creation of the European Coal and Steel Community in 1951. This was greeted with horror by the government establishment, with civil servants and politicians alike angry that Britain had been in the dark while it was planned, dismissive of its operational potential, and horrified at the idea of having to sell anything like it to the public. Herbert Morrison, who served as Churchill's Home Secretary during the war and helped mastermind Labour's 1945 victory over

Churchill, declared memorably, "We can't do it. The Durham miners will never wear it." When Churchill was restored to office in 1951, after an election in which Europe hardly featured, his attention strayed from the implementation of the grand visions he had offered in the immediate postwar years. He was focused on Cold War summitry and on demonstrating his physical fitness for the rigors of office. Elsewhere in his administration, Anthony Eden and Rab Butler exemplified the prevailing dismissal of European integrationist pretensions; their attitude made *de haut en bas* seem like a demotic expression coined in the English language. Their stance became all the more pronounced as the six founding states of the putative European Union negotiated their way toward agreement on the Treaty of Rome, the legal basis for the Common Market, with first Eden's and then Macmillan's governments curling their lips at the whole doomed enterprise or, somewhat contradictorily, conspiring to wreck it. Believers in the alleged British tradition of wise and disinterested civil service advice would not come up with many scraps of supporting evidence from a trawl through the official papers of the period. But some did see clearly what was coming, expressing the sort of opinions that normally in Britain earn the description "unsound" for their authors. As early as 1949, Sir Henry Tizard, chief scientific adviser at the ministry of defense, set out the true nature of Britain's position with withering accuracy: "We persist in regarding ourselves as a Great Power capable of everything and only temporarily handicapped by economic difficulties. We are not a Great Power and never will be again. We are a great nation, but if we continue to behave like a Great Power we shall soon cease to be a great nation." His argument was dismissed. As is so often the case in politics, it was the emperor who was the last to notice that he was in the buff.

Even relative British economic success in the 1950s, triggered by the postwar bonfire of controls, failed to generate a sense that the country was fast equipping itself for the modern world. In John Osborne's 1957 play, *The Entertainer*, the comedian Archie Rice advises the audience, "Don't clap too hard . . . it's a very old building." As that decade rolled into the next, not only did the building seem pretty decrepit—with its caretakers the butt of the young satirists of the age—but the economy began to slow, and we came to realize that the derided Common Market was catching up with us and even perhaps leaving us behind. The United Kingdom hastily set up a loose free trade area of our own (the EFTA), made up of the seven neighbors who traded most with us (supplying much of our food), but it was no match for the dynamic economy of the six Common Market countries. The relative importance of the Common Market and our dominion partners, Australia and New Zealand, as sources of imports and markets for exports shifted substantially in favor of the former. Britain was literally at "sixes and sevens" in its European policy. With America's encouragement, and with a clear recognition that what he was doing could split the Conservative Party as surely as Peel had torn it asunder over free trade in the nineteenth century, Macmillan took the plunge and sued for membership terms in the 1960s.

Thus we embarked on courtship, rejection, betrothal, and finally marriage of the sort that brings complaints about the noise level from the neighbors and much employment for social workers and family mediators. Britain's initial application, famously rejected by President de Gaulle in 1963, was squeezed reluctantly out of a nation that felt bewildered by the sense that we had won the war but somehow lost the peace. Who did these Europeans think they were to sit in judgment on our claims to join their club in our own time and on our own terms? These were the same countries that we had vanquished or saved, and now we had to go cap in hand to them. Since we were manifestly better than they, how come this odd role reversal? In the forty years since, exactly the same British attitudes and prejudices have been predominant; the basic assumption is that no substantial initiative Europe proposes is ever going to work. Even more balanced and moderate political leaders like John Major have been sucked into this syndrome, as happened with his denunciations of the prospects for economic and monetary union. In the recent negotiations on the proposed constitutional treaty, British ministers scampered under heavy media fire from the announcement of red lines around policy positions that, like First World War trenches, we said we would defend to the death, to protestations that the whole business was about as significant as discussing the London telephone directory. In attack we are diplomatic lions; in occasional and necessary retreat we are chartered accountants, claiming that nothing significant has been surrendered—just the odd decimal point adjusted in the bottom line. No wonder the British public is confused.

The equally bemused continent with which we have to deal is still regarded with suspicion as a pretty dangerous place by many Britons. During the war years, the hand of God helped to repel the Nazi hordes—an understandable identification of our lonely battle with the defense of Christian civilization. We had long felt that even if God was not actually a British passport holder, He had a particular affinity for the people of the isles. We never seemed to notice that the Germans had already laid claim to Him, even inscribing *"Gott mit Uns"* on their soldiers' belt buckles. This squabble over God's favor inspired J. C. Squire's 1915 poem:

> God heard the embattled nations sing and shout
> "Gott strafe England" and "God save the king!"
> God this, God that, and God the other thing—
> "Good God," said God, "I've got my work cut out."

We British regarded ourselves almost as clearly a chosen people as many Americans have believed themselves to be. Until recent years, this divine British patriot was pretty clearly Protestant. As a Catholic politician, I can honestly say that I have never been aware of discrimination, though certainly back in the 1950s Catholics were regarded as just a little exotic, like Freemasons with incense and our very own dead tongue mumbojumbo. But the identification of the European Union with the Catholic Church and Catholic political and social teaching has always made it a harder sell in Britain than it might otherwise have been. Alf Garnet's view of history did, after all, reflect a widespread view. "God told Henry to ignore the Pope and to build His . . . Kingdom on earth here in England," and it was from then on that England began "to win the world and rule it for its own good." Pope Pius XII's wartime prevarications over Nazi wickedness could not have endeared European Catholicism to the British, and there has always been a sense that Catholic countries are a bit unreliable when it comes to supporting democracy. The Archbishop of Canterbury William Temple's concern, expressed in a letter in

1943, that an authoritarian organization of religion was always bound to be drawn to authoritarian politics caught the mood. Catholic social policy has also caused anxiety, mixing (as it often does) waffling, well-meaning, and incompatible aims with a dirigiste instinct increasingly out of sympathy with the times. The lilies of the field neither toil nor spin, so one should not be too dismissive of attempts to turn the New Testament parables and homilies into policy wonkery. But there is no question that this brand of Christian Democracy is not very marketable in Britain.

Germany and France can be even tougher to hawk. "I tries 'ard," Ernest Bevin told the commander of the British occupation forces in Germany after the war, "but I 'ates the Germans." And when was that sense of Germanophobia mined to exhaustion? "France surrenders. We're in the Finals," read the wartime newspaper billboard, and the joke continues to today. It is much funnier if you are not a German. John Cleese's goose-step; the *Daily Mail* on the morning of the 1966 World Cup Final—"If Germany beat us at Wembley this afternoon at our national sport, we can always point out to them that we have recently beaten them at theirs"; the *Sun* newspaper's successful campaign to prevent German soldiers from taking part in V-E anniversary celebrations in London—"The Sun Bans the Hun": after sixty years all these echoes of wartime start to seem less reflections of pride than unhealthy obsessions, unhealthy because we Britons need to make new history, not live with our memories and trophies. To be blunt, if France after all its humiliations at Germany's hands can move on—at least in regard to its neighbor across the Rhine—why can't we?

There is a more serious side to all this. In 1945 A. J. P. Taylor produced *The Course of German History*, which was commissioned during the war years to explain the "German Problem" to a British audience. What exactly *was* the problem? Taylor set it out clearly in the first paragraph of the book:

> The history of the Germans is a history of extremes. It contains everything except moderation, and in the course of a thousand years the Germans have experienced everything except normality. They have dominated Europe, and they have been the hopeless victims of the domination of others. . . . Only the normal person, not particularly

good, not particularly bad, healthy, sane, moderate—he has never set his stamp on German history. . . . Nothing is normal in German history except violent oscillations.

However accurate his historical judgment, Taylor's predictive powers have been proved wrong. History does not always repeat itself, but British policy has sometimes been dominated by the contrary point of view. Germany was governed after the war by a succession of very "normal" people, "not particularly good, not particularly bad, healthy, sane, moderate," and their country became a triumph for the healing powers of democracy and socially responsible market economics. They coped with their history with a mixture of brave honesty and calculated amnesia. The fall of the Berlin Wall, one of the defining moments in our postwar world, and the subsequent reunification of Germany were handled brilliantly by Chancellor Kohl and his colleagues. Retrospective criticism of the generosity of the terms with which the west of the country welcomed the east to a single nationhood seems to me absurd. You cannot reunite a family on the basis of two different notions of law, welfare, and commerce. What should have been regarded as a moment for celebration by British politicians, whose country in the 1940s had helped to set Germany on its successful way, was regarded by some as a cause for gloomy foreboding. Could we stop reunification? How could we deal with its worrying consequences?

Though public opinion in Britain seemed from the opinion polls gratifyingly supportive of allowing the Germans to sort out their own future, Prime Minister Thatcher tried hard herself to derail this historic project, with brief initial support from President Mitterrand. Her behavior was diplomatically crass and morally wrong. Even the truth was bent to try to prove her *Sun*-headline instincts about Germany correct. The leaked record of a seminar at Chequers, held with a small group of historians to help inform her about a subject on which her prejudices were unshakable, was drafted to reflect her own views rather than theirs. While his remarks probably came close to reflecting her private opinion, the then trade and industry minister Nicholas Ridley, who had begun his political career (like the arch-opponent of EU membership, Enoch

Powell) as a European federalist, stepped over the line of diplomatic acceptability when he allowed himself to be quoted as saying that the European Union was "a German racket designed to take over the whole of Europe. . . . I'm not against giving up sovereignty in principle, but not to this lot. You might as well give it to Adolf Hitler, frankly. . . . I'm not sure I wouldn't rather have the shelters and the chance to fight back than simply being taken over by economics." Almost fifty years after the war's end, it was back to fighting them on the beaches and the landing grounds, in the streets and in the hills. It was difficult to believe that we were talking about one of our most important friends and allies, who— to its credit—simply turned the other cheek, perhaps not so much with pain or suffering as with growing contempt and pity, which is worse.

Francophobia has a long pedigree in Britain—the stuff of war, envy, slights, commercial competition. It has invariably gone hand-in-hand with quiet admiration—for the French quality of life, for intellectual achievement, and even (in some quarters) for the reverence shown for the state and its institutions. There are also a few closet British Bona-partists, admiring the longevity of centralized institutions, such as the education system. I must say that is not my own taste; it jars against my preference for the clutter of liberalism. We make great efforts to over-come the natural elbowing and barging that come inevitably when two very opinionated peoples share the same neighborhood. When we signed the entente cordiale in 1904, it was only six years after the Fashoda Inci-dent in Sudan had almost provoked a full-scale war between our two countries. We make our regular obeisance to it. During the centenary celebrations of the friendship treaty in Britain, I spoke at two meetings— one with President Chirac, the other with one of his predecessors, Valéry Giscard d'Estaing. Giscard spoke of fly-fishing and P. G. Wodehouse, the upper-class Frenchman's admiration for a Britain of well-cut tweed and worldly-wise understatement. President Chirac's message was dif-ferent. Seated in the hall of Rhodes House in Oxford, the sun streaming through the high windows on the symbols of empire in Sir Herbert Baker's best effort at Cotswold colonial, Chirac counted off in his beau-tifully modulated French all the contemporary links between the two countries—the French working in Britain, the British in France; the exports and the imports; the investments and the sporting contacts. It was the real world of Arsene Wenger, the French coach of North London's steamrolling soccer club, and of the vacation homes in Gascony and the Dordogne. Chirac noted how many of the villages near his own home in the mountainous Corrèze were being saved by British residents restoring the old houses they had bought and putting life back into villages and hamlets. I still recall the sight of the British Harrier pilot in the first Gulf War, reading a copy of one of Peter Mayle's awful books about life in Provence while waiting to take off. It was the British dream—a little slice of paradise in the French countryside, even if the natives did not all say "zis" and "zat" like Mayle's characters.

So we ask for Weetabix and Marmite in our vacation *épiciers*, bring home local cheeses that run all over the car, but still assume the worst of our French neighbors whenever we get the chance. This is the country with which we generously came close to merging our destiny in the darkest days of defeat in the last war, as Churchill himself proposed. So why do Britons still distrust the French? It is largely, I think, because France's rather tiresome exceptionalism cuts across our own bumptious certainty of our good intentions. How could anyone imagine that the British are not working for everyone else's best interests? Since France and Britain are, even allowing for German global commercialism, the only two countries with worldwide political and economic interests (though some are perhaps more illusory than real), there is a large stage on which we can discover each other's perfidy. This is unlikely to change. While the French government was clearly correct in its assessment of the case for the invasion of Iraq and was equally correct about the likely results, and while it was both absurd and dishonest for the British government to lay the blame for the failure of the UN Security Council resolution on President Chirac, I am more frequently in the camp that criticizes French policy, for example, its ideological obsession with limiting NATO's role because of America's leadership of the organization. Yet I remain a Francophile like so many of my fellow citizens, and as former Lord Chancellor Elwyn Jones put it, would regard a year without a stay in France as disappointing as a day without sunshine.

So whether it is France or Germany with whom we compare Britain, let alone any of the other European Union member states, we regard ourselves as fundamentally different from them—different and ultimately superior. Margaret Thatcher conceded in her famous Bruges speech in 1988 that links with Europe had been "the dominant factor in our history," but she and many others still looked back, to borrow a phrase from John Major, "to a golden age that never was." Golden and gloriously insular, "this blessed plot" (the punning title of Hugo Young's masterly book on Britain and Europe which he had once thought of calling "this skeptic isle") had a longer and deeper tradition of liberty, parliamentary democracy, and the law than our European neighbors; we had twice saved them in thirty years; we were outward looking, independent-spirited, and entrepreneurial. And it took a deep sense of magnanimity on our part to forgive them for being, well, foreign. As the British wits Michael Flanders and Donald Swann sang:

> The English, the English, the English are best
> I wouldn't give tuppence for all of the rest.

We have in recent years—principally through the dour oratory of Britain's Chancellor of the Exchequer, Gordon Brown—trumpeted our economic superiority. Badly performing European economies are compared with pluperfect Britain. From time to time I have concluded that the only halfway adequate response to these comparisons between a golden period in Britain and the grim problems that allegedly crowd in on the eurozone economies is to send food parcels. But British productivity levels are behind those in most eurozone countries, and the gap between Britain's and France's, as just one example, has been growing. Several of these countries trade a substantially larger share of their GDP than Britain does, and the eurozone has been running a trade surplus against a trade deficit in the United Kingdom. British household debt and consumption have run ahead of European figures, not precisely a sign of the United Kingdom's economic good health. Britain has done much better in recent years, thanks, as economic historians note, to Gordon Brown not squandering the legacy of the Major and Clarke years. He deserves credit for that. We do have in Britain a good macroeconomic policy framework and more liberalized markets, and have been able as a result to catch up to and overtake some other European economies. This does not justify what Britain's present European Commissioner, Peter Mandelson, called "gloating." Looking from overall economic performance to what it pays for, it would strain public credulity to claim that Britain's public services are superior to those in most other parts of Europe. Perhaps we have a few lessons to learn from them.

But what sort of people do we British think we are? Our identification as British has undoubtedly weakened as the Scottish and Welsh have asserted their own identities, and as they have become more suspicious of what they regard as English attempts to define Britishness in our own terms. It is interesting that Margaret Thatcher's assertion that she was involved in a battle royale to protect the British way of life was accompanied by a remorseless weakening of the Conservative Party's position in Scotland that eventually led to its obliteration there in the 1990s.

We in Britain—all the combines of our British state, separately and together—have a great history. We are the heirs to a great intellectual, political, and literary tradition. No thanks to successive governments, we have fine universities, the second-best tertiary education system in the world. Our armed forces are as effectively professional as they are overstretched. We speak and write what has become the world's most used and most popular language. All that, and much more, is true. We count for something in the world and, whether through the BBC World Service or the British Council, or our aid programs, our trading instincts, or our diplomatic services, we make ourselves felt. To recycle an old saw, we punch above our weight. So, as James Bond says to Tiger Tanaka in *You Only Live Twice*, "England may have been bled pretty thin by a couple of world wars" (note the use of "England"), "our welfare state politics may have made us expect too much for free, and the liberation of our colonies may have gone too fast, but we still climb Everest and beat plenty of the world at sport, and win plenty of Nobel Prizes. . . . There's nothing wrong with the British people." The sentiments, for all their period charm, are not wholly misplaced, and we have at least continued to win over forty Nobel Prizes in the last forty years alone, with Trinity College, Cambridge, winning more than France.

Where we get into trouble is when we give the impression, in the words of Noel Coward (admittedly writing a lyric about "the pillars of London society"), that "nature selected us / protected us," and that we are "firmly convinced our position is really unique." Others have pushed to escape from the traumas of their own history. Understandably, Britain does not feel the need to do that. But neither should we be trapped by our history in a cocoon of claustrophobic self-regard. We cannot live happily ever after within the covers of Arthur Bryant's *History of Britain*, the citizens of "Freedom's Own Island," "Set in a Silver Sea."

Consider only the most quantifiable of the relevant comparisons. What do the economic figures tell us? British GDP is now a little ahead of that in France. Fine. But Germany's is still more than a third greater, Japan's more than twice as large, and the United States' almost seven times bigger. No great surprise, perhaps; Britain is getting used to that. Looking to the future, however, it would do well to notice that China's economy, currently growing at close to double figures per year, is already four times the size of the United Kingdom's. Even India, once the jewel in Britain's crown, has an economy about twice the size of its former colonizer, with predicted growth rates that will rapidly increase the differential. It is no counsel of despair to observe that Thatcher's and Blair's Britain weighs in globally below Churchill's and Macmillan's of the 1950s and 1960s, and that their Britain was relatively less strong than Neville Chamberlain's prewar country. Britain is middleweight not heavyweight, and we need to think through the implications of that.

Two arguments which are directly relevant to such an analysis will be dealt with in the next two chapters. First, there is the issue of national sovereignty, a matter that has fueled the debate in the Conservative Party even if it does not entirely explain that party's flirtation with political suicide. Second, there is the debate about whether the United Kingdom's destiny lies primarily with America or with our continental neighbors. This is the issue that has rewritten Tony Blair's role in history, and which left us, bruised and bleeding in what Winston Churchill called "the thankless deserts of Mesopotamia," protesting Britain's good faith and honor before a skeptical world. We need a return of British political nerve, because the results of running before the wind, as we shall see, are dire.

4

NATIONAL SOVEREIGNTY AND
THE DESCENT OF CONSERVATISM

"I've got a sort of idea," said Pooh at last, "but I don't suppose it's
a very good one."

"I don't suppose it is either," said Eeyore.

—A. A. Milne, *Winnie the Pooh*

The British Conservative Party got an idea into its head in the 1990s. It was an idea that helped to wreck its prospects, delivering Britain into the hands of a Labour government shorn of principled strategic direction but rich in personal rivalry. The idea was to reverse the international posture it had first warmly embraced thirty years before when it had become a pro-European party. Labour had flip-flopped on the European issue—against, under the party leadership of Hugh Gaitskell in the late 1950s; more or less for, under Prime Minister Harold Wilson in the 1960s and '70s; split and then against, under Michael Foot in the early 1980s; increasingly for again in recent years, under Neil Kinnock, John Smith, and then Prime Minister Tony Blair. The simple rule: when Labour ran the government and won elections, it supported EU membership. Surely there was a lesson for Conservatives in this. Instead, some Conservatives worked assiduously to saddle the party with a policy—or, more accurately, an attitude—against Europe, and in the process jettisoned electoral success, unless I suppose you take the bleak view that

Conservatism's predicament would be even worse without the European albatross wrapped around its neck.

In the Conservative Party, as in other political formations, it is not necessary to have an intellectual basis for a policy, for a prevailing senti-ment, or for a political squawk. Indeed, Conservatives have rather prided themselves on being wise if slow-witted as opposed to clever and silly. The Tory stalwart Lord Salisbury's criticism of his fellow Conservative Iain Macleod for being too clever by half reflects the party's distaste for intellectualism, though it does scant justice to a tradition that embraces David Hume, Edmund Burke (in whose writings, as Coleridge observed, can be found "the germs of almost all political truths"), and Michael Oakeshott. But in the case of the European project, it was not deemed sufficient to have sniffed out error almost accidentally, to have stumbled on it in a belated journey back to first principles and deepest roots. There had to be a reason—an intellectual argument—for the historic change of course. So Conservatives woke up to discover that Britain's sovereignty had been pilfered in the night, as surely as though bits had been removed by vandals from the Albert Memorial. Sovereignty, our ability to rule ourselves, had been seized by Europe and had to be restored.

This discovery swept through large swathes of the party in the 1990s, while I was far from the scene. The Conservative Party was reelected against the odds during a recession in 1992, with the negative equity borne by many homeowners having added a second impediment to their victory. Yet under John Major, Conservatives polled more votes than any party in British political history before or since—half a million more than Tony Blair won in Labour's 1997 landslide, and a third of a million more than Margaret Thatcher in 1987. We led Labour in share of the vote by over 7 percent. Unfortunately, this large plurality did not bring with it an equivalent harvest of seats. John Major's overall majority in parliament was only twenty-one seats, and I was among those Conserva-tives who did not return to the house. Instead, I went to Hong Kong, leaving behind a party that had enthusiastically endorsed the Major-negotiated Treaty of Maastricht and warmly embraced the treaty in its manifesto, but hardly mentioned Europe during the whole election campaign.

Observing the Conservative Party's subsequent suicidal flirtation with "restoring" sovereignty from the distant Chinese coast was pretty surreal. Sovereignty was a rum concept to think about in Hong Kong. We were managing the last significant redoubt of empire under the sovereign authority of the Queen, although we could not say as much to the Chinese. What was for us land in part ceded for all time, and in part leased for ninety-nine years, was for them territory snatched by imperialists from a dynasty whose feebleness enabled the robbery to be endorsed in unequal (that is, unacceptable if not downright illegal) treaties. Britain held Hong Kong because China allowed us. Not even the gallantry of a small garrison of Gurkhas and Black Watch was expected to be able to hold off the ranks of the People's Liberation Army, were they to drive south from Guangdong into the New Territories, striking toward the governor's country mansion and its encircling golf courses at Fanling. The only bunkers in this colony were full of sand. So sensitive was this issue of sovereignty that the Joint Declaration of 1984 that set out the terms of Hong Kong's return to China delicately sidestepped the question of its location. Was it here? Was it there? We simply could not say. Further, Hong Kong's senior civil servants, let alone its politicians, had to be kept at one remove from those actually negotiating the transfer of power on behalf of the British government. For the British, then, there was no doubt about our legal authority (even if we had to keep quiet about it), while the Chinese conceded de facto sovereignty until such time as suited them—and what suited them, when they were pressed for an answer, was 1997.

I was exposed to other challenges to the ideas of sovereignty during my governorship. I remember in particular a couple of hedge-fund assaults on the peg that joined the Hong Kong dollar to the American. The currency peg was an important foundation of the colony's stability during the years of transition. I did not want Hong Kong to be cast adrift on high seas, blown this way and that by financial gales, but avoiding that fate sometimes meant occasional turbulence. With billions in traded currency crashing across the exchanges at the click of computers in London, Frankfurt, and New York, I sometimes questioned what it meant to be sovereign in global markets where technology has speeded and amplified every economic activity.

We survived, and Hong Kong made it successfully through to the transition to Chinese sovereignty from whatever it was that had existed before. My family packed our bags. We embarked on the royal yacht *Britannia* and sailed through a storm of fireworks out of the harbor into the South China Sea. We joined the largest fleet assembled by Britain east of Suez since the closure of the naval base in Singapore in the 1960s. For the last time, since *Britannia* was shortly to be decommissioned (the government thought it was too expensive to refurbish the vessel—and anyway wanted to get on with building the Millennium Dome), a royal yacht sailed majestically—literally, since the Prince of Wales was on board—through the fleet. We cruised on, accompanied by dolphins, flying fish, and seventeen ships of the line to Manila, where we were greeted by a twenty-one-gun salute from the Philippine navy (using, we were told afterward, live rounds). We flew back to London, prosaically ending the British empire in the queue for a taxi at Heathrow's Terminal Three.

I was greeted back home by a political landscape totally transformed over five years by "New" Labour's political sorcery and the Conservative Party's stupidity. Expressing my consternation at the prevailing scene in an early conversation with a young Conservative MP, he told me that I had lost the plot. Clearly I had, and at the same time the Conservative Party, which has always been my political home, had written itself out of the script. The great benefit of the old plot, unlike the new one, was that it usually seemed to end happily for Conservatives, an outcome too often regarded these days as a secondary consideration.

What had happened to the Conservative Party and the conservative enterprise in Britain? Conspiracy and mutiny had been followed by division, division by fratricidal conflict, conflict by defeat, defeat by the imposition of a new orthodoxy, followed by more defeats. It is not the first time that the Conservative Party has torn itself to pieces in this sort of way. But in the past, the biggest splits were either over issues that touched real financial interests, or over rival and coherent visions of Britain's place in the world. When Conservatives were divided over Peel's repeal of the Corn Laws in the mid-1840s, the country gentlemen who opposed him at least had the excuse of defending their pockets. They had more time subsequently for country pursuits, spending all but five of the next thirty years out of office. In the early years of the last century, tariff reform split the Conservative Party into three. Its proponents saw it at the heart of a great scheme for imperial unity and industrial survival. Where is the real interest threatened in the case of Britain's membership in the European Union? Where is the coherent alternative conception of Britain's role that can be compared with present policies—a conception that can be examined, debated, argued over, preferred, rejected? All that we can really get our teeth into is the accusation that British sovereignty is being whittled away; indeed the whittling may have already reduced our sovereignty to dust.

The ballyhoo about sovereignty in Britain owes much to its slide from superpower to medium-sized power. We associated imperial rule over a large part of the globe—even when I began to attend school in the late 1940s, much of the world map on the classroom wall was painted pink to denote our colonial reach—with the development of the most perfect system of self-rule in history. The Whigs had taught us that we were free men governing our own affairs as no others had been quite so able to do. The Tories taught us that we could bestow this political culture on races less blessed than we were ourselves—the English language, an uncorrupt civil service, a bicameral legislature, independent courts. British rule over others and self-rule at home were tied up in the same bundle, and when occasionally we were crossed we could send in the navy to restore the normal order of things. A decline in power exacerbated the hurt felt at the discovery of how limited in the modern world was our ability to do whatever we wished. Americans may find this argument about sovereignty particularly poignant, since even without losing its potency their country has again and again bumped up against the limits of its dominion and the realization that even a superpower cannot sit astride its sovereignty and tell the rest of the world how to behave.

Sovereignty is a notoriously slippery idea. In feudal times, the position was clear enough. Sovereignty rested with God. Royal or baronial critics of this would have done well to reflect on the meeting they would have sooner or later with their Maker, who would sit in final and unappealable judgment on them, sending some to a fate whose torments were explicitly detailed on the walls of every church. For Aquinas in the thirteenth century, human law was derived—by reason or revelation—from divine law. Valid law could not be created by an act of will.

Later, following successful assaults on ultramontanism by a scattering of kings and princes, God was good enough to delegate. Following the Act of Supremacy in 1536, sovereignty in Britain, for example, resided with the King-in-Parliament, a point that King James I sought to dispute. In a speech to Parliament in 1610, he said, "The state of monarchy is the supremest thing upon earth; for Kings are not only God's lieutenants . . . but even by God himself they are called gods." This theory of absolute monarchy never recovered from the blow that struck off Charles I's head. The Bill of Rights in 1689 asserted that it was illegal for the King to pretend [he had] the "power of suspending of laws, or the execution of laws . . . without consent of Parliament." While the monarch could refuse consent or dismiss a government, Parliament was in effect sovereign. And that sovereignty was no longer an expression of the will of God, but the will of the people.

As Geoffrey Howe argued in a seminal lecture at the London School of Economics in 1990, well before Conservatism's present troubles, sovereignty is customarily defined in three ways. There is, first, the notion of "parliamentary sovereignty," according to which the U.K. Parliament has untrammeled authority, recognized by the courts, to make or amend any law. This has always seemed to me pretty far-fetched since it recognizes no geographical boundary nor constitutional limit. Could this sovereign Parliament—at least outside wartime—abolish our courts or scrap general elections? Second, there is the notion of "a sovereign authority" that appears to cover, unhelpfully if uncontentiously, all who are involved in the exercise of supreme authority in the state—monarch, parliament, courts, people. Third, there is what Howe called "state sovereignty," which he defined as the "notion that a country has the unique right to control its own destiny, and that its sovereignty is infringed if any other country or outside pressure exercises an unauthorised influence on its affairs." Under this definition, the Soviet Union's sovereignty, for example, was clearly curtailed by the agreement in the Helsinki Final Act in 1975 to allow other countries to assert their concerns about human rights within its borders.

Howe's central proposition was that legalistic notions of sovereignty do not capture its real practical meaning. After all, what do the concepts that he accurately set out really portend? What do we learn from the statement, for example, that parliament is sovereign? Sovereign to do what exactly? To safeguard the quality of the air we breathe, and of the "azure main" around our "scepter'd isle"? To roll back protectionist measures in American markets? To prevent the nation from going to war in Iraq for reasons that were at best spurious and at worst fraudulent? To hold the cabinet, let alone the prime minister, to account? What makes the concept of sovereignty such a difficult one is the confusion between sovereignty *de jure*—the supreme legal authority, often defined in ways that defy fifty years of British political history—and sovereignty *de facto*— the ability to induce men and women to take a desired course of action and to deal with the problems that beset every nation-state.

Hotspur understood the difference. In Shakespeare's *Henry IV, Part One*, Glendower says to him, "I can call spirits from the very deep." "Aye," replies Hotspur, "and so can I. Or so can any man. But will they come when you do call for them?" My favorite example from history comes later and in another country. In 1793, French Jacobins egged on by Robespierre turned violently against the more moderate Girondins, urging the arrest of that faction's leaders and wheeling cannons up to the convention's door to underline their sovereign Rousseauian rights of participatory democracy. The president of the convention, asserting his own sovereign legislative authority, sent a message to the armed sansculottes outside the building urging them to end their intimidation of the elect within. The commander of the mob sent back a simple response. "Tell your fucking President that he and his Assembly can go fuck themselves, and if within one hour the Twenty-Two are not delivered, we will blow them all up." The deputies tried to escape, but every exit was blocked. So they returned to the chamber and exercised their sovereign legislative authority to arrest their Girondin colleagues.

The reluctance in Britain to confront this difference between the notional and the real betrays perhaps some of our illusions about our own importance in the world, and this in turn finds its symbols in our romantic view of how we are governed. Unlike the United States and all other European countries, we have no written constitution, and so we today deride any attempts to spell out in detailed treaty language the way in which sovereignty is to be shared within the European Union. When the European Constitutional Treaty was still alive and—rather gently— kicking, many argued that we should not for the first time in our history be saddled with a constitution. We needed no such continental device. We were free men and women with arrangements for self-government that had grown from the first Saxon acorn like a great oak. While we praise Westminster, parliamentary sovereignty, our independent judiciary, and our own brand of civil society, what do we actually put up with? We have an electoral system riddled with unfairness; a bicameral legislative structure that the government reorganizes at regular intervals on the back of an envelope; courts whose judges are attacked by the executive because it does not care for the way they seek to protect our liberties; an executive that displays under both Labour and Conservative leadership the attributes of what Lord Hailsham once memorably called an "elective dictatorship"; local government gutted by manic centralism (a process in which I played an ignoble part); a quangocracy that spirits responsibility away from those elected to exercise it; and a populist endorsement of referendums that undermine such authority as parliament has left to it. Are these really the sacrosanct instruments of self-rule that need to be preserved and protected against European assault, if such an assault is really taking place?

Maybe the argument made more sense forty or fifty years ago when the United Kingdom first confronted the consequences of membership in the European club. A supporter of membership, the Lord Chancellor of the day, Lord Kilmuir, explained quite openly to the House of Lords that both courts and Parliament would be operating in a new world, with the former obliged to defer to the European Court on matters covered in the treaty. This meant a greater loss of sovereignty than had previously been involved in joining NATO or the United Nations. It was contractual and would represent "an unprecedented step." But, in private, Lord Kilmuir conveyed much deeper reservations in a letter to the government's chief negotiator of the treaty, Edward Heath. The constitutional objections were "serious" though not in his view "conclusive." He concluded, "I am sure it would be a great mistake to underestimate the force of the objections. . . . But these objections ought to be brought out into the open now because, if we attempt to gloss over them at this stage, those who are opposed to the whole idea of joining the Community will certainly seize on them with more damaging effect later on." The real charge against supporters of entering the European Community is not that they covered up what was involved—remember Edward Heath's remarks in 1966—but that they did not enthusiastically take up this wise advice, partly I imagine because they too were imprisoned in a sentimental mythology of the British system of self-rule.

From the outset, the European Community (now the Union) has had the power to make laws that are binding on the citizens of all its member states. This has always been hotly debated and strongly contested. Tory Derek Walker-Smith argued that British citizens would lose part of their birthright, including "real things, deeply felt, instinctively understood and traditionally cherished by the British people." On the other side, Hugh Gaitskell spoke for many before and since when he asserted in 1962 that membership "meant the end of Britain as an independent state. The end of a thousand years of history." This is an argument we often hear these days, and it is plainly not new. What *is* new, however, is that many who opposed Gaitskell's views at the time have come around to echoing them—despite forty years of history that demonstrate that Britain remains Britain even with a stronger Europe. Gaitskell would surely have recoiled from the embrace of his xenophobic disciples today.

The 1967 white paper on European membership asserted that "the constitutional innovation would lie in the acceptance in advance as part of the law of the U.K. of provisions to be made in the future by instruments issued by Community institutions—a situation for which there is no precedent in this country." Four years later, explaining the content of British negotiations for membership, another white paper stated more coyly that there would not be "any erosion of essential national sovereignty." This begged several questions. The word *essential*, of course, lays claim to weasel status. Yet what is above all ducked is the issue of the virtual and the real—de facto versus de jure sovereignty. Yes, the United Kingdom was to give up notional authority in some areas, but it would gain real power elsewhere. Britain's reluctance to join the early movement to establish the European Community in the 1940s and '50s had been scuttled by the desire to preserve national sovereignty. It was all very well for the rest of Europe to combine forces and to develop supranational institutions—indeed it was probably a good thing—but Britain should remain "master of her fate and captain of her soul." Licentious foreigners could engage in increasingly federastic practices, but we should preserve our virginity. Yet by standing back at that time, by seeking to preserve Britain's de jure sovereignty, did we maximize our de facto sovereignty—our influence over our own destiny? Plainly not. By staying out, we allowed the European Community to take shape without us, drawing on principles that in some cases were alien to us. We abdicated our role as a serious European player.

Similar things could be said of the debate in France over the adoption of the Maastricht Treaty in 1991. Opponents demanded *l'indépendence de la politique monetaire*—or de jure sovereignty. But the franc fort already belonged to the deutschmark zone. So the best means of maintaining and maximizing de facto sovereignty was embrace of the euro. The Bundesbank, quite rightly, takes account only of German interests and cared only about the value of the deutschmark. But the French hold a seat on the European Central Bank, which has to look to their interests, too. This indeed is the logic of the whole European project. Its nations, by sharing de jure sovereignty, gain de facto sovereignty, or far greater mastery of their destiny.

So why do shared sovereignty and common policies often seem so intrusive? The reason is a simple one. If all of Europe is, for instance, to make a single market work, then we need to remove all the obstacles, and that involves detailed legislative intervention. As a consequence, ministers spend twenty-odd years considering a lawn mower–noise directive since such regulations are precisely the sorts of issues that can later be misused as a non-tariff barrier to trade. What else might a British lawn mower manufacturer discover on trying to sell its product to France? Doubtless it would find that the lawn mower breached scores of French regulations. Maybe the engine was too loud, and there were safety concerns. So each machine had to be tested in Perpignan. Perhaps the paint contained a forbidden ingredient, or was the wrong green. Moreover, it would be necessary to change the counterclockwise cutting motions of the blade because this contravened an ancient French right to clockwise cutting. All this may sound absurd unless you are a lawn mower manufacturer keen to sell your product! (As I considered whether this example might be deemed a little far-fetched, I heard a radio report of complaints by British caravanners that European legislation did not cover the material used to make the sofas in European motorhomes.) So you need laws:

laws that Britain—which has stood aside from continental practices for centuries, glorying in our differences—now has to obey; laws that every European member state has to obey. What happens each time you agree to such a law, from environmental pollution to the regulation of financial services? If you treat sovereignty as some mystical absolute, a birthright (to follow Walker-Smith) of every Britain, handed down through the generations like a sacred flame, invisible and unalterable, then every European issue has to be resolved by answering one simple question: Does the proposal on the table require Britain to surrender any more of its birthright? In this conception, the country is giving itself away, piece by piece, "drifting ever closer to its own destruction," to quote from a Conservative pamphlet from 2000.

The Conservative leader who gave this drift to destruction its greatest momentum was Margaret Thatcher, who argued for, negotiated, and in 1986–87 secured the legislative passage of the Single European Act (SEA). If you define sovereignty in the salami-slicing way described above—here a slice of birthright, there a slice of birthright—then SEA resembles hacking more than slicing. Britain (and other European parties) surrendered hunks of parliamentary sovereignty. It was all in an excellent cause, and followed the wise insight offered by the same Margaret Thatcher in a speech during the 1975 referendum campaign that "almost every major nation has been obliged by the pressures of the postwar world to pool significant areas of sovereignty so as to create more effective political units." In this case, we were trying to achieve a principal national objective, turning a customs union into a genuine single market.

Only a small minority in the Conservative Party battled away in the birthright's cause. The legislative enactment of the SEA, for example, was driven through parliament against scant opposition. The party as a whole still bore the stamp of Churchill's wisdom. In the parliamentary debate on the original plan for a European Coal and Steel Community that would operate under a supranational authority, the old hero had bellowed:

> We are asked in a challenging way: "Are you prepared to part with any degree of national sovereignty in any circumstances for the sake of a larger synthesis?" The Conservative and Liberal Parties say, without

hesitation, that we are prepared to consider, and if convinced to accept, the abrogation of national sovereignty, provided that we are satisfied with the conditions and safeguards. . . . [we] declare that national sovereignty is not inviolable, and that it may be resolutely diminished for the sake of all men in all the lands finding their way home together.

And so proclaimed (nearly) all of us in the Conservative Party, until the arrival—or more precisely, the departure—of one formidable Conservative leader.

The figure and views of Margaret Thatcher infuse every part of the European debate in the Conservative Party and in Britain. She was a towering figure about whom it is virtually impossible to find a neutral opinion. She is loved or hated, extravagantly adored or wildly scorned. She changed much of what she touched, not content to survive in office but determined to leave an impression and an impact. (Though the word *make* may be more accurate than *leave* since I do not believe she thought much about political life post-Thatcher.) As Denis Healey once observed, she was not a tree under whose shadowing branches much else was encouraged to grow.

Personally kind and remarkably and agreeably uncensorious about personal conduct—like many women, she was not surprised by the frailty of men—she was nevertheless a political bruiser, who understood the importance of an element of fear in political leadership. Thatcher's habit of summing up the conclusions of meetings at the outset required small acts of political courage from her opponents if they were to deflect her from her preferred political course; courage plus as much—or more— knowledge about the issue under discussion as she possessed herself. Different colleagues pursued their own ways of trying to deal with her force of nature. Peter Carrington, Thatcher's foreign minister until the invasion of the Falklands forced his resignation, made it clear to her in private that he was not prepared to be shouted at in meetings. She took the point. Geoffrey Howe, who stood in her cabinets as both a treasury and foreign minister, opted for patient and—on his side at least—quiet debate. Watching him courteously approaching again and again her intellectual mangle was a little like seeing a pained country solicitor with a difficult and aggressive client.

Thatcher's career demonstrates the importance of ideas in politics.

She was never satisfied to fight political wars over the terrain inherited from the social democracy of previous years. She wanted to shift, and to a considerable extent succeeded in shifting, the political battlefield to the right—where she would comfortably argue for lower taxes, less regulation, privatization, and a curb on abusive union power. There is not really a settled political philosophy called "Thatcherism"; the "ism" is the aggregate of what she did. Privatizing the railways was described as a "Thatcherite" policy. But I doubt whether she would have pursued it—too messy and likely to be too unpopular. She favored big ideas, but invariably (until near the end) pursued them pretty cautiously, carefully testing and preparing the ground, declining for instance to do battle with the miners until she had in place all the pieces necessary for success.

Big ideas were accompanied by a simple and clear narrative. Like Ronald Reagan, she understood that most people have little interest in politics and scant knowledge of what individual politicians stand for. She managed to weave together, as neo-Marxists have pointed out, a compelling story—at least outside Scotland and Wales—in which her instinctive feel for some of the issues of national identity helped to sell the case for a leaner, smaller state. Her idea of a state in which homeowners and small businesses were encouraged, taxes were cut, and enterprise unleashed, public spending was slashed (oddly, more in rhetoric than reality), and the armed forces and the police held in the highest esteem was the political expression of a nation of sturdy individualists, law-abiding, God-fearing, commonsensical, making two and two equal four, grumpy about nannying from Westminster, patriotic, prepared wearily from time to time to put aside the plowshares and take up the sword to save our untrustworthy neighbors from themselves. In her handbag, among the scraps of paper containing a few lines of wisdom from a variety of sages, you would usually have found something from Rudyard Kipling, perhaps "The Glory of the Garden" or "Norman and Saxon":

> The Saxon is not like us Normans. His manners are not so polite.
> But he never means anything serious till he talks about justice and right,
> When he stands like an ox in the furrow with his sullen set eyes on
> your own,
> And grumbles, "This isn't fair dealing, my son, leave the Saxon alone."

This was Thatcher's narrative, and though she appeared to know little history she had a real feel for at least one simple version of the story of our island home.

Thatcher was also a lucky politician. True, successful politicians to some extent make their own luck. Whether it was her own intervention in the Conservative leadership election of 1975 and her handbagging of her male opponents, or Tony Blair's expert garroting of Gordon Brown in a North London restaurant in 1994, there are moments when, if politicians are to succeed, they have to seize the moment. But like Blair, she was fortunate in her opponents, who became obsessed by her artifice and chutzpah, much like the Conservative fixation today with Blair. Both Thatcher and Blair were able to take advantage of such political turns, while other politicians were trapped like rabbits in the headlights of their prime-ministerial bandwagon. In the 1980s Labour was divided—over Europe, over defense, over how socialist it wished to be. It was infiltrated by extremists, whose relentless assiduity drove many traditional activists out of politics altogether. Several of its most popular leaders abandoned the party to start another, a fetal New Labour. Thatcher made the most of the disarray. Thatcher would have been sensible to have ridden her luck for two terms and then made way for a successor. But few political leaders are wise enough—think too of Tony Blair—to set themselves, as José María Aznar did in Spain, a two-term limit. When John Major faced his own first election as Conservative Party leader, he confronted an opposition brought back from the dead by Neil Kinnock, an electoral system quite sharply tilted against the Conservatives, and the beginning of tactical voting by opposition Labourites and the Liberal Democrats in marginal seats to knock Conservatives out (this is how I lost my own seat). It makes Major's triumph all the more remarkable, explaining also why his victory secured only a small parliamentary majority. Major was not as lucky as his predecessor.

The Conservative philosopher Michael Oakeshott favored continuity, disliked ideology, regarded politics as a secondary activity, and approved a harmonious sense of community. Those of us who rather agree with him inevitably found Margaret Thatcher a shock. To be fair, Thatcher— and a shock—was exactly what Britain needed at the time, and it is why my own view of her is on the whole positive. What would the Conservative creed of continuity and consensus have meant in 1979? Through the 1970s, Britain had become virtually ungovernable. The trade unions made governments—and brought them down. Parties scrambled to deliver gifts to the unions that should never have been offered as tribute to the unions for commitments that they never intended to keep. The country needed a good shaking. Being a very small "*c*" conservative society, it probably also required a leader prepared to go way out in front of what had previously been deemed the consensus, and shout very loudly. At first, Britons took a few hesitant steps in Thatcher's direction. She got a serious hearing from many of the influential and intelligent liberal commentators of the day. Peter Jenkins had mapped Britain's decline, and found that what had been relative could easily become absolute unless we made fundamental changes; Hugo Young disapproved mightily of Thatcher's shrill nationalism but gave her the credit of being serious and principled. So she generally was. While her government's initial policies arguably squeezed the overall economy and even some competitive industries too hard (the concurrent tripling of world oil prices seemed to be willfully disregarded), a combination of tax cuts, public spending restraint, privatization of state-owned industries, union reform, and deregulation of markets turned the economy around. There was no economic miracle. Yet the foundations were laid for an improved economic performance and for some advance in competitiveness, though productivity still fell short of our neighbors'.

Much more important, Britain had a government that could govern again, and could invigorate our sense of sovereignty. We took the moment to rescue from the broom cupboard all sorts of ideas about markets, taxes, incentives, and competition. While Tony Blair was still a young Labour candidate, hugging to his bosom Clause 4 of the Labour Party's constitution (a clause that committed it to nationalization) and wearing a "Campaign for Nuclear Disarmament" badge on his lapel, Thatcher was making his eventual ascendancy possible. Her Conservative principles blazed the trail for Blair's (mostly) skilled opportunism.

By and large Thatcher was surely—to use the terminology of W. C. Sellars and R. J. Yeatman in *1066 and All That*—"a good thing." I disagreed with her from time to time, publicly and privately. She got quite a lot wrong. She had no feel for institutional pluralism, took a sledgehammer to local government, and ignored the growing financial difficulties of our great universities. She could not see the point of the international outreach of the British Council and disliked the BBC, particularly its marvelous World Service, which attracted the wrath of some of her foreign friends, like Kenya's Daniel Arap Moi. She had no feel for Scotland, defining her sense of Britishness in terms so English as to infuriate electors north of the border, whose aspirations for a measure of self-government she spurned. She was equally truculent about the sensitivities of Irish nationalism, though in 1985 she did reluctantly sign the Hillsborough agreement, which pointed the way to an eventual political deal in Northern Ireland more than a decade later. Despite all this, I liked her personally and admired her politically, and took comfortably in my stride her occasional joshing about my "wetness," that is, my implacably moderate-conservative opinions. She was always much more agreeable than most of her unofficial right-wing court, which with only one or two exceptions acted as a sycophantic echo chamber for her more extreme views.

Before she assumed the premiership, the subject of Europe had not featured much in Thatcher's speeches. She attacked the referendum on Europe in her maiden parliamentary speech as party leader, spoke in support of a "yes" vote in the campaign for membership, and occasionally called for greater European political and security solidarity, not least in face of the continued belligerent existence of the Soviet empire. As prime minister, she hurled herself into the debate over Britain's budgetary rebate with undiplomatic passion and focused fury to the discomfort of colleagues and the disdain of other European leaders. She got most of what she wanted, which may or may not have been more than could have been achieved using more tact and guile. She got on surprisingly well with France's socialist president, François Mitterrand, and badly with Germany's Christian Democrat chancellor, Helmut Kohl. Other leaders came and went. She was not a federalist and wished to explore every argument for further integration before accepting it. But an increasing number of Europe's other leaders were only federalists or integrationalists on occasional Sundays, if at all; they went to church from time to time but few, as it were, believed in God. The bad luck all around was that her most nationalist sentiments came to the fore at the moment when the tide of integration washed further up the beach than ever before or since. Like King Canute, she scolded the waves, and her acolytes do to this day, even though they have long since ceased to advance.

The speech that Thatcher made in Bruges in September 1988 to an audience of stunned Europhiles is rightly seen as a watershed in the debate about British sovereignty and the European project. Incensed by the evidence that an activist European Commission president, and a socialist to boot, was determined to press for a "social Europe" alongside the "economic Europe" achieved through the single market, and concerned that others were moving with remarkable concord toward the creation of an economic and monetary union to underpin that single market, she determined to give the continentals an uncensored piece of her mind. It was the first time Thatcher criticized not the policies that came out of Brussels but the institutional structure that produced them. Her argument that Brussels was potentially hostile to U.K. interests destroyed at a stroke the traditional British relationship with Europe, which had essentially been a matter of tinkering toward the right coalition, behind the right agenda, to maximize the United Kingdom's influence. Suddenly, the Conservative Party was dominated by a nightmare vision of Europe—the imminent arrival of the superstate—that still prevails in the party today. National sovereignty was praised; socialism crushed underfoot. It was potent stuff, given more potency still by the aggressive media spinning afterward. The rapid obsolescence of Thatcher's main argument requires the quotation of the three passages that she herself singles out for particular mention in her memoirs, by which time (they were published in 1993) it should have been obvious even to its author how out of date this proposition was.

Thatcher began by reminding her audience that the European Community and its member states were not the only manifestation of Europe's identity. To the east, other proud nations were struggling for their independence. In the west of the continent, we had much to learn from their experience:

> It is ironic that just when those countries, such as the Soviet Union, which have tried to run everything from the centre, are learning that success depends on dispersing power and decisions away from the centre, some in the Community seem to want to move in the opposite

direction. We have not successfully rolled back the frontiers of the state in Britain only to see them reimposed at a European level, with a European superstate exercising a new dominance from Brussels. . . .

Willing and active cooperation between independent sovereign states is the best way to build a successful European Community. . . . Europe will be stronger precisely because it has France as France, Spain as Spain, Britain as Britain, each with its own customs, traditions and identity. It would be folly to try to fit them into some form of identikit European personality.

She began her closing peroration by declaring uncontroversially, "Let Europe be a family of nations, understanding each other better, appreciating each other more, doing more together, but relishing our national identity no less than our Common European endeavor."

Most of the countries that Thatcher praised and helped (I exclude Russia and several of the former members of the Soviet Union) have given their answer. In Warsaw, Prague, and Budapest, they praised her support for their struggle for national identity and national sovereignty. And what did they do as soon as they had acquired that sovereignty? They applied to become members of the European Union. Did they believe that they were giving up their identity as Poles, Hungarians, Czechs, Slovaks, Estonians, Latvians, Lithuanians, and Slovenes to be fitted into a European identikit? Do they believe that they have exchanged commissars in Moscow for commissars in Brussels? Yes, Europe is a family of nations, and our continent has more nation-states within its geographical borders than ever before; indeed, the nation-state remains the main focus of communal loyalty and affection among the citizens of Europe. Yet this family of nation-states has a common goal. Almost everyone is already a member of the European Union or wishes to join. The enlargement of the European Union in May 2004 was the most forceful rebuff to Thatcher's argument at Bruges, but also shows why, even with further enlargement of the Union on the horizon, the horrors predicted by Margaret Thatcher will not come. The new idea of Europe has allowed nation-states to pool and share their sovereignty in unique and unprecedented ways while retaining their national identities. They recognize that "closer political union," as Winston Churchill said to the

Congress of Europe in 1948, "involves some sacrifice or merger of national sovereignty." They believe that this sacrifice might be viewed, as he went on to say, as "the gradual assumption by all the nations concerned of that larger sovereignty which can alone protect their diverse and distinctive customs and characteristics of their national traditions."

The Bruges speech marked the beginning of the last act of the Thatcher era. It was followed by tumultuous arguments over whether Britain should join the European Exchange Rate Mechanism (ERM), a forerunner of the euro zone that most Conservatives had favored when it was first discussed in the mid-1980s. A year later came the rows over German reunification—a once sovereign nation bound together again. Then in 1990 came the agreement at the Rome summit on monetary union, derided by Thatcher as "being taken for a ride" to "cloud cuckoo land." There would never be a single currency. Her critics, however, could console themselves that just three weeks earlier Thatcher had finally agreed—too late and at a worryingly uncompetitive exchange rate—to Britain's entry into the ERM. But disaster struck. After the Rome summit, Thatcher reported to the House of Commons with a denunciation of Europe and all its works and pomps. An election challenge followed; Thatcher failed conclusively to beat back her competitor, Michael Heseltine, for the premiership in the first ballot and the trapdoor opened. (For the record, I voted for her on the first round.) When the cabinet was summoned one by one to advise her after this setback, I told her that her position was unsustainable, that even if she were to squeak home in the next ballot (which was by no means certain), the result would be a humiliation, and that she should resign with dignity.

Not only was Thatcher's elevation of national sovereignty and the vilification of sovereignty sharing curiously ill-timed given what was happening elsewhere in Europe, but it also seems in retrospect particularly paradoxical given what we know has happened across the globe in the years since. When Frederick the Great of Prussia saw the portrait of a man for whom he had very little time hanging on a wall, he is said to have declared, *"Niedriger hängen"* ("Hang it lower"). That would appear good advice to Conservatives—and others—who were and are considering national sovereignty in a period when interdependence seems more obligatory than ever. The 1990s saw an upsurge in the manifestations and consequences of what we call globalization—an even bigger opening up of markets than occurred in the century before, with the results augmented and expedited by technology. In the last two decades of the twentieth century, turnover on the world's foreign exchange markets rose fifty-fold. In the last fifteen years of the century, foreign direct investment increased sixteen-fold. In their book, *Future Perfect*, John Micklethwaite and Adrian Wooldridge note that "by 1998, the world boasted 60,000 transnational companies with 500,000 affiliates, compared with 37,000 transnationals and 170,000 affiliates in 1990." Money, goods, tourists, and technology flatten borders. I will return later to this point; it is enough here to note that prosperity and security—the things people care about most—can only be secured though international cooperation. Even an island nation-state like Britain finds that its borders are porous when it comes to combating drugs, crime, environmental threats, illegal migration, epidemic disease, and, painfully, terrorism. That is why interdependence through sovereignty sharing makes sense, and it is why leaders in Asia, Latin America, and Africa have taken careful note of the sorts of cooperation we have pioneered in Europe and are starting to copy them. Whatever else you say about the nation-state—and I concede its preponderant ability to attract loyalty and affection—it is difficult to conclude that its inviolate virtues constitute the basis of sensible domestic or international policies at the beginning of the twenty-first century.

Why did these arguments cut so little ice with British Conservatives over the last dozen or so years? Why did the Conservative Party sign up to a view of Europe that contradicted its history and desolated its future? Why did Conservatives deny the logical outcome of the policies embraced under Thatcher: the erosion of state sovereignty and the building of a borderless world through free trade, open economies, and competition? Why did they fear the consequences in Europe of their own economic liberalism? Why did Conservatives work so sedulously from 1992 to 1997 to make themselves unelectable, and then insist on playing the same lousy hand again and again? Why did Conservatives sitting in the opposition despair of the fact that Washington seemed on balance to favor Labour's pro-European sentiments and hunt for evidence that America deep down really disliked European integration? How could they become so unsophisticated in the field of foreign policy, where they had traditionally thought themselves supreme? To unravel these questions, we have to return to the defenestration of Margaret Thatcher, for it is that fact above all else that explains the dramatic disintegration of conservatism as a credible electoral force and the temporary end of Conservatives as thoughtful contributors to the European debate.

Margaret Thatcher's removal from the seat of prime minister by a portion of her own party in the House of Commons did not seem at the time quite such a calamitous act of regicide as it has subsequently appeared. Conservatives did not believe the party could win an election under Thatcher's stewardship and deemed her behavior increasingly and damagingly erratic. I do not myself believe we could have won another election under her. But should we have invited defeat, reckoning on an early rebound to office? As a member of Parliament, my seat was up too, of course, but since the previous election in 1987 I had felt certain that I was likely to be a "goner" the next time and had even turned down approaches to move to another, much safer seat, an act I regarded as distasteful carpet-bagging. So my personal prospects were inconsequential. The real issue was the future of the Conservative Party, and I did not see how anyone could happily build a strategy on the likelihood of electoral failure. It is never wise to be too smart in politics, and plotting a victory at the next election through a defeat in the current one is plain silly. In order to survive in office, the tribe thus turned on its leader.

But this was a leader with a difference. Thatcher had been the first leader from the right of the party for as long as anyone could remember. Moreover, a little like Ronald Reagan in America, she had given the Right the confidence to believe that their own prejudices and opinions ran with the grain of the nation's character and interests. Not for her the task of reining in their instincts; she loosened the reins and gave them their heads. Second, she had attracted a praetorian guard of fellow-thinking ideologues in the media, several of whom were converts from the Left and felt a loyalty to her but not to the Conservative Party itself. Third, she used a good deal of her political capital in the late 1980s, at Bruges and afterward, to drag the party into a more critical posture on

Europe. This issue helped to bring her down, but her fall left behind supporters for whom any mutiny over Europe was in effect a gesture of pious loyalty to her own blessed memory.

The election of John Major brought to Number 10 the candidate who was thought by many to come closest to wearing Thatcher's colors, but Major had never been a Thatcher acolyte. Presumably one thing that particularly pleased Thatcher about him was that he was not a smooth man; he was not the product of a public school, Oxbridge, or the elite Brooks's or White's clubs, and his opinions were therefore considered less suspicious and malleable to the potent mixture of privilege, guilt, and ambition—today a Thatcherite, tomorrow an apostate. I doubt whether she knew him very well. But what she did know was that he had done everything she had asked him to do very effectively, and so he was her choice. Moreover, from Thatcher's point of view, Major had the inestimable advantage that he was not one of her long-term critics.

But John Major was not Margaret Thatcher, either. Two in a row might have been terminally exhausting. Where she had driven the government over potholed roads and around hairpin bends at breakneck pace, he returned to a more traditional and measured style of government. Strangely, what had to some extent held together when driven at a lick started to fall to pieces as soon as the pace slowed. Major was prime minister for seven largely unhappy years that ended with terrible defeat despite a period (latterly) of pretty successful economic management. It is reasonable to ask how much he can be blamed for Conservative misfortunes.

John Major is a nice man, a point that is sometimes made as though it were a criticism. But just as do-gooding has always struck me as preferable to do-badding, so being nice is better than being nasty. To be absolutely accurate, Major is certainly one of the nicest men I have ever met and arguably the nicest prime minister in my political life. What do I mean by nice? He is honest, generous, kindhearted, and inclined to think too well of others. Machiavelli would disapprove, but I quite like political leaders to be nice. Major is also a clever man, much cleverer than he thinks, much cleverer than others assume can possibly be the case for someone touched by so little formal education. When he was chief secretary of the treasury, other departmental ministers used to have to negotiate their annual budget settlements with him. It was always a pretty intimidating meeting, which tested among other things a minister's grasp of his own responsibilities. Major would always ask politely whether you would prefer to dispense with civil service advisers and negotiate with him face-to-face. Waiting for such a meeting, in an anteroom surrounded by photographs of all his predecessors, I asked a senior treasury mandarin, "Who has been the best of them?" "That one," he said, gesturing at Major's door. The lack of much by way of secondary education, and nothing by way of university education, had not made Major less intelligent, only less confident about his intellectual authority and social skills. He was sensitive about patronizing criticism, and sufficiently self-knowing to understand that he should not be. A thicker skin, a bit more ruthlessness, and the willingness to trade on the tough background from which he had shot to political stardom would together have made him a happier man and probably a more successful prime minister. But I would not have liked him so much.

Major loved the Conservative Party, or at least his rather romantic idea of the party. It had been a home for him as well as a ladder, a ladder that had taken him from Brixton, garden gnomes, and clerical jobs to Downing Street, the youngest prime minister since the liberal Lord Rosebery in the nineteenth century. He believed it was imperative to hold the Conservative Party together; to avoid divisions and splits; to achieve success through unity—where Thatcher's first challenger and Major's rival, Michael Heseltine, had been said by his supporters to offer unity through success. The trouble was not that Major tried to hold the party together, but that it did not want to be held together, and fate dealt him an election result in 1992 that gave mutineers and troublemakers the Westminster arithmetic most favorable to their mischief.

It was, of course, Major who managed the Maastricht negotiations with great skill. Those were still the days when he rather enjoyed meetings in Europe. They were a showcase for his skills—greater mastery of detail than others in the room possessed, courteous but firm argument, a perhaps excessive belief in his ability to read body language, a clear sense of what he wanted and what he could get. But an objective secured at Maastricht would haunt him. He masterfully negotiated an opt-out for Britain from the so-called social chapter concerning employment and welfare rights, on the insistence of Michael Howard, then his labor secretary, and others that it would be a ball and chain around the ankle of competitive British industry. The argument was probably exaggerated; having opted back in to the chapter in 1997, it seems clear that British economic progress was not hindered in any significant way (though we occasionally had to fight, as over the Working Time Directive, to retain a sensible measure of flexibility in our labor market arrangements). The social chapter, however, was anathema to the Euroskeptics in the Conservative right, and to more mainstream Conservatives, too, and it had to be thrown overboard. Major followed them.

During the 1992 election campaign, Europe (to quote from the regular Nuffield election study) "which a few months earlier, in the days of Mrs. Thatcher and of Maastricht, had seemed so important, attracted little notice. Once it was over, nothing attracted more." With a slim majority of twenty-one, Conservative anti-Europeans, deploying all the sovereignist arguments of the superstate and the loss of Britain's birthright, could achieve real and damaging leverage, and they did so straightaway against the bill to ratify Maastricht. When I was party chairman, we had thought that we could perhaps push the legislation through Parliament before the spring general election. But Major and I concluded that the attempt might constrain our election timing options. When the bill was put to the House of Commons in the summer, opponents seized on the fact that the Danish had voted down the treaty in their own referendum and insisted that Parliament's scrutiny be delayed. Fatally they were heeded, and by the time debate resumed, Britain had been ejected from the Exchange Rate Mechanism, a humiliating setback. In retrospect it is easy to see what had gone wrong with the ERM. We went too late into the system, which set the trading level of British sterling within prescribed limits against other European currencies; we entered at an uncompetitive rate; that rate became ever more uncompetitive as the costs of German reunification were borne by everyone in the system; and any possibility of realignment was halted by clumsy financial diplomacy on the British side and insensitive intransigence on the German. Shortly afterward, the Germans bailed out the French, who were themselves in difficulty, though they had failed to do the same for the United Kingdom. The government's reputation for competent economic management was swept away. The most valuable asset any government holds is the benefit of the doubt. With the ERM debacle, the Major government lost that benefit—over the economy, Europe, and most other issues—and its subsequent splits and rows ensured that it never recovered this vital ingredient of success.

The chaotic financial crisis of the resulting "Black Wednesday" emboldened the anti-Europeans, who made hay as the Maastricht legislation stumbled from one parliamentary crisis to another. In the early 1970s, Edward Heath had been able to call on bipartisan support to move the legislation on the terms of our accession agreement through Parliament. Roy Jenkins had led a group of pro-European Labour members into the government lobbies whenever it was crucial to do so. No such support came from Labour's pro-Europeans this time. Taking as a reason or a pretext for the opt-out from the social chapter, Labour instead worked to maximize the government's embarrassment. Conservative rebels plotted with Labour whips to damage the government at every opportunity. With the bill eventually concluded, there was no collective sigh of relief or a determination to return to normal. With the Conservative government in retreat, the Tory rebels (including the brief and very unsuccessful party leader, Iain Duncan Smith) hounded ministers to move Britain in an ever more Euroskeptic direction. The descent into shambles continued through to the election and the party's overwhelming defeat. The ERM disaster made it look as though the anti-European argument might be correct across the board.

Dissent was driven by the mad, the bad, and those beyond ambition. There were the longtime anti-Europeans. There was a group of new young members—the so-called Thatcher's children—who were regularly encouraged in private by their political matron to demonstrate their principles by voting against the Major government. There were those who had failed as ministers and discovered their own consciences in dismissal from office, and there were those who grew disillusioned because they felt they had gained no advancement after thirteen years in office. Any party after a long period in office builds up such a residue of the disenchanted. It is not easy to manage. Major was always preoccupied with the risk of splitting the party like Peel. He did not want to be remembered for bringing down his own government.

The trouble is that once you start bargaining with extremists, once you start accommodating and playing for time, the slope opens up steeply in front of you. Major promoted his opponents, "the bastards" as he accurately called them; they behaved like even bigger bastards, leaking and plotting against him. He tossed out concessions on policy, until Britain's posture on Europe turned into an ineffective and even embarrassing parody of Thatcherism. We blocked the nomination of the Belgian prime minister, Jean Luc Dehaene, as president of the European Commission, and got instead a Luxembourger who was less able and arguably more federalist than the wily Belgian. We tied ourselves in knots over voting rights and enlargement. We courted humiliation over mad cows and British beef—provided it did not kill you—the tabloid papers' hero of the hour in the land of the chicken tikka. The Conservatives even conceded a referendum on the euro, with no discernible impact in stemming the tide of voter desertion. And then we had the gall to send the foreign secretary, Malcolm Rifkind—a smart and wonderfully articulate Scot—around Europe to lecture our fellow member states on the sort of Europe they really wanted if only they woke up and realized it, though Conservative Euroskeptics and anti-Europeans had (and have) no idea what to offer in place of the arrangements against which they railed, except the argument that the British really know what is best for the rest of Europe.

Do the most outspoken Conservative Euroskeptics really want Britain to stay in the European Union at all? Some say they want no more than a free trade area. But, as I have discussed, we have tried that and found it wanting. And why should the United Kingdom be able to achieve a negotiated disengagement from Europe tailor-made for all our priorities and presumably downgrading everyone else's? Some advocate that we should join Norway, Iceland, and Lichtenstein in the European Economic Area, or follow the lead of Switzerland, which has negotiated its own bilateral commercial arrangements with the European Union. They argue that we should preserve the most insular version of our sovereignty and give up any chance of leading Europe, by opting for life as a sort of Switzerland—with the bomb.

In my job as a European commissioner I was responsible for relations with Norway, Switzerland, and the rest. My conclusion was clear. They enjoyed all the enhanced sovereignty that comes with staying at home while the decisions that intimately affected their own economic life were made by their neighbors in Brussels. The European Union put a diplomatic gloss on it, of course, but to enjoy the EU market, they had to follow our rules: rules they did not make or share in making. Norway, for example, must follow all the single market rules in order to export to the Union, and makes as great a budgetary contribution to Brussels as EU member Denmark, without receiving any financial support in return. When we enlarged the European Union, these outer-ring countries had to pay into the funds that we make available to help the poorer new members. I remember a Swiss negotiator telephoning me to plead that this subscription should be presented as a voluntary donation for development in the deprived parts of Europe, not an additional fee for access to the larger market. I was happy to oblige. But we both knew what the truth was. De facto sovereignty or de jure?

There are also some Conservatives who want Britain out of Europe altogether. Their position is no different from that of the United Kingdom Independence Party. Some of them drifted in and out of Jimmy Goldsmith's populist Referendum Party, and they dwell permanently in the xenophobic twilight, hating Europe and not much liking the United States, either. Unfortunately, it looks as though they will continue to obstruct the efforts to drag the Conservative Party back into a more sensible and comprehensible European posture.

For the time being, these Conservatives can hawk their attachment to national sovereignty, a vociferous commitment to the continuation of a millennium of glorious independence and a hostility to the ambitions of the nightmarish superstate. Theirs is a program whose main achievement has been to exclude from all hope of the party leadership, the one man—former treasury secretary and Europhile Kenneth Clarke—most able to exercise it in a way likely to restore the party's fortunes. Others with similar views to his are driven to the outer fringes of conservatism, to watch with dismay the continued infatuation of the party they love with a ruinous fantasy. Such a pity, not to understand the new plot.

5

POODLE OR PARTNER?

Entreat me not to leave thee, or to return
from following after thee;
for whither thou goest, I will go;
and where thou lodgest, I will lodge.

—The Old Testament, Ruth 1:16

The most famous speech about postwar British foreign policy was made by an American, Dean Acheson, the former U.S. secretary of state and one of the founding fathers of the world order shaped under President Harry S. Truman's leadership. Acheson was, in the words of the British ambassador at the time, David Ormsby-Gore, an "old and true friend of the United Kingdom." He was also a strong supporter of European political and economic integration, believing with most of the other paladins of Washington's foreign policy establishment that America needed a genuine partnership of equals with a resurgent Western Europe. Acheson's speech in December 1962 to the West Point Military Academy raised questions about Britain's international role that remain unanswered to this day.

"Great Britain," Acheson noted, "has lost an empire and not yet found a role. The attempt to play a separate power role—that is, a role apart from Europe, a role based on a 'special relationship' with the United States, a role based on being the head of a 'commonwealth' which has no political structure, or unity, or strength and enjoys a fragile and precarious economic relationship by means of the sterling area and preferences in the British market—this role is about played out." The truth, hot and strong, is rarely well received in diplomacy, though in my view one should not conclude from this that the word *diplomacy* is generally a synonym for casuistry and polite obfuscation. Certainly on this occasion, umbrage was taken in large British spoonfuls; the nation's dignity had been outraged. The British prime minister, Harold Macmillan, replied in terms with which Margaret Thatcher would have sympathized. "Insofar as he appeared to denigrate the resolution and will of Britain and the British people, Mr. Acheson has fallen into an error which has been made by quite a lot of people in the course of the last four hundred years, including Philip of Spain, Louis the Fourteenth, Napoleon, the Kaiser, and Hitler." Macmillan went on to criticize Acheson for failing to understand the powerful role of the newly reorganized commonwealth in world affairs.

Within weeks, two decisions were taken that demonstrated both the limits and the potential of the special relationship, as well as the effect of that perceived relationship on others. Britain was still struggling to remain a military nuclear power of sorts. The original choice of the next generation of weaponry, the British Blue Streak, had already been scrapped in favor of a cheaper joint venture with the Americans, Sky Bolt. Now the Americans decided to cancel Sky Bolt and Britain was left begging for permission to purchase the American Polaris at a knocked-down price. Reluctantly, the Americans agreed, largely it seemed because President John F. Kennedy wanted to help Macmillan out of a hole; his Conservative government had nuclear ambitions but no adequate weapon and growing hostility to trying to purchase one. So Britain stayed in the nuclear club, with a deterrent that was anything but independent, and enraged General Charles de Gaulle, who felt confirmed in his instinctive suspicion that Britain was tied to Washington's apron strings. The episode helped to provoke his infamous "non" to the British bid for membership in the European Common Market. America had helped to abort what it wanted—an unequivocal British commitment to European integration—by allowing what it did not greatly favor—the prolongation of Britain's nuclear role. It stands as one of the few examples of the special relationship being allowed to affect America's judgment about its own national interest.

Like much else in Britain's twentieth-century story, the special relationship was largely the creation of Winston Churchill, whose mother of course was American. It became a mantra for successive British governments that American presidents are occasionally prevailed upon to mention with appropriate reverence. For Churchill, it incorporated both the sentimental ties that bound together Britain and its most famous former colony—ties forged out of shared enlightenment values and the bonding of "kith and kin"; tested in battle; and expressed in a common language—and a guileful geostrategic ambition. Initially, Churchill hoped that a close partnership with America would help Britain to hang on to some of its empire, or at least its status as a world power. In the former case, his hopes were rapidly dashed; in the latter, Britain managed most of the time to get its bottom onto a seat at the top table where big strategic issues were being discussed.

At its most wholesome, British enthusiasm for the American connection reflected admiration for American vigor and optimism. Churchill himself gave voice to this when, in a 1941 radio broadcast, he quoted Arthur Hugh Clough's famous lines:

> For while the tired waves, vainly breaking,
> Seem here no painful inch to gain,
> For back, through creeks and inlets making,
> Comes silent, flooding in, the main,
> And not by eastern windows only,
> When daylight comes, comes in the light,
> In front, the sun climbs slow, how slowly,
> But westward, look, the land is bright.

"Bright," perhaps, but not always very knowledgeable about the "old" country. I recall almost twenty years ago the poll taken at Pennsylvania State University, shortly before the actor Roy Dotrice performed his one-man show about Winston Churchill there, which showed that only one-third of the students had ever heard of the great man. What would the figures be today?

At its worst, British mush about America has contained a large helping of condescension. During the Bretton Woods negotiations in 1944, when America was firmly putting Britain in its place in the postwar economic world, British negotiators comforted themselves with the lines:

> In Washington Lord Halifax,
> Once whispered to Lord Keynes:
> "It's true *they* have the money bags,
> But *we* have all the brains."

Speaking to the Labour politician Richard Crossman in 1944 about America's leadership of the Allies, Harold Macmillan observed, "We, my dear Crossman, are Greeks in this American empire. You will find the Americans much as the Greeks found the Romans—great big, vulgar, bustling people, more vigorous than we are and also more idle, with more unspoiled virtues but also more corrupt. We must run [the Allied forces headquarters] as the Greek slaves ran the operations of the Emperor Claudius." The analogy of a once powerful empire, fallen on hard times, now playing the role of wise if world-weary friend and mentor to its youthful, unsophisticated successor has been a constant theme in Britain's transatlantic relationship since the 1940s, and we can still hear echoes of it today, albeit without Macmillan's mastery of the classical comparisons.

It says much for Britain's American friends that they have by and large put up with this sort of maudlin and supercilious nonsense. At least French arrogance comes unvarnished, without the hand-wringing servility of an Edwardian retainer. David Cannadine has pointed out in his book, *In Churchill's Shadow*, that Ian Fleming's James Bond has an eerily similar relationship with the CIA's Felix Leiter. While Bond is notionally subservient to America's secret service, he is the agent who inflicts the real damage on the enemies of Western democracy. It is, as Bond explains to Leiter in *Thunderball*, the United Kingdom that is most prominent in the front line defending the West. "Perhaps it's just that in England we don't feel quite as secure as you do in America. The war just doesn't seem to have ended for us. Berlin, Cyprus, Kenya, Suez. . . . There always seems to be something building up somewhere." Americans occasionally play up to the corniness themselves. "The Special Relationship," wrote the American intellectual and former government official Eugene Rostow, "is not a policy but a fact—a fact of history which reflects not only a shared devotion to Shakespeare and Jane Austen but the congruent interests of Great Britain and the United States in world politics." Is this how the average American would see things?

It is nice to think of American and British citizens joined culturally at the hip. Where this is so, literature is less likely to be the agent of adhesion than film, popular music, or fashion. And "national interest" is usually of more importance to Americans than anything else. As the former American ambassador in London Ray Seitz has argued in his memoir, *Over Here*, relations between states are not often advanced by sentimentality. "Nations pursue their interests, and important interests tend to remain stable," he writes. "This is how nations behave."

During these years of the special relationship, a brass plate that Ambassador Seitz declined to polish, America has rightly and invariably pursued its own national interest, and Britain has invariably, and not always rightly, assumed that its own national interest was to line up dutifully behind America. This is called being an "Atlanticist" and a "believer" in the transatlantic relationship. The idea that occasional disagreement might make that relationship stronger does not appear to be worth serious consideration. Defining *Atlanticism* entirely in terms of unqualified support for whatever America says at one time or another is in its national interest is to twist the concept into a shape that leaves no place for partnership. Good friends should give each other the benefit of the doubt; they should eschew rivalry, but one should not demand or expect subordination from the other.

America fought beside Britain in two world wars, understandably coming late to the slaughterhouse each time but hugely welcome and essential as an ally in the struggle to overcome the worst effects of European nationalism. It took the Japanese attack on Pearl Harbor and Hitler's declaration of war on America to bring it into the second war. Polls showed that as late as October 1941, only 17 percent of Americans favored fighting Germany. Americans, including their president, feared that Britain would use its most powerful ally to help it hang on to its empire. The editors of *Life* magazine wrote an open letter "to the people of England" in October 1942 in which they said, "One thing we are sure we are not fighting for is to hold the British Empire together. We don't like to put the matter so bluntly, but we don't want you to have any illusions." Mohandas Gandhi had told Franklin Roosevelt in 1942 that "if India becomes free, the rest will follow," and the president had no interest whatsoever in helping Britain and the other colonial powers to retain "the archaic, medieval Empire idea." Scolding Churchill for the suspicions he harbored about Stalin, Roosevelt said, "You have four hundred years of acquisitive instinct in your blood and you just don't understand how a country might not want to acquire land somewhere if they can get it." Roosevelt even tried to get the British to give up Hong Kong to the Chinese as a gesture of goodwill at the end of the war. The Americans did not hit the bull's-eye in that case, but elsewhere they were more successful in helping to speed the exit from empire by the colonial powers, while not always liking (as in Indochina) the consequences.

Before the war's end, the future institutions of global governance had been planned—the United Nations at the San Francisco conference and the International Monetary Fund and the World Bank at the meetings in Bretton Woods, New Hampshire. Anyone who thinks that sentimentality gets a look-in when America is negotiating about money and commerce should read Robert Skidelsky's biography of John Maynard Keynes, the head of the British delegation at the economic conference. "The Agreement was shaped," Skidelsky notes, "not by Keynes' 'General Theory,' but by the U.S. desire for an updated gold standard as a means of liberalizing trade. If there was an underlying ideology, it was [the American treasury secretary] Morgenthau's determination to concentrate financial power in Washington." Skidelsky goes on to quote the assessment of the newspaper *The Commercial and Financial Chronicle*, which reported that "the delegates did not reach an 'agreement.' They merely signed a piece of paper which looked like an agreement." One Bank of England official called Bretton Woods "a swindle"; another said it was "the greatest blow to Britain next to the war." It certainly ended London's days as *the* financial center of the world. The empire went, and our position as the premier financial player went as well (although several decades later, London has established itself again as one of the most important financial marketplaces).

Britain and America worked hand in hand in the construction of the postwar world order. For America, part of the new order was a politically and economically integrated Western Europe. There was a recognition, in the words of a State Department report in 1943, that "like the little girl in the nursery rhyme, a European Union, from the point of view of our long-run economic interests, can either be very, very good, or horrid." But by the Truman presidency, officials had come down heavily on the side of the benefits of European integration. Both President Dwight D. Eisenhower and President Kennedy called explicitly for a partnership of equals, with Eisenhower himself anticipating gains for peace from a "third-force Europe" that he hoped would establish "an industrial complex comparable to the United States, having, in fact, more skilled laborers than the U.S." Pascaline Winand, in her study *Eisenhower, Kennedy and the United States of Europe*, describes a two-part American program:

> First, European energies should be concentrated on building a European political community solidly rooted in economic integration. This would give Europe greater influence in world councils and reduce the attraction of nationalism. Western Europe would therefore become the economic and political equal of the United States. Second, the potential of the European co-equal should be harnessed to that of the United States for two common enterprises—world economic development and military defense.

There was never any doubt in American minds that Britain should be a wholehearted member of this enterprise, committed to its political purposes and not hedging every pro-European gesture with qualifications and caveats. When, for example, Britain refused to participate in the discussions about the establishment of the Coal and Steel Community, there was much grumbling in Congress, with some members seeking to cut off Marshall aid to Britain if it persisted in opposing membership.

American enthusiasm for British cooperation in Europe rested on a number of considerations. First, there was no sympathy for Britain's delusion that it could retain the stature of a great power based on a few shards of empire and the creation of the commonwealth, even as Harold

Macmillan, the most Europhile cabinet minister in the early 1950s, was declaring unequivocally, "the Empire must always have first preference. Europe must come second." But for Britain, what was involved was both mission and status. As Anthony Eden explained, "These are our family ties. That is our life; without it we should be no more than some millions of people, living on an island off the coast of Europe, in which nobody wants to take any particular interest." Yet the empire was melting away, and the family ties were growing weaker. While the appeals for commonwealth solidarity as a reason to resist European integration still had some resonance in the 1960s, Americans surely perceived more swiftly than Britain's own leaders that the days of British empire were over—and brought to a reasonably successful conclusion by the old imperial power— and that the commonwealth added little political weight to Britain's status. British governments were never able to transfer the public enthusiasm that had been generated by the empire to the commonwealth, and the curtailment of immigration from the Caribbean and South Asia made nonsense of efforts to suggest that the commonwealth bestowed a common citizenship and common rights on those who had once dwelled under the Union flag. Even in the 1990s, many Conservatives and much of the British media resisted any idea that we should be moderately generous in the award of citizenship to some of those who had lived in Hong Kong (often directly serving the colonial power), and deserved a guarantee that, if necessary, they could look to Britain for a home after 1997. *Civis Romanus sum* was not to be translated into a modern British obligation. In contrast, Australia and Canada, both of course commonwealth countries, were much more generous in granting citizenship to Hong Kong residents. They were a lot more maternal than the so-called mother country, and have benefited greatly from the migrants that Britain turned away.

Second, Americans undoubtedly felt that Britain would provide the European integration process with the benefits of its experiences and good sense—better to have Britain helping to steer in the front seat, rather than simply offering advice and criticism from the back. This sentiment could easily shade into seeing Britain as a potential American Trojan horse in Europe, able to ensure that Western Europe did not embrace policies inimical to American interests; de Gaulle especially feared that Britain would get its marching orders from Washington and see every European issue from the American viewpoint. It is not an entirely fair assessment of America's intentions, but there is a bit of truth in it—and even as a suspicion rather than an accurate assessment of diplomatic tactics, it can have a potentially toxic effect on the United Kingdom's involvement in Europe.

Third, Americans believed that American trade would benefit if Britain joined the European Common Market. Britain's growth rate, which then lagged behind that of the six Common Market countries, would most likely be stimulated, increasing American opportunities for trade and investment.

The fact that America supported British membership in the European Community was one of the reasons why much of the British political establishment was so lukewarm about the idea. Clearly, it was felt, America wanted Britain placed firmly in the second division, a middle-ranking European country rather than a world-class player standing with the United States. This suspicion was strengthened by Britain's lamentable Suez expedition of 1956, one of several examples in the years since the 1938 meeting in Munich (Iraq was the most recent) of the alleged lessons of that humiliating negotiation being used to justify a disastrous foreign policy initiative. But Munich did not prove that negotiation with a bully is always wrong and always a sign of weakness. In the view of Harold Macmillan, at that time the Chancellor of the Exchequer, the Egyptian leader, Colonel Gamal Abdel Nasser, was "an Asiatic Mussolini," and Britain and France must cut him down to size before he destabilized the entire Middle East. The Americans, it was reckoned in London, would look the other way, allowing Britain and France to go on acting like imperial powers. "I know Ike," said Macmillan, "he'll lie doggo." The miscalculation could not have been greater. The Americans were horrified, not least by the impact of the invasion in radicalizing opinion in the Arab world and increasing hostility to the West. At the United Nations, the United States demanded British and French withdrawal, and threatened to kick away the props under the British economy and the pound unless Britain complied. There was no choice: the economy was too weak for Britain to defy America, and the sterling area—a last vestige of world power—had to be preserved. Britain backed off, reminded with bruising force of its real status in the world.

While the British government moved quickly to try to repair the special relationship, there is no doubt that it took a heavy hit as a result of the Suez fiasco. Noel Coward spoke for many in Britain when he argued that the Americans had "behaved vilely." There had, of course, always been an undertow of anti-Americanism in wartime and postwar Britain, directed initially against those GIs who were "overpaid, oversexed and" (thank heavens) "over here." Anti-Americanism was to be found on the right, for instance in the novels of Evelyn Waugh, and on the left, in the work of Graham Greene. American "betrayal" at Suez stoked it up; some shopkeepers put up signs, "No Americans served here." Macmillan worried that it would increase an isolationalist mood in Britain, which was already directed against Europe, whose postwar success was regarded by some with dismay. Some of the anti-Americanism was cultural. There was a worry that the United Kingdom was being swamped by American values, exemplified above all by Hollywood's domination of the cinema. We tried to protect our own filmmakers with subsidies, quotas, and levies, but despite the efforts of the Ealing film studios, the Californian tide of glamour, sex, and violence continued to wash over us. Concerns about the Americanization of the British way of life were at the heart of the debate in the 1950s about the introduction of commercial television.

By the late 1960s anti-Americanism was more associated with the political Left than the Right. Vietnam was the cause, with the young in particular identifying with the poor Asian peasants who withstood whatever tonnage of munitions American B-52s dropped on them. Around the world, America's enemies attained heroic status on the left. This produced some stomach-turning results, such as the lionizing of Cuba's wretched dictator, Fidel Castro. What began in Vietnam and Cambodia was continued in Chile and Central America. The Sandinista Left became a significant element in British municipal socialism. A Prince Valiant of this movement was David Blunkett, later to become the hammer of civil libertarians in Tony Blair's Labour government. Interviewed in 1983 about the tradition of raising the American flag on July Fourth over the city hall in Sheffield, where he presided over a council of comrades, he responded, "Independence Day. It would be nice if we were independent of the United States, wouldn't it?" I should note that Blunkett deserves some sort of recognition for having made the journey from populist left to authoritarian right without being touched by even the shadows of the European liberal tradition.

But despite it all, the special relationship lived on. It survived the British withdrawal from east of Suez in 1967, the biggest military recognition yet of our reduced circumstances. It was battered by Labour Prime Minister Harold Wilson's sensible refusal to commit British troops to the American side in the Vietnam War, and by American snubbing of his piddling efforts to mediate between them and the North Vietnamese. It leapfrogged the Edward Heath years of 1970–74, when that short-lived and ill-starred prime minister declined to reach for the old familiar comfort blanket and made it clear that he was a European prime minister above all, not an American surrogate. But then it came roaring back to life again during the Thatcher years when, despite rows over the American invasion of Grenada, public hostility to the bombing of Libya, American pressure to curtail European dependence on Soviet energy supplies, and concerns in London about President Reagan's flirtation with Mikhail Gorbachev over nuclear disarmament, the relationship was sprinkled with stardust and put to music. Ronald Reagan and Margaret Thatcher got on conspicuously well. On a photograph of Thatcher speaking at a dinner in his honor at 10 Downing Street in 1988, Reagan wrote, describing the look of bewitched admiration on his own face, "as you can see, I agree with every word you were saying. I always do." Ideological soul mates, the president and the prime minister sensed that together they were cresting a wave of anti-Communism and free-market economics. Perhaps their joint resolve to stand up to Soviet pressure and to assert the moral superiority of the Western cause, coupled with their recognition that Gorbachev was a different sort of Soviet leader, helped to quicken the collapse of Russia's Communist empire in Europe. Elsewhere the "special" fruits of the special relationship were difficult to spot, though at least the Americans—after considerable initial misgivings and hesitations—provided some intelligence and logistical support as Britain sought (rightly) to preserve the last remnants of empire in the South Atlantic from Argentinean rapacity.

Before the Iraq war, conventional wisdom had it that whatever was left of the special relationship had largely disappeared with the end of the Cold War and the fundamental shift that this engineered in America's geostrategic interests. Ray Seitz saw the successful coalition politics of the first Gulf War as "the last hurrah of the old regime." He regarded disagreements and misunderstandings about Bosnia in the subsequent years as a sign of changed times. Before turning to the most recent manifestation of Britain's understanding of its relationship with America, and America's views on what is required of its junior partner, it is worth reviewing how in practice each side has seen the relationship.

For America, it has been useful to have a dependable ally that never strays far from Washington's own strategic interests. Britain and others are allowed to depart from the script when issues such as trade, the environment, and economics are concerned. But anything touching on security brings with it a three-line whip. And on the whole, America has believed that its interests are best served with Britain inside Europe rather than outside. European integration matters more in Washington than British sensitivities about a loss of sovereignty. However, British membership in the European Union can complicate the relationship with Washington, often in ways that Washington finds difficult to understand since it still tends to confuse a union, in which sovereignty is shared at a deep and comprehensive level, with an alliance. But while membership can snarl up the relationship (for example, over trade issues), it is vital to it. British withdrawal from the European Union, even semidetachment, would greatly worry most of America's foreign policy establishment. America also feels that it is entitled to intervene in British politics on the Irish issue, and has been encouraged to do so, with the aim of both pushing forward the peace process and securing its outcome. (I wonder myself how much payback has been received from American investment in Gerry Adams and Sinn Fein. I suspect that Adams has got more out of Washington than London and Dublin have got out of him. Maybe I allow myself to be excessively influenced by a personal distaste for those who have fudged the distinction between politics, murder, and crime.)

What counts in the scales on the British side? We persuade ourselves that we can influence our most powerful ally in ways that are presumably beneficial to our national interest. Since the days when Churchill's efforts to broker agreements between the United States and the Soviet Union were brushed aside by Washington, the influence has been much exaggerated. Where substance is important to America, the most that Britain can usually do is to affect process. In return for the prospect of influence, Britain provides a sign to the world that America is not unilateralist. Britain is a multilateral emblem to pin in America's lapel. Perhaps our privileged status as friend of first resort underpins our positions in NATO and on the UN Security Council. We have access to intelligence, particularly through global eavesdropping, that would otherwise be denied us, and who knows what errands we perform to earn this status? This is as valuable as intelligence ever is, for, as the former cabinet secretary Lord Butler has said, intelligence is uniquely worthy of skepticism. We are also a nuclear power thanks to American largesse. In general, British officials usually find it easier to deal with their American cousins, though this is not always the case as any trade negotiator will attest. An exaggerated combination of the sentiments in this paragraph submerges two simple propositions. First, Britain will usually agree with the United States on security issues. Where we and our friends in Europe do not do so, it is sensible and in the interests of Britain, Europe, America (and usually the world) to work to try to reach agreement. But if Britain announces at the outset that it will stand beside America whatever it decides to do, Britain ceases to serve its own national interest and in the long run does few favors to America. Second, foreign policy should not be a brain-free zone. "Feel" is no substitute for cerebral activity; hearts and flowers should not take precedence over reason.

As we have seen, it has been a constant theme of American foreign policy for the past sixty years that Britain should be a part of the process of European integration. It has equally been a constant in British policy that we should be an influential player in both Brussels and Washington; it has even been argued that playing the European game hobbles Britain internationally and as an independent partner of America. We search desperately for an answer to Dean Acheson's question—an answer that avoids any clear choice. The dilemma is well illustrated in Richard Weight's superb history of postwar Britain, *Patriots*. Drawing on the work of film historian Nick Cull, Weight takes the classic British-made film *The Italian Job* as a metaphor for the British problem. In the film, a gang of typical British characters shows what chumps the continent's "bloody foreigners" are. The gang plans and carries out successfully a gold bullion robbery in Turin, masterminded by a patriotic convict played by Noel Coward (who, just six years before the film was made in 1969, had told the annual dinner of the Battle of Britain veterans, "England has become a third-rate power . . . we are vulgarized by American values"). Their intention is to use the bullion's theft to help tackle Britain's balance of payment crisis. The gang makes its escape from Turin in a fleet of Minis, the last mass-market favorites of the British car industry, soon to be as dead as Mr. Cleese's parrot (long before their recent resurrection). The robbers change from their cars to a bus that, racing through the Alps, takes a bend too fast and only just manages to stop with the front end on the road and the back, containing the stolen gold, hanging over a precipice. Every move toward the gold by the gangsters jeopardizes the delicate balance of the coach. As the credits roll, the gang leader, Michael Caine, says, "Er, hang on a minute, lads, I've got a great idea." The great idea for Britain has been . . . what? To go it alone? To seek a comfortable berth in Washington's back pocket? To throw in our lot with our European partners? Can we confound those who tiresomely insist, like the late Mr. Acheson, that we really have to choose, and show them how Britain can bridge the Atlantic, a solid and dependable link that can carry traffic in both directions?

It is a point that brings us rather obviously to Prime Minister Tony Blair, President George W. Bush, and Iraq. There is already a rich and angry literature on Prime Minister Blair and the calamitous military invasion of Iraq. It includes some first-class journalistic history and two official reports—an absurd contribution by a former senior judge, Lord Hutton, and a subtle critique of the way Blair conducts his government by the former cabinet secretary Lord Butler. I do not intend to add much to these pickings, least of all to try to establish—like the author of a country-house mystery—who did what to whom, where the bodies are buried, and whether there are any fingerprints on the weapon. My own starting point insofar as the United Kingdom, the United States, and the Iraq controversy are concerned is the closing chapter of the first Gulf War.

In the last days of February 1991, the fighting was rapidly coming to an end. Iraqi forces were streaming back from Kuwait City to Basra along what was called the Highway of Death. John Major had asked me, as party chairman, to have dinner with him at Downing Street to discuss political tactics for the coming months and whether we should listen to the advice to call an early election, taking advantage of his own political honeymoon (he had only been in office a few months) and of the successful prosecution of the war. To his credit, Major made it absolutely clear that he had no intention of playing politics with a military triumph that had been supported, in any event, by the main opposition parties. I agreed with him that it would be a tacky thing to do, and almost certainly bad politics as well. We were sitting after supper on our own in his drawing room, surrounded by cricketing memorabilia and copies of Trollope, when the telephone rang. It was the duty clerk from his office downstairs to say that President George H. W. Bush wanted to speak to him. The gist of the conversation was clear. On the advice of his military commanders, the president wanted to call off the fighting, which had spiraled into a one-sided slaughter. The president and prime minister went through all the main issues, with Major asking tough questions about the consequences of letting Saddam Hussein off the hook. They discussed the terms of the UN resolution that had launched the coalition, the prospect of the coalition fracturing, and the problems associated with pressing on to Baghdad. I recall the president's clinching argument—"If we chase Saddam all the way to Baghdad, we'll own the place"—which, it became clear, was the last thing he wanted to do.

Indeed, the older President Bush spelled this point out in *A World Transformed*, a book that he wrote with his former national security adviser, Brent Scowcroft, in 1998:

> Trying to eliminate Saddam . . . would have incurred incalculable human and political costs. . . . We would have been forced to occupy Baghdad and, in effect, rule Iraq. . . . There was no viable "exit strategy" we could see, violating another of our principles. Furthermore, we had been self-consciously trying to set a pattern for handling aggression in the post–Cold War world. Going in and occupying Iraq, thus unilaterally exceeding the United Nations' mandate, would have destroyed the precedent of international response to aggression that we hoped to establish.

Bush also saw the danger that the whole Arab world could be turned against America and that young American soldiers would be condemned "to fight in what would be an unwinnable urban guerrilla war." Writing in the journal *Foreign Affairs* in 1992, Colin Powell, from his vantage as chairman of the Joint Chiefs of Staff in the Gulf War, noted that occupying Baghdad would involve "an unpardonable expense in terms of money, lives lost, and ruined regional relationships." I may be unimaginative, but I have never moved much beyond these wise arguments.

Further, the collateral damage of the fixation on Iraq included the failure to finish the job that was begun in Afghanistan with the unseating of the Taliban regime there. In order to build a new nation in that desperately poor country, it was essential first to provide the security on which political authority and development depend. That has never been achieved. The military commitment was kept to a minimum throughout 2002, presumably so as not to impinge on the buildup for an invasion of Iraq. European countries, including the United Kingdom, found it all too comfortable to shelter behind America's security assessment and keep their own military deployments there, principally in the international security force, to a minimum. We all kidded ourselves that we had bought the warlords, whereas it swiftly became apparent that we had only rented them. Poppy growing and opium production mushroomed as the American and European troops were discouraged from interdicting the manufacture and trafficking of heroin. With up to 90 percent of the heroin on the streets of Europe's capitals originating in Afghanistan, we created a particularly malign version of the Common Agricultural Policy. Demand exploded and no serious effort was made to control supply. The warlords profited hugely from the proceeds of a trade that brought together, as in Colombia, terrorism, organized criminality, and the sapping of the state's authority. At the Tokyo donors' conference held after the fall of Kabul, I pledged on behalf of the European Commission a minimum contribution to Afghanistan's development of one billion euros over five years. (We have actually been spending more than this—not just committing the money, but, in a dangerous environment, contracting and spending it as well.) I stretched the elastic of my political authority about as far as it would go in making a pledge from the European community budget of this size, and had to withstand a good deal of tiresome criticism from the French delegation at the conference as a result. What became increasingly frustrating through 2002–04 was to see such development funds exceeded by the warlords' drugs income, and to watch as President Hamid Karzai's government stood paralyzed as the dangerous security situation inhibited its authority and the maximum use of development assistance. Indeed, there were times when it seemed that the government's authority did not run very far outside battered Kabul. A focused multilateral force could have started to build far more rapidly a modern nation in Afghanistan—poor but decent. America and Europe shall now have our work cut out to avoid the establishment of a narco-state, exporting terrorism as well as drugs.

The former British Conservative defense minister Sir John Stanley has observed that the Iraq invasion was the first time that a British government has gone to war "specifically on the strength of intelligence assessments." The dossier that collected those assessments together in September 2002 has turned out to be a turkey. As John Kampfner (*Blair's Wars*) has noted, none of the nine main conclusions in that report has been proven. Whether or not the prime minister connived at squeezing out of the intelligence services the answers he wanted, it is at the very least true that he overstated evidence which he himself described as "extensive, detailed, and authoritative," and which Lord Butler much more accurately assessed as "very thin." It also seems clear that Blair had concluded from the time that he met President Bush at Crawford, Texas, in the spring of 2002 that the Americans were not to be deflected from invading Iraq and that Britain could not leave them to act on their own. Britain went to war because America chose to go to war. Blair told his cabinet and Parliament, and perhaps convinced himself, that his reasons were other than this—to track down weapons of mass destruction, to prevent their proliferation or use, to strengthen the authority of the United Nations by insisting on compliance with Security Council resolutions, to get rid of a wicked tyrant and serial abuser on a massive scale of human rights. This is, I suspect, an example of what an unnamed American official called "rolling rationalization [that] is one of the less attractive features of British foreign policy." We are now led to believe that the prime minister had always been preoccupied by the dangers represented by Saddam Hussein, though his interest in Iraq (like that of many American officials) does not seem to go back to the days when Western countries were arming its dictator and looking the other way as he gassed, murdered, and tortured Iraqis. In those days, the infamous tyrant was on "our" side: silly, really, that he failed to understand how we play the game of an ethical foreign policy, or perhaps he understood it for most of his career all too well.

I have never myself had to make decisions directly that send young men and women to face danger and perhaps death, though I shared in the collective decisions the British cabinet took in 1990 to join the coalition in the Gulf War. I remember saying to John Major at the time that this sort of decision was particularly difficult for politicians of our generation—the first in Britain that had not had to fight in a war themselves. In that sense we are different from Americans of our age group, though a surprising number of those who are most enthusiastic these days about sending in the Blackhawks and Humvees had, in Vice President Dick Cheney's apposite phrase, "other priorities" than military service during the Vietnam War. Awareness of the gravity of the decisions taken about life, death, maiming, war—particularly, I repeat, by those who have never themselves had to go through the fire of armed conflict—makes me reluctant to assign base motives or assume a frivolous lack of moral anxiety on the part of those who reach different conclusions from my own about the necessity of going to war. So what is it about Prime Minister Blair, who is manifestly not a bad man, that enabled him to convince himself that what he was doing was right, and right for Britain, and indeed that his real motives were those that he expressed with such power and eloquence?

There is no dispute about Blair's political ability, on display to extraordinary effect during the week in July 2005 when he helped secure the Olympic Games for London in 2012, presided over the Gleneagles G8 summit, and dealt with the appalling terrorist bombings in London. But there is a debate about whether the prime minister has any convictions. His friend and rather generous mentor Roy Jenkins concluded that, if anything, he had too many and held them too strongly, especially when dealing with the world beyond Britain. "He is," Lord Jenkins noted, "too Manicheean for my perhaps now jaded taste, seeing matters in stark terms of good and evil, black and white, and with a consequent belief that if evil is cut down, good will inevitably follow." Jenkins concluded that the color gray seemed to be missing from Blair's political palette. On the other side, there are those who regard him as a meretricious chancer, supremely gifted at what the Americans call triangulation: touching all the political bases—yes, no, maybe—at the same time squaring circles, finding the color gray, and painting it in a brighter hue. Such critics are likely to judge the "third way," a nebulous all-things-to-all-men political style much associated with Blair and other successful politicians of the center-left, as, in Tony Judt's felicitous description, "opportunism with a human face." Blair regards his own early years as a Campaign for Nuclear Disarmament anti-European as part of a necessary phase on his way to becoming a senior Labour figure in a position to change his party into a more electable and sensible political vehicle. Most political sophisticates buy this—an example of acceptable careerism justified by such a satisfactory outcome. Perhaps I am too romantic about politics, but I find myself sucking my teeth a bit about it. I warm much more to careers that have a more principled core, though I hesitate to exaggerate the point lest I drift into sanctimoniousness.

My own view is that Tony Blair, a usually likable man, has convictions to which he holds strongly—while he holds them. His convictions change on issues as disparate as hunting, nuclear weapons, civil liberties, the constitution, the euro, and the reasons for going to war, partly to reflect what he believes to be prevailing, convenient opinion. I do not for a moment deny that from time to time Blair has had to show considerable courage in defending a policy he has decided to pursue. Iraq fell squarely into this category, though the prime minister and his advisers probably assumed with Bush and other American officials that an early victory would turn European and world opinion around and that the invasion would be seen as the liberation of a tyrannized people rather than the descent, in 2003–04, into a bloody quagmire. But whatever his changing positions, Blair and his supporters insist that his actions should be seen to have the seamless and principled continuity that you would expect of "a regular kind of guy." This is where he is at his most dangerous. There can be no questioning his integrity. His veracity, decency, and dedication to a higher good (not vulgar pragmatism) must be explicitly conceded.

The convictions that drive the Blair government do not always seem well considered. Let us take, for example, his Gladstonian instinct to root out wickedness and install good in its stead. I have considerable sympathy for the notion that foreign policy should not be devoid of ethical considerations, and reckon that there is frequently an overlap between expedience and morality. But I am unclear when exactly Prime Minister Blair came to this conviction and how much he has worked out some of its implications. When in 1997 Robin Cook, Blair's first foreign minister (who died in 2005), produced his mission statement for the Foreign Office arguing the case for an ethical foreign policy, I do not recall much echoing enthusiasm from 10 Downing Street. Cook, with all his fussiness about arms sales and with his manifest concern for Palestinian human rights, was clearly regarded as rather tiresome. You also have to be a little careful about just how strongly you associate what you are doing with a higher morality in foreign policy. America and Britain have had to assemble a pretty eclectic group of partners to prosecute the cause of democracy and good governance in Afghanistan and Iraq. An embarrassingly large number of them have dubious human rights records, not, admittedly, as bad as Saddam Hussein's, but certainly not up to the minimum standards that would come close to satisfying Amnesty International or Human Rights Watch. The mission, however virtuous, makes the coalition, but the coalition is not always very virtuous. I wonder, too, whether there is not an embarrassing disproportion between the Gladstonian rhetoric and the power that Britain can actually deploy today, a fraction of what was available to our Victorian forebears. Even Zimbabwe's Robert Mugabe, a tin-pot tyrant if ever there was one, can snap his fingers at Britain and tell us to go hang. Time was when he would have lasted as long as it took to send in the king's African Rifles.

Tony Blair also has an even stronger belief than most leaders in personal diplomacy and in his ability to shape other leaders' perceptions of their own national interest. I am very doubtful about this general approach, which too often sucks much of the intelligence and consistency out of the conduct of foreign policy, a point that I shall argue later in relation to our French and German colleagues in Europe. Before either of those countries had taken up with Russia, Blair was all over Vladimir Putin; Putin was offered "best friend" status, a central place in the fellowship of leaders that Blair hopes he can orchestrate to Britain's advantage. Gladstone or no Gladstone, Chechnya and the destruction of Grozny do not seem to have featured much in the early Blair-Putin conversations. What started so propitiously turned sour as Putin went his own way on Iraq, publicly humiliating Blair in Moscow, and joining Jacques Chirac and Gerhard Schröder (both of whom the prime minister seems to have misread) in opposing the Iraq war. Sir Christopher Meyer, Britain's ambassador to Washington during the buildup to the war, has added his own gloss to an analysis of Blair's personal diplomacy, arguing that the prime minister did not argue his case sufficiently strongly with President Bush and his entourage. I always doubted myself how much bad news Blair would be happy to impart to Bush and the American political establishment once he had been given a hero's reception in Congress.

Before turning to some of the substantive consequences of the policies followed, and of the reasons for them, I want to mention one further question of governing style. Before he became prime minister, Tony Blair had never been in government. This seems to have exacerbated his contempt for the existing institutions of government, the traditional approach to decision making, and relations between politicians and civil servants. Power was concentrated in his private office and entourage, who rampaged across the Whitehall bureaucracy. Part of the quite astonishing naïveté of the Hutton Report is the assumption that seems to underlie it that the evidence before the judge conveyed the workings of a normal government. It had certainly never been "normal" before for the head of communications in Downing Street to get involved in the presentation of intelligence. The concentration of power in No. 10 completed the destruction of the cabinet office as the official conductor and progress chaser of government, a process begun, alas, under Margaret Thatcher. This has reduced the competence of government in Britain, and been a main part of the dismantling of the barriers of discretion and seemliness between politicians and civil servants.

One of the government departments most affected by the accumulation of power in Downing Street has been the Foreign Office. The position of this department today recalls the letter written by its permanent secretary to Lord Salisbury (who was then foreign secretary but absent from the office) at a time when the prime minister, Arthur Balfour, was in temporary charge of it. "I am now," wrote Sir Thomas Sanderson, "a sort of standing dish at Arthur Balfour's breakfast. When his attention is divided, as it was this morning, between me and a fresh herring, there are alternately moments of distraction when he is concentrating on the herring, and moments of danger when he is concentrating on foreign affairs." The appointment of a senior foreign policy adviser to the prime minister is not new; what has been novel is the number of such advisers at the prime minister's right hand, regardless of their skill and decency, and their direct role in overseeing foreign policy on the key issues. For a prime minister with no previous experience in foreign policy, and with an excessive regard for his own "feel" for the subject, to take on so much himself is unwise and dangerous. Where is British policy on the Middle East made today—in No. 10 or the Foreign Office? Who handles the most sophisticated traffic between London and Washington? It also raises questions about the role of the foreign secretary. Is he to regard himself as the prime minister's senior adviser and policy implementer on the big issues of the day or should he occupy himself with those issues that do not hit the prime minister's radar screen? It cannot have been helpful in the buildup to the Iraq war and in its aftermath that the prime minister was divorced from the informed skepticism that the Foreign Office would have brought to a discussion of the available policy options. Certainly making policy over the heads of the State Department and the Foreign Office has not been conspicuously successful.

Blair's principal aims in foreign and security policy are admirable. He wants a strong alliance with the United States, the only superpower, which he hopes Britain can influence in the way that America exercises its global leadership. He wishes to see a strengthened United Nations, which can provide legitimacy for international intervention in the affairs of sovereign states to protect the human rights of their citizens and to deal with real threats to the security of our own. He would like Britain to take a leading role in the affairs of the European Union, and to lay to rest our ambivalence about EU membership. How has the Iraq war advanced these goals?

Blair committed Britain and British soldiers to the American side in Iraq because he believed that it would be perilous for us, indeed for all America's allies, to leave our friend to fight alone. He also felt that we would be able to influence America in Iraq and elsewhere if we were pre-pared to fight alongside. With Britain in the bag, America was able to build a "coalition of the willing" (or "billing," as one wag called it, point-ing to the favors promised to the ragbag of allies in the adventure). Without Britain could America have invaded? The answer is that it probably would have done so, but the enterprise would have been more politically hazardous and British hesitation might have encouraged doubts in the American establishment and in the United States more generally. Even if this is an absurd speculation, would Britain have damaged its own interests or America's by warning the Bush administration exactly what was likely to happen, repeating the warnings of the president's father and his father's senior advisers? Choking off our own grave doubts, the sort that Foreign Secretary Jack Straw evidently put to Prime Minister Blair at the eleventh hour, did Washington no favors. Moreover, did fighting alongside America deepen the sentimental attachment to the trans-atlantic relationship or weaken it? Is it really the role of a good friend to suppress anxieties rather than express them candidly? In my own politi-cal lifetime I have never known a situation where there has been so much criticism of the United States in Britain and so much resentment about the closeness of our relationship. Supporting the Bush invasion of Iraq is probably the worst service we have paid America, and may even make it more difficult politically for us in Britain to line up beside our old ally when there are bigger and better causes to pursue together in the future.

The British have honored the special relationship in part as a means of maintaining some outsized influence over the United States. What influence did Britain buy for itself by going along with this ill-judged adventure? From the Crawford meeting in the spring of 2002, Blair had given Bush and his senior advisers to understand that, whatever hap-pened, if there was fighting the United Kingdom would stand shoulder to shoulder with the United States. According to Peter Riddell (*Hug Them Close*), Lewis "Scooter" Libby, Vice President Cheney's chief of staff, asked a senior British official in the autumn why Blair was so worked up about the United Nations when he was "going to be with us anyway." What influence did the special relationship provide to Britain in determining the prosecution of the war, the governance of Iraq when the war formally ended, or even the decision to announce the "mission accomplished" when history and intelligence would show that the fatalities would only mount?

As a senior official of the European Union, I visited Baghdad in September 2003 to discuss the assistance Europe could provide for reconstruction of the country. After an exciting flight in to the city, with our RAF plane diving and weaving into its approach like a Welsh wing-three quarter dashing down the touch-line, and an equally thrilling helicopter ride to the safe-ish "green zone" via the bombed UN headquarters where my friend Sergio Vieira de Mello had died, we spent forty minutes with the cocky, clever, confident American Paul Bremer. He told us how much the security position was improving, a reassuring message that was somewhat undermined by the fact that we had been refused permission to stay overnight in Baghdad for reasons that owed nothing to the shortage or expense of hotel accommodation. We then walked twenty yards down a long corridor in what had once been one of Hussein's palaces to talk to Bremer's deputy, the former British ambassador to the United Nations, Sir Jeremy Greenstock. He was painstakingly loyal to the official line while delivering it with more subtlety and less unqualified self-assurance. But what influence was this wise diplomat able to bring to the shaping of decisions by Bremer and his bosses in the Pentagon? To what extent was he part of the governance of Iraq? It is revealing that whatever the disastrous mistakes made by the occupying power—the purging of Ba'athists, the employment of the sort of military overkill tactics used by the Israel Defense Forces, the Grozny-ization of Fallujah and other towns—no one has ever pointed the finger of blame at the British. No one holds Britain to account because no one thinks for a nanosecond that Britain is implicated in the decisions. Britain is there as part of the feudal host, not as a serious decision-sharing partner.

Britain has also been assured that it has been influential in persuading President Bush and his colleagues to become more involved in pushing forward the peace process in the Middle East. Conceivably one day this will be true. But in the years when I personally saw the process deliberately driven into a cul-de-sac, Britain's principal role was to find excuses for American inaction, not prods for American action. During the Danish presidency of the European Union in 2002, Europe—not America—produced the first part of the so-called road map for rescuing Israel and

Palestine from continuing bloody mayhem. In the past, Israel had argued (and still does, in defiance of the central principle of the plan) that it would only move on political issues such as the settlements once the Palestinians had delivered complete security on the ground. Now Europe pressed for both sides to take parallel rather than sequential steps toward a peace. The road map was discussed in the so-called Quartet of major diplomatic players—the United States, the United Nations, the Russian Federation, and the European Union—and, after a few perfectly reasonable tweaks, the U.S. State Department bought it. But what of the White House, where President Bush had just appointed a well-known Likud-supporting hawk, Elliott Abrams, as his principal Middle East adviser? We went to see the president and vice president in late 2002 to discuss the plan. Bush assured us of his extremely welcome commitment to a Palestinian state, and to what he explicitly called "a" road map. But he urged us against early publication. The imaginative Dutch draft was put away in the locker. The United States eventually "allowed" us to publish it in 2003. Despite numerous meetings and much froth, nothing much happened. Some of our moderate Arab friends understandably began to refer to "the Quartet, *sans trois*." Moreover, the essential element of the road map's approach—the rejection of sequentialism—never became a part of American policy.

This must have been a grave disappointment to Prime Minister Blair, who had promised in his party conference speech in 2002 that "final status" talks on the Middle East would start by the end of that year. He presumably continued to nag away at Washington about the Middle East. In the spring of 2004 he got his reward when he visited Washington two days after Ariel Sharon and was told that President Bush had bought the Israeli prime minister's plan for Gaza withdrawal, the retention of settlements in the West Bank, and no right of return to Israel for Palestinian refugees. Yet this sharp change in American policy brought no word of disapproval from Blair. We were apparently to welcome the policy shift as a step forward along the road to peace, entirely consistent with the road map. Shortly after the Bush-Blair meeting, a weekend European foreign ministers' meeting brought the strains to the surface. The Irish, who then held the EU presidency, had been consistently sensible about the Middle East, refusing to allow anyone to pretend that progress was being made when all that could be charted was continuing murderous failure, and their foreign minister, Brian Cowen, who was the host of the retreat, raised the argument. We were all a little surprised to hear Jack Straw, poor man, proclaiming the party line that nothing had really changed in Washington or, if it had, we should welcome it as a breakthrough. Such was the influence exercised through Britain's very special relationship.

I often wondered how our British, and European, failure to speak out more eloquently on the Middle East and related issues must have undermined the position in Washington of Colin Powell and other sensible moderates. Powell, of course, had to contend in Washington with those whom James Naughtie, the author of *The Accidental American*, tells us Powell himself described as the "fucking crazies," a description one assumes of the neoconservatives and their assertive nationalist allies like Vice President Cheney and Defense Secretary Donald Rumsfeld. In an interview with Naughtie for his book, Blair surprised the author by declaring, "I never quite understand what people mean by this neo-con thing." If this really does represent Blair's state of ignorance about the febrile political atmosphere in Washington, then perhaps he also failed to study "The National Security Strategy of the United States of America" issued by the White House in 2002, which asserts, to quote the great American historian Arthur M. Schlesinger, Jr., "the revolutionary idea of preventive war as the basis of U.S. foreign policy." The Iraq war was such an engagement. It did not preempt an imminent threat; it prevented a speculative threat. If Prime Minister Blair has signed up to this worldview, in which preventive wars are acceptable for America, the global hegemon, but for no one else, and in which America can follow its own rules and not others', then he has done immeasurable (though not necessarily permanent) damage to our historical relationship with the United States, the values on which it is based, and our previous shared commitment to the international rule of law.

Blair is right to argue that the Treaty of Westphalia in 1648 no longer provides an adequate basis for international law. That treaty, which brought to an end the Thirty Years' War and inaugurated the modern European state system, also concluded that one state should only take up arms against another and intervene in its affairs if it were itself to be attacked by that state. That is plainly no longer sufficient as a central assumption in international law. How does a state deal with threats to it, or attacks on it, by a non-state actor (like a terrorist group) that is supported by a state? How do states deal with a state whose institutions of government have broken down, resulting in chaos and threatening the stability and security of others? (Both these hypotheticals were relevant in the case of Afghanistan.) How do states prevent the manufacture, threatened use, and proliferation of weapons of mass destruction? Do states have no obligation to intervene in a state that is abusing the human rights of its citizens? If there is not a right to intervene, is there not at least, as the former Australian foreign minister Gareth Evans and others have argued, "a responsibility to protect citizens of other states whose human rights are being abused"? How should we cope with Rwanda, Kosovo, Sudan? Is it only states that have rights and not their citizens?

Blair feels strongly that there should be an international consensus, rooted in the practices and principles of the United Nations, that can legitimize armed intervention in the sort of cases I have mentioned, where other efforts to prevent a crisis fail. He set out his views on intervention in a 1999 speech in Chicago, entitled "Doctrines of International Community," in which he considered the five main justifications for interventions to prevent "threats to international peace and security." Were we—that is, the international community as well as Britain—sure of our case? Had we exhausted all diplomatic options? Were there military options that would be undertaken prudently? Were we prepared to stick things out for the long term? Were British national interests involved? Did Blair think that his tests were met in the case of Iraq? Going to war in a democracy on these sorts of grounds—with the goal of preempting danger, for example, by stopping a destabilizing flow of refugees that results from an attempted genocide—depends crucially on trust. Electors are asked to trust their leaders. They are not faced with an armed intervention across their border that they have to resist; the danger is less immediate and less personal. And with each such preemptive use of force, the voters are taught whether to trust their leaders the next time around. What have they learned from Iraq? Do they feel they were told the truth? Were they told the truth? Was the intervention based on sensible judgments? Has the invasion and occupation increased the dangers of terrorist attack on free and independent states or has that danger been abated? Blair's policy on Iraq has certainly made it more difficult to put in place a policy of preemptive intervention based on and backed by international law and the strength of public opinion in European societies.

Tony Blair is clearly committed to a Britain that holds a strong position in Europe. He has worked hard with France (beginning with the Saint-Malo Summit in 1998) to develop a more effective European defense capability, and this has fluttered the dovecotes in Washington. Americans want Europe to do more for itself in the field of security, but they are reluctant to see the development of capacity lead to any loss of American control in the chain of command. Blair is right to worry that at the moment Europe dwells in the worst of all worlds: our pretensions worry the Americans without giving us much additional ability to work with them to make the world safer.

Unfortunately, Blair's European ambitions have been thwarted in Iraq. Maybe he could have been more effective in bridging the Atlantic—representing Europe to America and America to Europe. But that would have taken a clearer and more outspoken determination to speak up for European doubts. Did Blair ever speak out against the American attacks on "the cheese-eating surrender monkeys of Europe" or their "axis of weasel"? Did he try to explain the strength of public opinion in Europe—far more united in hostility to the Iraq adventure than Europe's governments ever were? Did he think twice before confirming Donald Rumsfeld's views about "old" and "new" Europe when he and a handful of other leaders coauthored a *Wall Street Journal* article supporting America's preemption? Did he protest against the suggestion that the Spanish election result in the wake of the Atocha bombings was the result of cowardice in the face of terrorist atrocities? What did he believe would be the benefits for Britain's European policy of blaming France and its president for the failure to pass a second Security Council resolution, an outcome that was never in the cards despite all Britain's efforts? Is it unfair to single out the British prime minister in this way? Is it playing the man rather than the ball? The problem is that in this case the man and the ball were pretty well identical. Even members of Blair's own party clearly doubt whether the British engagement in Iraq would have developed in the same way without him. Would a Labour government led by anyone else have gone to war for the same reasons? Now we must hope and work for a peaceful democratic future for Iraq. We can at least support Mr. Blair in that. But we cannot forget the journey that brought us here, and that could shape Britain's relationship to Europe and America for the next generation.

Blair flew to Crawford and to Washington. He told George Bush, "Whither thou goest, I will go." He went to Iraq. He drove France and Germany into each other's arms (the reverse of what should be Britain's abiding European strategy). He subordinated Britain's national interest to American interests and raised serious questions about the exercise of Britain's de facto and de jure sovereignty. Politically weakened by Iraq, he surrendered to populist media pressure for a referendum on the European constitutional treaty. As his weak posting in the 2005 general election campaign showed, he sacrificed the public trust that would have been necessary to win that referendum if it had ever taken place. He weakened his position as well in Europe, so that at precisely the time when the referendum votes in France and the Netherlands and the political problems of Gerhard Schröder and Silvio Berlusconi gave him the chance to seize and shape the European agenda, he had less political authority to do so. A victim of his own interpretation of the special relationship, Blair is all too likely to be judged by history as a leader who was braver in defending the Bush agenda in Iraq than he was in standing up for his own, and Britain's, strategic objectives in Europe.

6

FROM BRUSSELS TO ISTANBUL

The Governor of She asked Confucius about government. The Master said, "Make the local people happy and attract migrants from afar."

—Confucius, *The Analects*

In a speech in 1960, General Charles de Gaulle argued, "To fancy one can build something effective in action and acceptable to the peoples, outside or above the States, is a chimera." Yet that is of course exactly what the European Union has been obliged to do. If you agree, as France and the other twenty-four states have done, to share sovereignty, then you need to establish institutions to manage that shared sovereignty as effectively as possible. Those in the United States who recognize the importance of working with Europe as a competent partner, one that can deliver what it promises, have a stake in the credibility and proficiency of those institutions. But they also need to comprehend that the authority of European institutions like the European Commission does not replace the authority of the individual member states, and that the whole European construction is inevitably imperfect, even ramshackle.

There is a tendency for the champions of the European Union to cover up its warts while advertising its winsome charms. Moreover, at least some of the hostility to the Union results from the habit, prevalent in particular in parts of the Brussels establishment, of implying in the first place that it stands above criticism, that its genesis and its works exist in a world beyond politics, that those who carp and censor must be motivated by base designs. The European idea may not, unlike the fated *Challenger* space shuttle, have touched the face of God, but it is certainly deemed to have felt the breeze as the dove of peace flew past.

The chords of Beethoven's "Ode to Joy" can animate a provocative light-headedness about the European project. I recall a colleague in the European Commission returning to one of our meetings from an inter-governmental conference of presidents, prime ministers, and foreign ministers to complain that there was no "European feeling" in the corridors. No carpet, no chairs—that I could understand, but no "European feeling"? If this meant anything at all, I suppose it indicated exasperation that the democratically elected leaders of twenty-five nation-states were disinclined to put what they perceived to be the interest of their own countries second to some more amorphous caprice. What this idea—if it really is an idea at all—overlooks is the fact that the original supra-national ambition was embraced because it suited national interests.

What "European feeling" did I detect during years of attending European summits? At these meetings, we were all seated (about forty in the late 1990s, sixty or so by the end of my tenure in 2004) at a hollow square of tables, each bearing the name of the country represented on inverted V-shaped cards that looked like the expensive chocolate bars at airport duty-free shops. Indeed, when we enlarged from fifteen to twenty-five, I half-expected to spot the prime minister of Toblerone in a distant corner. In the center of the tables there would usually be a halfhearted floral display, a few funereal ferns, and the occasional dusty begonia. The Swedes once presented us with an exhibition that looked like a tropical rain forest (doubtless there had just been a meeting of environment ministers) and I recall another floral tableau that bore an uncanny resemblance to the topography inhabited by the Teletubbies, complete with big yellow daisies, mock toadstools, and dinky green hillocks. The true depth of European feeling would be tested as Jan Peter Balkenende, the Dutch prime minister who looks exactly like Harry Potter, nagged away (doubtless in a European spirit) at some detailed textual amendment to a draft communiqué on the workings of the internal market, or when the rival merits of the possible sites for some new European agencies were canvassed (not much European feeling there) by their national champions. Should the new Food Standards Agency be sited in Parma (Italy's idea) or in Helsinki (Finland's idea)? If the proposals had been the other way around, it really would have represented the death of the national interest.

Observing President Jacques Chirac at such meetings provided hours of innocent entertainment; he is to body language what Shakespeare is to the spoken word. Like President François Mitterrand before him, he usually made a point of arriving late, surrounded by saturnine courtiers from the Elysée Palace, molded from the best clay that the École Nationale d'Administration could provide. A uniformed aide-de-camp always hovered by his side carrying a large briefcase. Did it contain the key to the *force de frappe* in case the president was minded to launch a preemptive nuclear strike against a hereditary foe, or was it merely carrying a little extra something for the president's lunch? Perhaps—though not, I reckoned, very probable—this was the man who, like the slave in a Roman victor's chariot, muttered "Memento Homo" ("Do not forget you are only human") in the capacious presidential ear. The president, whose appetite is legendary, would invariably sit deep in contemplation of a pile of sale-room catalogues for Asian artifacts, his long fingers hovering like birds of prey over the jars of mints and trays of biscuits that were berthed between the bottles of mineral water and pots of coffee. Intervening in debates, Chirac was part emperor, part ham, carrying all before him—or at least conveying that impression even when his audience had plainly come to a conclusion that completely contradicted his own. In my early years, poor Lionel Jospin was locked in cohabitation with Chirac as his Socialist prime minister. In the president's company, Jospin, a nice, courteous man, always looked as though he was wincing even when good manners dictated otherwise, and bore a look of stoic disapproval. I recall a working dinner in Stockholm when Chirac, who usually made a clamorous point of drinking the local alcoholic brew, forced a bottle of Aquavit on his reluctant prime minister. Jospin passed me a note across the table, "Have you seen your British film, *Saturday Night, Sunday Morning?*" he inquired, referring to a film that, as I recalled, depicted another particularly stormy cohabitation. The Chirac-Jospin marriage was not one made in heaven.

Kant once observed, "Out of the crooked timber of humanity, no straight thing was ever made." That is as true of the European Union as of every other institution I have come across. In politics, where aspiration is so exaggerated, the gilt never stays long on the gingerbread. Walking into the chamber of the House of Commons for the first time, I was excited and a little misty-eyed; speaking for the first time there, I could smell my own fear, just like it said in the books. Joining the cabinet, being sworn of the Privy Council (historically, the group of advisers closest to the monarchy), were emotional experiences. But it was not long before the romance wore off, and I could detect like others the weaknesses in our system of parliamentary democracy and the trumpery of much that is claimed these days for cabinet government. The fact that I could see what I thought was wrong did not mean that I concluded that we should throw parliamentary democracy and cabinet government overboard. Nor does my criticism of the way the European Union works mean that I think it is fundamentally flawed and that we should seek a rapid exit. Recognizing the blemishes, I remain convinced that the European Union provides the best forum in which to pursue Britain's national interest and that of its other members. But it does need to change.

As I have noted before, the European Union evolved naturally from our continent's response to the bloodiest century in our history. Europeans believe in knocking down barriers to trade because we recall the results of dog-eat-dog protectionism in the years between the world wars—the slump, the unemployment, the misery, the revolutions. We seek to institutionalize reconciliation because we know that for all our self-puffery about European values we have in the recent past used our creativity to bring technology to the service of mass murder. We believe in accommodation, consensus, cooperation, and international rules that apply equally to everyone, because without these things we have suffered and we have caused suffering. When the American polemicist Robert Kagan distinguished between the Mars of America and the Venus of Europe, he touched one or two partial truths. In Europe these days, it is fair comment that we are less comfortable with the use of force to support our view of how the world should be ordered than Americans are— and sometimes we are wrong to be so nervous about the need for armed might to sustain the international rule of law. It is also true that our European preference for nonviolent options to the world's problems, and our enthusiasm for any analysis that sustains this sort of choice, is partly a result of our military weakness. If we packed a larger punch, we might well be more prepared to get into fights. But this is to a great extent explained by our past. After all, we once followed Mars—and learned some hard lessons. I recall debating in the Presidential Palace in Prague with the leading American neoconservative, Richard Perle, who clearly rather enjoyed the sobriquet "the prince of darkness," which he had earned through a lifetime's attachment to military options in and out of both government and the better-compensated employment of Conrad Black. As I listened to Perle's sophisticated advocacy of aggression, I wondered how Americans would feel if similar views were being expressed nowadays by a German. Europeans have learned to be deeply suspicious of the terrible romantic temptations of leather and bayonets.

Creating a peaceful and stable continent has never required the death of the nation-state. I do not deny that there are some who have always taken a contrary view. For them the nation-state is an outmoded concept, discredited by war, fading away under the pressures of globalization from above and of multiculturalism and regional revivals from below. While global challenges and threats and the porous nature of frontiers require nation-states to work together to share their sovereignty, they do not dispose of the fact that nations are—despite the pressures on them—the largest units (for the time being) to which people will willingly accord emotional allegiance. That looks unlikely to change for the foreseeable future, which is no bad thing. It is after all the differences within Europe—our various histories, languages, traditions, and patterns of thought—that give Europe its depth and fascination. The European Union should not aspire to eliminate those differences; nor could it do so, even if it wished, as its development thus far has shown. Instead, it is seeking a supranational polity that combines the strengths of each nation while overcoming what separated them in the past: extreme nationalism, xenophobia, mutually destructive trade and monetary policies, unstable balance of power politics, and above all war. The European Union should seek, in short, to contain nationalism while retaining and indeed welcoming patriotism.

When you mention the nation-states' central invigorating importance in Europe, you are invariably described as a Gaullist, in or out of the closet. But most of us *are* in the strictest sense Gaullist. When the colonies in North America met in Philadelphia to agree to a constitution, they were subnational communities trying to become one nation. In each of the treaties that provide the legal base for the European Union, and in the latest discussions of 2003–05 on a constitutional treaty, we have witnessed ancient nation-states laying down the ground rules for sharing sovereignty. They were not creating a new nation or new state. They proposed (but then, unfortunately, rejected) a constitutional *treaty* for Europe, with the heads of the participating nation-states signing their names to a treaty on constitutional issues between the individual states, not to a constitution for a single state. The power that is transferred in Europe's laws and treaties flows from the democratically elected parliaments and governments of the nation-states to the European institutions established to manage their shared sovereignty. "What are the pillars on which Europe can be built?" asked de Gaulle in 1960. He answered correctly, "In truth they are the states, states that are certainly very different from one another, each having its soul, its history and its language, its glories and ambitions, but states that are the only entities with the right to give orders and the power to be obeyed."

The political classes spend a great deal of time in Europe discussing the institutions of government and the relationships between them—parliament, council, commission, and so on—and not enough time thinking of the ones that matter the most, the governments and the parliaments of the member states. It is the strength or weakness of the governments of the member states that determines the strength or weakness of Europe. Strong national leaders produce a strong sense of direction in Europe; the reverse is also true. Take the European stability and growth pact as an example. It sought to establish a fiscal framework for the eurozone and to avoid the profligacy of some countries attempting a free ride in the financial markets, paid for by the hair-shirted prudence of their colleagues. The initial rules were tough, reflecting a traditional German concern to ensure a strong currency and to prevent weaker economies from being carried on German coattails. In changed times, with a different government, the Germans themselves found the rules too tight and joined the French in a push to relax them. Let us be clear what happened. Two of the largest EU member states decided the rules were too strict for their countries, so the rules were changed. There was not much sign of a superstate here. Further, there was little that the European Commission could do to stop it, try as it might to retain the credibility of the system. We had anxious discussions in commission meetings about how to handle this bad behavior. The responsible commissioner, Pedro Solbes—the former and future finance minister of Spain—denounced the backsliding. But member states are the ultimate arbiters of how they run their own economies. There is no question that it would have been better for European economic performance if the commission had been able to get its way; democratic reality pointed in another direction. This raises questions that de Gaulle's answer does not adequately meet. We have in fact created institutions—principally the European Commission— to manage pretty effectively "in action" the sovereignty that we have agreed to share, but not in a way that is very "acceptable to the peoples."

We have shared sovereignty in Europe for reasons that are mundane as well as exalted. Of course, the creators of the old Coal and Steel Community wanted an end to war and the ability of individual European nations to compete in building the instruments of death; they also had an eye to the industrial needs of Alsace-Lorraine and of the Ruhr. To persuade France to join the Common Market enthusiastically, it had to be offered a high external tariff, exchange controls, the association of its colonies, and subsidies for its farmers through the Common Agricultural Policy. The CAP has eaten up (and still does so) a very large share of the EU's financial resources. It has been right to help poor farmers and rural development. But this policy, created primarily for French aims, discriminates against the products of poor developing countries, burdens European consumers, and causes rows between EU member states. It is a complicated monstrosity that squats at the heart of the European Union. We came back again and again to CAP reform in our commission discussions and put forward on several occasions more liberal and far-ranging reforms than ministers (led by the French) were prepared to accept. One result was that our reform proposals were stripped of their most meaningful suggestions for ending the unfairness to poor countries, a point that Prime Minister Blair once put very courteously to the French president at a European Council meeting. I had a front row seat for Chirac's explosive finger-wagging reaction. It was a case of precision targeting of a very raw nerve. Until the French face up to the impact on poor farmers in poor countries of their implacable support for an unre-formed CAP, much of their eloquent concern about development in Africa and elsewhere is heavily sauced with hypocrisy. Thankfully, on other fronts reform is eroding the CAP's worst features and its end is now more or less in distant sight. Like President Chirac, it will not—it is reasonable to assume—be with us forever.

Sovereignty sharing has, therefore, its costs as well as its benefits. How much of it do we want? How much is required by Europe's nation-states? How much will their citizens bear? The original Treaty of Rome committed the member states to work for "an ever closer union among the peoples of Europe." Is this a mandate for Brussels gobbling up everything, pushing back the bounds of national sovereignty as far as possible, as often as possible? Does it point the way eventually to a fed-eral Europe, in which powers are transferred from "we, the people" of the member states to a central political authority that then passes back powers, as it sees fit, to the governing institutions of those member states at the national or regional level? This would, indeed, be a superstate, a "United States of Europe" or a new country, "Europe." There are some who argue for this, as well as those who give the impression that they would like such an outcome to sneak up on us without much debate. For example, Jean-Claude Juncker, the long-serving, chain-smoking prime minister of Luxembourg, has said, according to *The Economist*, that "we decide on something, leave it lying around, and wait and see what hap-pens. If no one kicks up a fuss, because most people don't know what has been decided, we continue step by step until there is no turning back." This is the sort of mission creep that has given Europe and democracy a bad name. It could doubtless be justified on the grounds that "more Europe" must be "better," even if most Europeans do not now see things that way. But the "better" is not often defined. A paradox about the coun-tries that have usually argued the "more must be better" line is that they are usually those that have the worst record in implementing the policies that have thus far been accepted as desirable at the European level.

Bureaucratic momentum has also been at the service of role inflation. The European Commission is the motor of the European Union. Estab-lished as an independent initiator of policy and legislation, it has come to manage too much and has aspired to manage even more. When a person becomes a member of the commission, as I did in 1999, he or she takes an oath to serve Europe's interests rather than his or her own country's, a reasonable requirement given that by joining the European Union each country declares the belief that their individual interests are best served through an effective union. During my tenure, members were surprisingly restrained (or discreet) in defending national positions, with one or two exceptions whose flag-waving diligence usually backfired. Nor was there much ideological dissension, though on economic issues there was a discernible divide between those who took more and those who took less liberal positions, with the distinctions often bearing only a confusing resemblance to the political labels worn by individual commissioners. Thanks to the friendly, avuncular style of Romano Prodi, the president of the commission, and to his willingness to delegate to colleagues, the commission was a pretty happy team with little acrimonious bickering or bureaucratic turf warfare.

During my years as a commissioner, and since then as well, I have rarely been able to get into a London taxi without receiving an earful of advice about the European Commission, which seems to provide a cathartic safety valve for the frustrations that taxi drivers and others feel about life as a whole. No subject save the whims and fancies of the London mayor, Ken Livingstone, so excites their interest. The commission clearly fulfills the same sort of role in British public life that is played by the United Nations in America (which is argument enough for laying out the facts). Very often the "taxi drivers" appear at dinner parties, too. I recall one evening being told by a companion at dinner how corrupt the commission is. "I suppose I should remind you that I work for it," I said. Rather lamely she struggled for a way out, murmuring, "How very brave of you." Writing about "nooks and crannies" in relation to European legislation could, I suppose, slide effortlessly into "crooks and nannies" when it comes to the commission. The European Commission is everyone's whipping boy. Insofar as the facts are likely to change perceptions and prejudices—gentle Irish rain falling on flint, I fear—what do they tell us?

The commission's overall management performance is not much better or worse than that of the governments of the member states. Indeed it is probably better than most. The EU's budget for 2004–05 was just over 70 billion pounds, less than that for Britain's department of health and about a quarter of total central government spending in the United Kingdom. About 6 percent is spent on administration. The commission, with a staff about the same size as a large British municipal authority, is responsible for implementing the budget, but 85 percent of it is spent through member-state governments and regional and subregional bodies, and it is this part of the budget whose handling has been regularly criticized. The commission depends on the member states to ensure that the money is spent according to the rules.

Alas, we in Britain can no longer lecture others on issues of governance. The handling of the mad cow and foot-and-mouth disease epidemics (problems that were handled slowly, secretively, and incompetently), the design of the poll tax, the management of the social security system and the Child Support Agency, successive computerization initiatives in Whitehall, the administration of immigration and asylum policies, even the British Treasury's inability to control let alone know the costs of refurbishment of its own buildings—none of these reflect well on the current standards of public sector management in Britain. How do figures for fraud compare in Brussels and London? It is reckoned that 1 percent (about 700 million pounds) is obtained fraudulently from the European Union, most of this through the portions of the budget managed by member states. There are shortfalls in revenues from taxes, levies, and duties, and subsidies are paid for crops that are not being grown or for land that is not being cultivated. Much of this money is recovered. What happens in Britain? The department of Work and Pensions loses 2 billion pounds a year in fraud and error in payments. (That is presumably why its accounts have been qualified by the National Audit Office for each of the last thirteen years.) The EU Court of Auditors is often called in evidence to show how badly the European Commission is run because it has failed to give a positive opinion on a part of the EU budget for ten years, but that part of the budget largely covers the money distributed by the member states for agriculture and support in the poorer regions. In their 2004 report, the Court of Auditors noted that "the consolidated accounts of the European Communities faithfully reflect the revenues and expenditures and the financial situation of the

Communities," tabling only one reservation concerning the treatment of debtors. This does not gives much support to the notion that the commission is run by the Mafia.

Yet there *has* been mismanagement and fraud in Brussels. That is totally reprehensible. We should, however, be rather less prejudiced and a little more factual in discussing it. My colleague Neil Kinnock had the demanding job of trying to reform the commission's management. Any fate that gives one man in his political lifetime the job of reforming both the Labour Party and the European Commission cannot be described as kind. He labored successfully—changing the accounting methods, for example, from a cash-based to an accruals system, and establishing a modern promotion and personnel policy. And much thanks he got for it! I passed much of my own period in Brussels trying to turn around the commission's performance in the management of foreign assistance programs, both conventional development aid to the poor and support for more obviously political purposes like reconstruction in the Balkans. I wanted as much as possible of the aid to be managed out in the field. It was uphill work. After five years we were reckoned (by the Organization for Economic Cooperation and Development and others) to have made significant improvements and were probably managing our funds about as well as the European Union average. Not that anyone outside seemed in the event to care very much—in Brussels more than anywhere else I have ever worked, unacknowledged success came first through the quiet avoidance of disaster.

There was one real downside to tackling EU mismanagement. Each new incident created new rules and regulations that made it more difficult to run things competently and to take decisions quickly. The cat's cradle of controls with which the commission was obliged to cope would have made it impossible in Hong Kong, to take the most obvious example from my own experience, to move as rapidly as we did to implement policy decisions—not least investments in infrastructure. I had been spoiled in Asia. Too many officials in Brussels, like those in many other bureaucracies, the United Nations included, now spend too much of their time covering their own backs. But it does not save them from the scourge of the press, especially in Germany and Britain.

By its very nature, the European Commission was bound to be greedy for more power unless it were to be deliberately steered in another direction. The founding treaty assigned to the commission the guardianship of its legal provisions, and this conferred a sense of responsibility for the legacy of Monnet and Schuman. The Commission tends to stand guard over that "European feeling" rather as the six Vestal Virgins in Rome preserved and protected the sacred flame of Aeneas. The awareness of this solemn duty has sanctified bureaucratic ambition. The commission already has plenty to do—initiating policy, drafting and implementing legislation, administering vast tracts of Europe-wide programs. It needs to pay more regard to Montesquieu's wise remark that unnecessary laws merely enfeeble necessary ones. Unfortunately, bureaucracies often talk about the need to do less; they are rarely as good as their word, and the European Union is no exception.

The concept that is supposed to determine what is done at which level of government is called *subsidiarity*. This is a word barely heard outside the debating chambers of the European Union, except by those who study the 1931 papal encyclical, "Quadragessimo Anno," in which Pius XI sought to maintain church authority against state encroachment, defining the appropriate roles for each. What it means in the European Union is that decisions should be taken at the most appropriate level—Brussels, national government, or regional and local authority. For some in the commission, the most appropriate level always seems to be Brussels. I recall a discussion on energy efficiency during which we solemnly agreed to specify how often ten-year-old boilers should be inspected. The great European idea had come to this.

Yet there is a real problem for the commission in deciding exactly what it should and should not do. The single market, for which Britain campaigned harder than any other country, is an engine for ever more regulation to iron out national differences in barriers to trade in an effort to create the desired if sometimes mythical "level playing field." Just as lobbyists shift the tides in national legislatures, the commission is endlessly being leaned on by, shall we say, the manufacturers of billiard-cue tips (or lawn mowers). They complain about some example of outrageous national protectionism. By the very logic of its mission, the commission feels duty-bound to respond. But one man's "level playing field" is another man's "nook and cranny" (I use the term the right way this time around) into which Europe infamously pokes its nose. It is genuinely difficult to know where to stop, and the boundary changes with the zeitgeist. Subsidiarity can never be an exact science. But while the commission's essential task is defined in ways that drive it forward, it cannot itself define the limits of its mission; that exercise in logic would carry the evolution of the European Union all the way to the establishment of a superstate. As Samuel Butler said, "Extremes alone are logical, and they are always absurd. The mean alone is practicable, and it is never logical."

Europe's difficulty in limiting itself in favor of shared sovereignty can only be dealt with by specifying legal limits on the process of centralization. This is what the much criticized constitutional treaty set out in part to do. It was the result of a novel experiment in European decision making. The first draft was produced by a representative convention led by the magisterial president Valéry Giscard d'Estaing and assisted by a wily Scottish diplomat, John Kerr, a very funny man who has not allowed the often necessary cynicism of his trade to destroy his remarkable creativity as a public official. Giscard and Kerr, though similar in intellectual firepower, were otherwise about as alike as Puligny-Montrachet and malt whiskey. These two men helped to craft a well-balanced treaty that drew all the lines in more or less the right and acceptable places (though it soon became the punching bag of everyone in Europe with a grouse about anything at all). Their work went to heads of government and foreign ministers in the intergovernmental conference for further manicuring. The draft even survived Silvio Berlusconi's eccentric presidency of the European Union. At the council meeting in December 2003 at which it had been hoped the treaty would be finalized, Berlusconi presided over rather desultory conversations. One session began with a long silence that was eventually broken by one of the Italian prime minister's flirtations with political incorrectness. "Well," he said, "if no one has anything to say about the treaty, why don't we talk about football or women? You start, Gerhard," he went on, gesturing to the German chancellor, "you know a lot about both." There was an embarrassed silence. It is fair, I think, to say that there is a sort of Berlusconi line across Europe, south of which he evidently does well but north of which he would not stand much chance of getting elected. It runs pretty close to the Alps.

The Italian presidency of the Union was followed in the first half of 2004 by the Irish, which brought that country's prime minister or *taoiseach*—to use his correct vernacular name—into the chair. The Irish steered the constitution through the intergovernmental conference with great skill. Bertie Ahern, their prime minister, is a canny operator whose calculatedly unsophisticated style masks a clear mind, a mastery of detail, and tactical wizardry. As often happens when a smaller member state has the task of presiding over the EU's affairs, the Irish were not encumbered by a host of national preoccupations. There was no Dublin wish list that took priority over Europe's agenda. They also had outstanding officials both in their Brussels team and back home. Perhaps one result of working in a smaller bureaucracy is that very good civil servants are more likely to be granted authority.

The constitutional treaty was widely regarded in the rest of Europe as a triumph for the predominately "British" view of how the European Union should work. I think it is fairer to say that the treaty recognized that Europe had gone about as far as we could or should in developing supranational policies and institutions. The real world of twenty-five nation-states and national parliaments had intervened. The supranational bargains already struck were not to be disparaged, but enough was enough. The treaty made clear that member-state governments, for example, had ultimate control of their budgetary, employment, and social security systems; and the European Union could neither tax nor borrow, which should have quashed the suggestion that Europe is intent on becoming a superstate. The debate swung strongly against encroachment into what were held to be member-state domestic policy areas. In the future, we will need to be more rigorous in determining when there is added value in running policy at the European level. Jacques Delors, once a leading proponent of a "Social Europe" (counterbalancing economic integration with social protection in the single market) had come to a different conclusion by 2000, stating, "I believe that areas like education, health, employment, and social security, in short everything that creates social cohesion, must remain within national competence." There is a simple democratic reason why this is wise. If powers that should be exercised at the national and local levels are appropriated by the European Union, voters are in effect disenfranchised. Of course, they are in a sense also disenfranchised, and certainly hoodwinked, if powers that can only effectively be exercised at the European level are retained by national and local politicians. (In Britain, successive national governments have been disenfranchising voters for years by destroying local government.)

The paradox of the treaty's rejection by French and Dutch voters—and others would have said "no" too, if given the chance—is this: the treaty sought rightly to draw a line in the sand as far as further integration is concerned, yet many of those most satisfied by the treaty's rejection sought precisely the outcome contained in the treaty. There is another irony. The preparation of the treaty through the initial convention was regarded as the most open attempt to involve the public in the reform of the EU's institutions that had ever been attempted, but voters gave the treaty a Wagnerian raspberry partly because they dislike the feeling that Europe is being constructed over their heads without their involvement or approval. Still, the reasons for rejection in France and the Netherlands were very different, and many of them seem to have had little to do with the treaty itself. However, in both countries, and elsewhere in Europe, there is clearly a sense that the European project—the centralizing of powers in Brussels—has gone too far, too fast for many of Europe's citizens; there is a sense, too, that Europe's political leaders have allowed the institutions that they themselves have created to drift away from the citizens that those same institutions are supposed to serve. There is no sufficiently convincing political narrative connecting the institutions to the voters, especially in the older member states where the workforce is encouraged by some populist politicians to take fright at the mythical threat of Polish plumbers rather than at the real competition coming from Asian workers. It is easy enough to see what we should stop doing—no more overreach, no pushing for more power here, there, and everywhere. We have to focus on what we need to do to improve the lives of our citizens in a world of competitive challenges and the sort of threats that individual countries cannot face on their own. But how do we make the European project more accountable? How do we improve the sense of democratic control in Europe when voters plainly do not feel they have much control over what is happening in their own countries let alone in the European Union as a whole? We should of course give more powers—as was proposed in the constitutional treaty—to national parliaments in order to police European legislation and subsidiarity, though those legislatures will need to take the job more seriously than they have in the past. The majority of national parliaments have failed for years to make full use of their existing powers, ducking the serious job of scrutiny of European policies and plans, which they could have performed much better. For the moment, I do not see how much more accountability can be achieved simply through Europe's democratic machinery, namely, its eponymous Parliament, rather than through the increased involvement of the member states.

There are several reasons for this, only a few of which fall on the shoulders of the European Parliament's members. The European parliamentarians always seemed to me rather similar to national parliamentarians. Working in two extraordinary buildings in Brussels and Strasbourg—one resembling a great glass jukebox, the other a modish vacuum cleaner—the Parliament contains some very hardworking and knowledgeable politicians, and the usual small minority of idle, expense-collecting layabouts, probably unemployable in any other walk of life. This is just like every other parliament, and is customarily said to be justifiable on the grounds that in a democracy everyone deserves to be represented, including the bums. In my area, external affairs, I worked with some real experts in parliament, was subjected to far more scrutiny than would have been the case at Westminster, and was particularly impressed by the mechanisms established to secure budgetary accountability. Fighting for my budget each year gave me the same sort of headaches that would have been experienced by a member of an American administration in Congress. During my years, the European budget committee was chaired by a wise and experienced Socialist, Terry Wynn. It is no disrespect to him to say that he was probably largely unknown outside the European Parliament; within it, he was as skillful a parliamentarian as I have encountered.

So the European Parliament largely does its best—and it has real and growing powers—but has not succeeded in avoiding the impression that it is a virtual parliament, debating in the virtual languages of interpretation, representing a virtual electorate, organized in virtual ideological groups, and disconnected from the political world at home. There are some things about which it can do very little. It cannot create a real

European electorate; there is none. Europe's *demos* is fractured. Goods may know no boundaries in Europe, but politics are locked firmly into national cultures, stereotypes, histories, and institutions. Attempts to cross frontiers—right, left, and center groupings on a European scale—are pretty superficial. Nor can it probably do very much about the fact that it is an itinerant body, obliged to travel between Brussels and Strasbourg each month in order to meet the terms of a deal done long ago with France, with which Britain, to its eternal shame, connived during the 1992 Edinburgh European Council in order to secure some assumed benefit elsewhere. Maybe parliamentarians should dig in their heels and make more of a fuss, rallying behind the old chant, "Hell, no, we won't go." As things stand, moving like a traveling circus every month "lock, stock and filing cabinet" is hardly conducive to the creation of a serious, well-run parliamentary body. If there is little they can do about these things, parliamentarians could at least reorganize their own procedures so that debates are not simply a procession of speakers in an ill-attended chamber. Members do like to pontificate, and like most parliamentarians are never happier than when expending hot air on subjects over which they have absolutely no control. They should also create more of a political career structure within the Parliament. There is a rapid and large turnover of members, presumably reflecting in part the fact that members of the European Parliament do not cut much of a dash in their own countries. Who knows who they are? How many people vote for them? Many of the ambitious ones move to national politics as soon as they can. Even so, service and competence should be more obviously and often rewarded in internal election to important offices. Above all, European parliamentarians should reform their indefensible system of expenses for travel and office costs, which so far have given them the not-undeserved reputation of riding a "béarnaise sauce train." You cannot pose effectively as a guardian of the taxpayers' interest if you are suspected of bending the rules for your bank account's benefit.

I fear, however, that no matter how much the institution is reformed, it will be difficult for the European Parliament to acquire for some time the democratic credentials needed to diminish popular alienation about Europe and to bridge the accountability gap. G. K. Chesterton once remarked that unity may be as simple as changing ten shillings into a ten-bob note or as absurd as trying to change ten terriers into a bulldog. As problems go, trying to turn twenty-five different political cultures into one parliamentary body and one electorate is at present nearer the bulldog end of the scale than the ten-bob note.

Here is another reason why Europe needs to draw breath before contemplating any further transfer of powers to the shared center. There are now twenty-five member states, with other aspirant members hammering on the door. The mere scale of the enterprise should set limits on the ambitions of those pushing for centralized power. There used to be a rather simplistic suggestion that there was a choice between broadening the European Union or deepening what it did. In practice we have broadened *and* deepened, but you cannot deepen everywhere. With twenty-five or thirty-five member states, the centralizers cannot continue to draw every concern and decision to Brussels. Political reality as much as political will have changed the game.

And it is about time. Unless we call a halt to the process of vacuuming powers, we will find people—not only in Britain, France, and the Netherlands—questioning their political obligation as well as voting "no" in referendums. If citizens in democracies (and in other societies) feel they have no say, or that policy is being made over their heads, or that the law is a scourge rather than a protection, they will eventually revolt. As Edmund Burke said, "People crushed by law have no hopes but from power. If laws are their enemies, they will be enemies to laws." Every time a referendum result goes wrong, every time a pro-European result gets home by a whisker, every time a pro-European proposal is rejected at the polling booths, every time turnouts in European elections fall to a new low, too many European politicians behave as though what has happened is an aberration, or—worse still—as though the European electorate does not deserve the wise leaders it has. Prime Minister Juncker produced a plum example of this attitude in his response to the French and Dutch referendums. "I do not believe," he said, that "the French and Dutch voters rejected the European constitution." This brings to mind Bertold Brecht's observation in *The Solution:* "After the uprising of the 17th June, the secretary of the Writers' Union had leaflets distributed in the Stalinallee stating that the people had forfeited the confidence of the Government and would win it back only by redoubled efforts. Would it not be easier in that case for the Government to dissolve the people and elect another?"

If a cricketer asks why he should obey the umpire who has called him out, you can answer by explaining the rules, and even the position of the governing body of the sport, the Marylebone Cricket Club. Beyond that there is nothing to be done but to say, "You must return to the pavilion because that is the rule of the game of cricket." That is the knock-down argument. You must obey because we are operating within an accepted set of procedures. The growing problem regarding perceptions of Europe in Britain and in several other parts of the European Union (and if only cricket were played elsewhere beyond the Netherlands in Europe, the metaphor might be better understood!) is that too many people are coming to think the game they are playing is "not cricket," in the sense that there is something unfair about what is going on. Cricket, they discover—or soccer, if you must—has sprouted all sorts of new rules while they were not looking. They pine for the game they used to play and love in which their own national political institutions stood proud and unchallenged at the center of debate and decision making. But that is like a conservative cosmologist during the Renaissance pining for the medieval model of the universe that was comfortably geocentric; when the planets moved in perfect circles; and when there were no loose ends. The game has moved on. We are still building the new model, and we have to be a lot more careful about how we involve our citizens in the task. But there is no going back to the old one.

Europe's great test thus is not how it configures its governing institutions, but what those institutions do and what they achieve. What are the results so far? For the first thirty years after the Second World War, the results in Western Europe were spectacular. Democracy rose from the ruins of fascism and authoritarianism, and with it came the freedoms that had been so often lauded in the nineteenth century but so often denied since. Helped by Marshall aid, growing trade between various states that opened their markets to one another, and the migration of cheap labor from the countryside and from former colonies, European economies took off. Annual growth in Western Europe from 1945 to 1975 ran at 4.5 percent, and GDP per capita rose at an only slightly lower rate. A French economic planner wrote a book that began by describing two seemingly different villages—one backward, the other developed; they turned out to be the same village transformed by what he described in the book's title, taking as his analogy the thirty glorious days of the July Revolution of 1830, *Les Trente Glorieuses ou la Révolution Invisible*. The "glorious thirty" gave their name to the whole period. In his excellent history of modern Europe, *The Struggle for Europe*, the young American historian William Hitchcock notes that "in narrowly economic terms . . . the Marshall Plan did not save Western Europe." But what it did do was to enable Europe to follow a path of industrial expansion and investment in heavy industry, "while at the same time putting into place a costly but essential welfare state." The $12.3 billion of Marshall aid between 1948 and 1951 helped give Europeans the chance to choose a mix of economic and social policies that proved to be mutually reinforcing. Economic growth paid for social policies, and the social policies helped to underpin the economic progress. The German economy was the strongest engine, and the Christian Democrat Ludwig Erhard gave the policy its philosophic raiment, "the social market economy." In the years immediately after war's end, 100 million people in Europe were undernourished to an extent that seriously damaged their health; even Britain's ascetic Chancellor of the Exchequer, Stafford Cripps during the freezing winter of 1947 thought that things were so bad that "the best place to be was in bed." Thirty years later both the quality and the standard of living had been transformed for most citizens in Western Europe; their standard of living roughly calculated in terms of GDP per capita had risen exponentially and stood at 70 percent of the American figures. Mae West once said that she used to be Snow White but she drifted. This was Europe's Snow White period.

The drift began with the two oil shocks of the 1970s. Unemployment and inflation rose; growth rates faltered; public finances deteriorated. Stuttering recovery was set back at the end of the 1980s by that glorious event, the reunification of Germany. Glorious but costly: transfers from Berlin to the eastern Lander have amounted to 1,250 billion euros since 1991. The 1990s were increasingly dominated by painful efforts to align the costs of the social policies that Europeans had come to take for granted with our desultory economic performance. Preparation for the creation of the eurozone applied a discipline to the member states to clean up their public finances. While they kept inflation low, unemployment in several countries remained worryingly high, with social costs and rigid labor markets inhibiting job creation.

Europe's economic problems are often exaggerated, just as our economic vitality was in the past oversold by economists like Lester Thurow, who confidently predicted that by now we would be knocking the socks off our American competitors. Comparisons with America are most frequently used to try to demonstrate that Europe is tapped out. It is true that the U.S. economy has grown more rapidly than Europe's, but that is largely the result of America's 1 percent annual population growth. Figures for per capita productivity and productivity growth tell a far more confused tale, partly because Europeans believe American statistical methods overstate U.S. performance. In the last few years, per capita GDP has arguably risen slightly faster in Europe, and if you measure GDP by the hours worked, Europe and America are equal. Moreover, America's far greater size gives it advantages that show up particularly in the wholesale and retail sectors, which can benefit from expansive physical layout and easier traffic flows. Some studies suggest that 60 percent of the difference between U.S. and European productivity in the last ten years is explained by the Wal-Mart or Home Depot factor—large shopping sheds on out-of-town green-field sites. Many Europeans would also question whether America's saving rate—less than 2 percent of household income—supports a fundamentally stronger economy (or society) than Europe's, which stands at six times that figure. All this said, it remains true that Europe has not continued to close the gap in the difference between American and European living standards, partly because Europeans choose to take much of our productivity gains in more leisure and less work. We are more inclined in Europe to take holidays than risks. In addition, where flexible labor markets in America have meant that the impact of new technology has raised levels of inequality while retaining high employment, inflexible markets in Europe have meant that we have lost jobs but have not experienced a big inequality gap. Europe's jobless figures would be unacceptable in America; America's inequality figures would be politically intolerable in much of Europe.

Measuring our economic performance against America is not the biggest challenge that Europe faces. We do need to improve our competitiveness in order to raise our growth rate; without that, it will be difficult to pay for that famous social model that provides bus and train passes and winter fuel allowances. In 2000, European governments declared an ambitious ten-year goal of turning the European Union into the most competitive and dynamic knowledge-based economy in the world. Dream on. This betrays a characteristic European tendency to prize the enunciation of rights, freedoms, and objectives (full employment, a cleaner environment, and so on) over more solid but unspectacular achievement. But there are three powerful reasons why we really do need to raise our game economically.

The first is demographic. It seems to be a universal truth that prosperity, female education, and easy, cheap, and acceptable access to reliable contraceptives lower fertility rates. That has happened dramatically in Europe. The fertility rate has fallen well below replacement levels in every European country except Albania, and is still falling. The countries with the lowest birthrates are those—like Italy—that have had the most traditional views of the role of women. Indeed, if you look at fertility rates in the larger Catholic countries—Italy, Spain, Poland—you cannot conclude that the teachings of the Catholic Church are having much impact on family life. So Europe has followed a baby boom with a baby bust. At the same time, people are living longer and there is no good reason to suppose that this trend is about to peter out for biological or health care reasons. The result is a rapid change in the dependency ratio, with fewer people in work supporting more people out of work. In the past, as Adair Turner, a British banker charged with the task of reorganizing the country's pension system, has argued, each generation has been larger than the one before. No longer. Europe's population is likely to fall by almost a fifth by midcentury, while the number in retirement compared with those of working age is predicted to double from 24 percent to almost 50 percent over the same period. This trend dwarfs even the U.S. trends. Unless we act urgently, Europe's shrinking population, and particularly the fall in working-age population, will force us into lower growth rates and a declining share of world output. To keep up with the United States and, as we will see, the rapidly emerging economies of China and India, Europe will have to make tough policy decisions. More Europeans will need to work and we will have to postpone our retirements and accept more flexible working conditions. We will have to pay more for the social provisions of health care and pensions that we take for granted. None of this should be impossible, but it will require social disruption in some countries and bold political leadership everywhere.

The second big challenge faced by Europe—even France—is globalization, and this can be expressed very simply. According to the economic historian Angus Maddison, between the years 1500 and 1800 the combined economies of China and India accounted for 50 percent of the world's gross domestic product. As the Industrial Revolution lifted economic performances elsewhere—in Britain, Germany, the United States, Japan, and so on—India's and China's combined GDP declined, by 1950 to about 8.7 percent of the world figures. Between 1820 and the early 1950s, the Chinese economy was growing by only about 0.2 percent a year compared with 3.8 percent in America and 1.7 percent in Europe and Japan. The two decades after the middle of the last century saw continuing stagnation in both China and India, but since then these countries have been transformed by rapid economic growth. By the century's end, they represented between 15 and 20 percent of world GDP, and with growth rates almost in double figures and with a combined population of well over two billion, they will rapidly become powerful economic players. Their wealth per capita still lags far behind American and European figures, so that while their overall economic size will increase exponentially their citizens will remain poorer than those in Western countries. They also face significant challenges that could throw them off course. But if they manage to sustain anything like their present performance, by 2050 the European Union's GDP could stand at just under half of China's and three-quarters of India's figures.

The rise of India and China, and of other Asian economies, is not necessarily a threat to Europe's prosperity. American and Japanese economic success has not taken place at the expense of Europe. On the contrary, it has certainly benefited us. Similarly, Indian and Chinese growth means new clients and new markets for European firms. In recent years, about a third of the increase in the volume of world imports has been accounted for by China. There are, however, two things that we need to bear in mind. First, even today, some of the competition from China and India is in areas where we have assumed that we have a technological advantage. In Hong Kong, the economy was transformed from a low-value-added manufacturing base—cheap textiles, toys, plastic flowers—to a sophisticated high-value-added competitor in much less than one industrial manager's lifetime. With technology speeding up change, we shall find that competition from India and China affects not only our cheaper service and manufacturing sectors. The growth in the number of Indian and Chinese engineering and information technology students (proportionately a far bigger figure than in America or Europe) also points toward more intense competition in the future. Second, at the very least the European Union, with its falling population and a share of world output that may almost halve over the first fifty years of the twenty-first century, is unlikely to have the same clout in economic or political matters that it has today. But if they work together, European countries will at least have more influence than if they were to try to manage on their own in glorious isolation.

The third big challenge facing the European Union is that enlargement also demands an improved economic performance. This would both meet the immediate difficulties of incorporating ten new member states and, in a way, highlight the principal conundrum we have to resolve: How do we cope with the consequences of our attractiveness to our neighbors? The enlargement in May 2004 increased the EU's population by 20 percent, but only added 5 percent to Europe's GDP and led to a drop in per capita output of 12.5 percent. The arrival of new member states in the past—for example, Greece, Spain, and Portugal—has brought a sharp pickup in their growth rates and a positive impact on the Union-wide economy. The same thing should happen again, and indeed the growth of output and productivity has quickened in all the new member states, whose performance over the last five years has outstripped that of the United States as well as the rest of the European Union. But the gap in the standard of living between the old and new members will require substantial shifts in resources if we are to establish a real sense of community from the Polish border to the Atlantic. The difference in wealth between East and West Europe is not simply the product of Soviet colonialism, though that greatly exacerbated it. Ever since the eighteenth-century partition of Poland by Austria, Prussia, and Russia, Central and Eastern Europe have been victims of Great Power politics, and that has carried an economic cost. Per capita incomes in the West were twice the figure of Central and Eastern Europe as long ago as 1870. The betrayal of Czechoslovakia at Munich in 1938 is part of a sad pattern of behavior, which also ignored the sacrifices of Central and Eastern Europe in the two European wars, overlooked their contributions to European civilization, and downplayed their aspirations for national independence during years of Soviet occupation. Central and Eastern Europeans were far more likely to regard the United States as their faithful friend during the dark decades of Communism than any Western European country (although Margaret Thatcher in the 1980s greatly earned their respect). Now we have welcomed Central and Eastern Europe home and we must not be too niggardly about the benefits they should enjoy as members of Europe's club.

For Europe to succeed, the relative poverty of the new members should not be regarded as an outrageous political and economic advantage. I am sure that most Slovakian or Estonian workers would happily exchange their own weekly pay slip for a German, French, or British one. Low pay and low corporate taxes in Central and Eastern Europe will inevitably attract investment from the old member states as well as some movement of jobs. The former French finance minister (recently reincarnated as interior minister) Nicolas Sarkozy and other Western Europeans have attacked this as unfair, and have called for less financial support for those countries that do not raise their tax rates to those that prevail in some Western European countries. Cutting taxes is described as tax dumping. The same attacks were made in the past on Ireland, which took no notice—and grew into the Celtic tiger as a result. The answer if a country is worried about the impact of tax cuts elsewhere is to cut taxes on its own businesses. High tax deters investment and job creation, and we should not criticize the new members for discovering and acting on this ancient verity. A better economic performance across the board in Europe will reduce the pressures of supporting poorer member countries. It is not Central and Eastern European workers who threaten the standard of living of Western Europe's workers, but politicians who obstruct reform and deny its necessity.

As the present phase of enlargement begins to bear fruit, our neighbors will be eager to join, too. The countries of southeastern Europe are already either on the train or at least the station platform, with Romania, Bulgaria, and Croatia negotiating membership and the countries of the western Balkans cherishing what the bureaucrats call "a membership perspective." What is happening in the Balkans is a reminder that the most potent instrument in European foreign policy—Europe's most effective instrument of soft power—is the offer of membership in the European Union. That talisman is driving reform in the war-torn region, and in earlier times it helped to consolidate democracy in Spain, Portugal, and Greece. The European Union also cemented the process of democratization and economic reform in the countries of Central and Eastern Europe after the collapse of the Soviet empire. It has proved itself to be an outstanding agent and sustainer of regime change in its own neighborhood, rather more effective in its approach than America for all its flamboyant and sometimes militaristic attachment to the notion. So we have stabilized our neighborhood and exported democracy and markets. When does the EU promise and potential reach its limit? Jacques Delors believed that something that was not quite membership could be offered to countries like Finland, Sweden, and Austria, maintaining the EU's political and economic coherence and yet extending its benefits and its reach. But the ambitions of those countries were not to be satisfied by a table in Europe's anteroom. They were not prepared to be bound by rules over which their citizens were denied a say. The democratic logic for their membership was inexorable.

The most worrying aspect of the "no" votes in the French and Dutch referendums was the evidence of opposition to the recent enlargement and of even greater antipathy to any future enlargement. The European Union has a lot of explaining to do if we are to carry public opinion with us on this issue. We cannot simply ride rough-shod over public sentiments. Nor can we throw in the towel. The issue is far too important. In the western Balkans, if the countries of Croatia, Bosnia, Albania, Serbia and Montenegro, Macedonia, and Kosovo deliver on their efforts to reform and meet EU standards, we must deliver on our promises to welcome them into the European Union; the European Union could make the difference, ultimately, between war and peace in that region. And it's not a matter of softheaded do-gooding as much as it's a matter of hardheaded security. Conflict in the Balkans—or elsewhere on the European periphery—means refugees on the streets of our cities and is likely to result in the need for costly and risky military intervention by the international community. Political leadership at its strongest seeks to mobilize opinion behind essential policies that voters may initially regard with suspicion or downright hostility. But if EU member states can persuade our citizens that enlargement should continue, where do we tell them that it should stop? Do we simply continue adding rings of friends and neighbors until we get to the Caspian Sea or the Pacific? What do we say when Israel, Iraq, or Azerbaijan come knocking on the door?

Plainly there has to be an end to the process somewhere, and we have tried to put it firmly in place with the so-called Neighborhood Policy. This seeks to establish a series of neighborhood agreements with the countries around the southern and eastern littoral of the Mediterranean and the countries to our east, including Ukraine, Moldova, Georgia, Armenia, and Azerbaijan. Russia stands out on its own, too big and grand to negotiate such a deal, though erratically enthusiastic about forging its own special relationship with the European Union. These agreements offer the countries that are parties to them a share in our market and in some of our policies (in areas such as research and the environment) in return for implementing democratic and economic reforms. But membership is not on the table. Our partners are welcome to set up a stall in the marketplace, but not to set foot in the town hall.

It is an imaginative try, but two events will make it difficult to hold this neighborhood line, demonstrating that politics is as much an arbiter of decisions on this issue as principle: first, the agreement in 2004 that Turkey can begin to negotiate membership in the European Union; and second, the "Orange Revolution" in the Ukraine. At my first ever meeting with a foreign minister of the Ukraine in 1999, he asked me—doubtless knowing my support even then for Turkey's membership—why I regarded Turkey as a European country but not Ukraine. "What," he asked, "is so special about Turkey's European vocation and so deficient about Ukraine's?" I stumbled through an unconvincing answer, one that convinced me even less in retrospect when I discovered that two of my officials present at the meeting had parents who had been born and worked in what is now Ukraine but which then had different borders.

The question of the further enlargement of the European Union arrives as the most important question of Europe's identity, of what Europe is to become, of what Europe will be in the world. Certainly, Europe cannot enlarge forever. But I do not believe it can stop yet. It has often been said of the European Union that managing it was rather like riding a bicycle; you had to go on adding to its tasks, peddling like fury, otherwise the bicycle would come to a halt and you would fall off. As metaphors go, it is far from perfect. After all, you *can* stop a bicycle without falling off. People do it every day. On my new snazzy two-wheeled roadster, complete with basket and bell, I even manage it myself in Oxford. Moreover, the aggregation of power in Brussels has necessarily come to a halt. But I believe we have to make progress in another sense, and that it is administratively possible to do so. The narrative of the European Union—its raison d'être—was to end war in Europe. We have done that on the whole (though we have been shamed by recent ethnic cleansing in the Balkans). We have also ended Europe's divisions; the barbed wire, the barricades, and the bunkers have had their day. No one of my daughters' ages—from mid-twenties to early thirties—can be blamed for taking all that for granted. "That's great, Dad. We haven't had a world war for sixty years. So what's next?" There has to be a "next"—a difficult "next" that will define our Europe, secure its stability, and confirm our place in the world as a post-Christian society with Christian roots, a secular society that takes its shared democratic values for granted. The "next" task will do more than anything else we could attempt to prevent that "clash of civilizations" predicted by Samuel Huntington and devoutly hoped for by extremists, especially (but not solely) Islamic ones. The reconciliation of France and Germany was the necessary and admirable European accomplishment of the twentieth century; reconciling the West and the Islamic world, with Europe acting as a hinge between the two, is a major task for the twenty-first.

The Turkish application for membership in the European Union rouses deep passions and turns up the heat under some of the most sensitive issues in European politics—for example, immigration and the need to build tolerant multireligious communities in our cities. Valéry Giscard d'Estaing argues that the entry of Turkey would mean the end of Europe. But which Europe does he mean? He is far too intelligent and cultivated to believe that Europe can only be properly depicted as a

Christian club, barring the advance of Islam into what the Polish historian Oscar Halecki called "nothing but a peninsula of Asia," just like the besieged citizens of Vienna in 1683. What is this Europe that Pope Benedict XVI, when a cardinal, identified almost exclusively with the Christian faith? The doctor in Chaucer's *Canterbury Tales* was learned in the works of scientists from Greece, Rome, and the medieval Islamic world. Math, astronomy, chemistry, and scientific experimentations were some of the things that Christian Europe brought back from its raids on Islamic civilization and that Moslem occupation seeded in Spain and elsewhere. Our identity as Europeans absorbed the heritage and influence of the ancient Greek and Roman worlds and of Islam, too. The beginnings of Christianity were rooted in Asia and Africa as well as Europe. Byzantium was as lineal a descendent of the Roman Empire as Western Europe. How should we seek to explain to the Metropolitan of the Syrian Orthodox Church and the Patriarchs of the Armenian Orthodox Church that they are outside the Christian club? Do we write the Orthodox churches out of Europe's history alongside the Moslems, and how do we pass over the extraordinary Jewish contribution—out of all proportion to their beleaguered, often vilified numbers—to what we call European civilization? The proposition that Europe can be defined by religion is not only false but dangerous. In many ways, the European Union is a reaction against the idea that we can define ourselves by ethnicity or religion, and thus define others as beyond consideration. And in some ways, Europe, more so than the immigrant "melting pot" of America, is pressed to find an answer.

Whether or not Turkey should be a member of the European Union surely depends on three things. First, is Turkey European? If we were simply to allow aspiration to be our guide, the answer would have to be a resounding "yes." Turkey has resolutely steered a European course ever since Ataturk decreed the end of the Sultanate in 1922. The feeling runs deep and has been promoted with unrelenting vigor by successive Turkish governments. The legacy of Ataturk, born in Thessaloniki and convinced—despite the condescension of the European powers of the day—that his country's future lay to the west, is ever present. And his presence is sometimes more than historical—any meeting in any Turkish government office takes place under the cool gaze of the Ghazi, immaculate in determinedly Western suit and tie. Does Turkey respect our principles—of democracy, liberty, respect for human rights and fundamental freedoms, and the rule of law? This is where substantial doubts have properly been raised in the past over the Turkish treatment of minorities and the role of the military in Turkish politics. Those questions were much more pertinent in 1963 when the then president of the European Commission signed an association agreement with Turkey, declaring, "Turkey is part of Europe. This is the deepest possible meaning of this operation which brings, in the most appropriate way conceivable in our time, the confirmation of a geographical reality as well as a historical truism that has been valid for several centuries." Many Turkish observers would be astonished if that was deemed to be less true now, under a government that has carried on and even redoubled a program of constitutional reform designed to entrench democracy, promote the protection of minorities, and limit the scope of the military in government. This helps make the Turks as reluctant as were Austrians, Finns, and Swedes to accept some status that denies them full membership in the European Union. In their eyes, Turkey has grappled with its existential question, against a background of economic uncertainty and terrorist activity, and has unequivocally chosen the European course. How, they ask, can some Europeans fail to recognize that?

America does not always make it easy to convince European doubters about Turkey's embrace of democratic values. It is aggravating that American presidents regularly offer Turkey EU membership, as though it was for them to bestow this gift, and that the diplomatic pressure from Washington—public and private—on Turkey's behalf is so relentless. But the real damage is done when it seems as though America's only interest is not democracy in Turkey, or the enhancement of the EU's role, but Washington's own security agenda. When, for example, Turkey's parliament in the run-up to the invasion of Iraq refused to accede to America's request to launch operations from southern Turkey, the then American deputy secretary for defense, Paul Wolfowitz, was dispatched to Ankara, where he scolded Turkey's military command for not taking a tougher line with their democratic leaders. Wolfowitz is too clever a fellow to think that this is the way democracies behave, and he does not presumably believe that the European Union would welcome as a member a country where the generals told the elected government what to do. Democracy should be respected even when it is inconvenient for the Pentagon. It was a particular surprise that Wolfowitz should have undertaken this mission, since he is one of those neoconservatives most closely associated with the argument that the Iraq war was the foundation stone of a broader strategy to spread democracy throughout the region.

The second issue to consider is that Turkey lies on the cusp between the current European Union and the Islamic world. Throughout its history, Istanbul—Constantinople, as it was—has been a bridge between worlds. At one time, and particularly when Western Europe itself was a more savage place, Turks and Turkey were admittedly the very incarnation of the threatening outsider. But that was when *Europe* and *Christendom* were (however imperfectly and inaccurately) synonymous. Is Europe to return to that exclusive and warped idea of who and what we are? Today there is a simple geopolitical question to answer: Can we afford to ignore the continuing importance of Turkey as a bridge between worlds? What message do we send out to the world beyond if we shun a neighbor that has demonstrated the falsity of the argument that Islam and democracy do not mix? Turkey has done pretty well all that we have asked of the Islamic world on our borders (much of which had been done already by our Islamic friends in South and Southeast Asia). What are the consequences for those countries around the Mediterranean, what effects will there be on the moderate activists for democracy and reform if we make it clear that regardless of our promises since 1963, and regardless of its own efforts (if they succeed) to become a pluralist democracy under the rule of law, Turkey is not welcome in our club because it is Islamic? We should make no mistake. However we would couch the message of rejection, that is how it would look, and if we are honest that is how it would in reality be.

Third, there is the question of Islam within our own borders. There are probably around 12 million Muslims living in Western Europe, with nearly 4 million in France, 2.5 million in Germany, and 1.75 million in the United Kingdom. Their religion is the fastest growing in the world. In some of our countries, Islamic religious observance outstrips that in the traditional Christian churches. I doubt whether this number is likely to be massively increased by immigration, and if Turkey were to join the

European Union their terms of membership in ten or twenty years would doubtless include some constraints on the speed with which they could exercise complete freedom of movement within our borders. Immigration to Europe raises questions about how much assistance we give our neighbors to grow and prosper, but above all it calls attention to what we can and are doing to encourage better community relations. I have no trouble with the argument that we should have tight border controls. Europe is far smaller than the United States and the pressure on available space is more intense, as anyone who lives in southeastern England will attest. (The population density of the five most densely populated northeastern states in America is 40 percent of England's.) We should encourage immigration for particular labor market requirements, but we should not kid ourselves that immigration could solve our demographic problems. The number of migrants required to improve significantly age-dependency ratios in Europe would be so large as to be unmanageable in political, environmental, social, and economic terms. But a firm hand on future immigration, and a generous approach to the economic requirements of our southern neighbors, is entirely consistent with our imaginative support for what Soheib Bencheikh, the grand mufti of Marseilles, has called "active cohabitation, not just a juxtaposition of closed communities."

Fear of the Islamic communities within the European Union has been exacerbated by the attacks of September 11, 2001, and the events following—for example, the discovery of "sleeper cells" of Al Qaeda and other terrorist groups in cities, including Hamburg, and the bombings in London in 2005. In the Netherlands and France, and in Britain, too, we have also seen assaults, not on the Christian nature of our European societies, but on something that has not always been synonymous with Christianity, the tolerance we prize above almost all else. It is the same tolerance that welcomes different ethnic, religious, and cultural groups to Europe and allows them to practice their own rites and customs, provided they do not assault the broader tolerance we prize and incorporate in our rule of law. This tolerance helps delineate our pluralism. But to convince doubters, to win the argument in the streets, in the homes, and in the mosques, we not only have to make the right economic and social policy choices in deprived areas, we also have to show that the standards

Europeans cherish, and on whose acceptance we insist, inform our relations with those outside as well as inside our frontiers. We will not win the battle for tolerance in Amsterdam or Paris or Manchester if we show signs of double standards in the way we deal with Islamic neighbors.

There is a tendency for some American commentators, when they witness tensions between the majority and minority Islamic communities in Europe—rows about head scarves, or freedom of speech—to react with a sort of "told you so" reproach. Now, they suggest, you see what we Americans are trying to do in the Middle East. But, damn it, this is our neighborhood that is being talked about, our neighborhood in which we have been painstakingly pursuing a reform agenda for years. What is geostrategically important for the United States is rather more simply and directly our own backyard. Throw petrol around there (excuse the appropriateness of the metaphor) and we in Europe are the first to get caught in the flames.

My plea, then, is for Europe to define itself as a symbol of tolerance—democratic, prosperous, and free—able to bridge civilizations, to prevent division (geographical and cultural) between the West and the Near East, and to demonstrate the way in which these shared values can transform societies with very different histories and cultures. Turkish accession should be seized as an opportunity to give the European Union a new dynamic and purpose.

We know that globalization destroys boundaries and in the process raises fears about the loss of our cultural anchors and identity. With the blurring of the geographical boundaries of nation-states, what else can continue to bind us together as citizens at ease with the identity of the community in which we live? Can we turn the tolerance of diversity in an open society into a bond far tighter than cultural introversion and the exclusion of difference? Can we make that the element that defines our European community, our "European feeling"? This is Europe's challenge in the next few years, bigger, more important, and far, far more difficult than spelling out competences and delineating institutional boundaries in a constitutional treaty. We can haggle and barter in Brussels, but it may be that it is in Istanbul that we shall write the next chapter in the European story.

7

STRONG NOUNS, WEAK VERBS

And on the issue of their charm depended
A land laid waste with all its young men slain,
Its women weeping, and its towns in terror.

—W. H. Auden, "Embassy," *Sonnets from China*

Returning home to Worcestershire on the train in the 1930s, Prime Minister Stanley Baldwin's study of the *Times* was interrupted by a question from a fellow traveler. "Weren't you at Harrow in the eighties?" he was asked. "Yes," replied Baldwin. "Thought so. So was I," said his Harrovian contemporary, who continued, "So what have you been doing with yourself since then?" It is a story with which I identify. Back in London after over five years incessantly circumnavigating the globe as Europe's Commissioner for External Affairs, I found that my years of service in the cause of CFSP—Common Foreign and Security Policy— were not uppermost in many people's recollections: "The C-what?" Admittedly, "Didn't you used to be Chris Patten?" was only said to me once, but it did catch the flavor of the moment. For most Britons, I had last been seen as their farewell governor of Hong Kong. Since then, there was hardly anywhere from which I had not departed—from Moscow to Montevideo—and sometimes my departure followed all too rapidly my arrival. I recall a crazy visit to Rio de Janeiro for a morning meeting to negotiate a deal (unsuccessfully as it turned out) with four Latin American foreign ministers. One night, there, south; the next night, north: no wonder I have a bad back. One year my scheduling princess—a young Welsh woman whose calm and boundless competence included a creative mastery of the world's air routes—calculated that I had got on and off over 180 airplanes. "Cabin crew—cross check, doors to manual," were the words I had heard more frequently on behalf of Europe than "Welcome home!"

For what purpose and to what end were these Odyssean travels made? They reflected in part the global interests of the aggregate of European states. When you added new members to the European Union, you also added the depth and experience of their existing bilateral relationships with nations around the world. So when Spain and Portugal joined up, the European Union's breadth of contacts with Latin America increased significantly. Poland's EU membership moved all of us closer—politically and economically, as well as geographically—to Ukraine. Imagine the consequences of Turkish membership in extending European interests and influence from Central Asia through the Caucasus to the Middle East. As a global partner of America, Europe does not, unlike the superpower, hold the military balance on every continent. Our military writ does not cover the world. But there is nowhere that Europe does not have some interest or influence, and in much of the world we are a bigger investor and trading partner than the United States.

But was Europe, let alone the world, better off for all my travels? What did that acronym, CFSP, for which I had consumed so many airline cashew nuts, really stand for, and what impact might it have on the lives of British or European citizens? By the mid-1990s, European governments had concluded that Europe had to aspire to a status greater than that of a glorified and successful customs union. That hope had in fact long been in the script. As one of the two most powerful economic and trade blocs in the world, European leaders had begun in the 1980s to discuss more honestly and seriously the gulf between the EU's economic and political strength. We described Europe in the self-lacerating cliché of the time as an economic giant but a political pygmy. This was not wholly true. The individual member states still counted for something in the world. Four of them, after all, were members of the industrialized consortium of the G7 cum G8, and two—France and Britain—had nuclear weapons and were members of the UN Security Council. Several were major aid donors and regular contributors of armed forces to UN peace-keeping. Most were members of NATO, whose battle-free triumph over Soviet imperialism was imminent. In different corners of the world, the clout of individual members mattered—Spain in Latin America, Belgium in Central Africa, and so on. But there was no distinctive EU voice or presence at the world's conference tables, nor specifically European contributions to crisis prevention and the resolution of conflicts. If European countries were able to act together, the argument went, Europe would be able to do more than the individual countries acting on their own; we could draw on our varied resources, reflecting our different experiences and histories, to promote solutions to global problems.

British politicians, including those on the right, like Prime Minister Margaret Thatcher and Michael Portillo, a defense secretary to Prime Minister John Major, urged Europeans to do more to share America's security burdens, and it had always been an American hope that an integrated Europe would help the United States to discharge its global responsibilities. Throughout the 1980s, ambitions were stirred but nothing much was achieved. The name for the "wannabe" European foreign policy was "European Political Cooperation." EPC meant that no major subject on the international political agenda could be safe from discussion by Europe's foreign ministers and their diplomats. There was no hiding place from Brussels' attention. Europe had an opinion on everything, though life being what it is, clever textual compromises between the different positions of sovereign states sometimes rendered these opinions bland and even feeble. Europe's policies were declared in the conclusions of the General Affairs Councils that brought foreign ministers together each month. Looking through these conclusions today, one is struck by the contrast between the strong adjectives and nouns and the weak verbs. Europe talked a passable game, but no one got their shorts muddy. We did not do too much harm—except in the Balkans—and we did not do much good.

Aspiration was transformed into action by a number of world-changing, conscience-arousing, bloody, and embarrassing events. First, there was the collapse of Russia's Communist empire in Europe and the immediate historic consequences. Europe could no longer define itself as freedom's vanguard against Marxist tyranny. All the old certainties provided by the barbarians at the gate melted away. Europe now had to cope instead with the ending of its division. We found a policy, the enlargement of the European Union, to support the emergence of open markets and democracy in Central and Eastern Europe. Indeed, this has been the most successful foreign policy pursued by Europe.

It was not only the swift collapse of Communism that pushed Europe to go beyond a foreign policy composed of communiqués. In one outpost of the Communist world, though not a former Soviet colony, the 1990s brought the sort of chaos that Europe believed had been laid to rest in our history books. Yugoslavia after Tito and Marxism reverted to that state recalled by Rebecca West as inseparable from her earliest memories of liberalism. As she leafed through piles of dusty Liberal pamphlets in secondhand bookshops, the subject of the Balkans would regularly recur. "Violence," she wrote in *Black Lamb and Grey Falcon*, was "all I knew of the Balkans," and "Balkan," she went on to note, was a term of abuse in France, suggesting a type of barbarism. The descent in the 1990s into war, primitive brutality, siege, ethnic cleansing, and the burning of families from their homes, and inside their homes, suggested that the French slang was all too accurate. All this was happening on the European Union's doorstep, in a country to which Europeans could drive in a matter of hours. Dubrovnik under siege, bombarded from the heights above by Serbian mortars and artillery, was where Europeans had browned themselves in the sun not long before. The massacres were not kept under wraps, only to be discovered well after the event by intrepid journalists; they were shown nightly on our televisions.

The hatreds that consumed Yugoslavia were cousins of the xenophobic nationalism that the European Union had in part come into existence to prevent. Here was a chance for Europe to exert itself, to show what it had become, to export and if necessary impose its values on another European country where their overthrow was so hideously destructive. We should not have needed America to give a lead, especially since for Washington this was a faraway country of which it knew little and wanted to know even less. Secretary of State James Baker did not believe America had "a dog in this fight," and his successor, Lawrence Eagleburger, opined in 1992 that "until the Bosnians, Serbs, and Croats decide to stop killing each other, there is nothing the outside world can do about it." So we were on our own and rather gloried in it. This was Europe's hour, as one foreign minister memorably observed—Europe's hour and Europe's humiliation.

What should we Europeans have done in the Balkans? Should we have tried to prevent the dismemberment of Yugoslavia, or sought to guide that process without conflict? Should we, we wondered, get involved or turn our backs, lest intervention sucked us into military commitments, casualties, and expense? Should we work to resolve this latest posing of the Eastern Question by another Congress of Berlin, negotiating new internal borders—a proposal put forward by the Dutch in 1991 but not taken up? We sent emissaries. They made recommendations. We ignored them. We rained communiqués down on the heads of Milošević and Tudjman and the war criminals who marauded across the country. We placed those of our forces who were deployed to protect civilians in the intolerable moral position of being silent witnesses to rape and murder. In Bosnia alone perhaps 220,000 people died. The concentration camp made a return visit to the continent that had invented it, or at least had borrowed the idea in a horribly big way from Britain's Boer War experience.

Because our foreign policy was solely declaratory—like the Pope we had no divisions—even sensible proposals had no traction. The fact that the United States was sitting on its hands was more important in the region than the EU's puny efforts. U.S. inactivity was decisive; EU activity was irrelevant. And ironically, the most damning critics of EU incapacity were the strongest opponents of European integration. Out of this debacle came one thing at least: the determination that Europe should not find itself in the same position again, a determination so far only tested at the margins and certainly not yet proven.

During the meetings of European leaders in Maastricht in 1991 and Amsterdam in 1997, Europe agreed to establish its Common Foreign and Security Policy. By the second of these meetings the Balkans were much on everyone's mind, as were the horrors of Rwanda and Somalia where, again, we and others had stood aside while crises turned predictably and savagely into disasters. The Amsterdam Council made the CFSP more actionable, with the decision to appoint a high representative for the policy with his own secretariat. The fact that the policy would be common but not, like the currency, single, and that the Council of

Foreign Ministers would be in the driver's seat, said something fundamental about the nature both of foreign policy and of the European Union. Foreign policy and security policy go right to the heart of what it means to be a nation-state, raising different issues from, say, trade policy. If foreign policy goes wrong, it may lead to decisions about the use of force; diplomacy can be the only alternative to death. As was pointed out by W. H. Auden in the sonnet quoted at the head of this chapter, and which should be inscribed over the door of every foreign ministry, diplomats in "a conversation of the highly trained" seek to avert crisis:

> Far off no matter what good they intended
> Two armies waited for a verbal error
> With well-made implements for causing pain.

When it comes to using those implements, the governments of Europe's nation-states make the key decisions and stand over the consequences. Trade policy, monetary policy, even—controversial though it is—the issue of a country's banknotes do not touch on the core of a nation's sense of community in the same way as a policy that can lead to men and women being asked to risk their lives. Parents would not be happy to allow their sons or daughters to risk injury or death on the say-so of a remote commissioner in Brussels. Europe is not a country. Citizens fight for America (or the promise of American citizenship). They fight for France, Germany, Spain, Britain. They do not fight for Europe.

On the other hand, countries in Europe may conclude that their national interests are best served by acting together; that way they have more influence, make more impact, achieve more. So they aim to work in common. To have a single policy, not a common one, would imply either a denial of the bonds that create a national sense of community or the fraying of those bonds and their replacement by a wider sense of loyalty and attachment. This may be a nice idea, but there is not much sign of it happening yet. For the foreseeable future, Europe will have twenty-five foreign ministers and twenty-five foreign ministries committed to trying to work together, but not trying to do themselves out of a job.

Two officials were responsible for implementing the common foreign policy: High Representative Javier Solana (a former Spanish foreign minister and NATO secretary general) and myself, the Commissioner for External Affairs. Solana was the representative of all the foreign ministers; I was in charge of the European Commission's external services, including development and cooperation programs and the coordination of all the activities that had a major bearing on other countries. As far as I was concerned, Solana occupied the front office and I the back office of European foreign policy. Some of my staff did not like this analogy. They would have preferred me to have made a grab for foreign policy, trying to bring as much of it as possible into the orbit of the commission. This always seemed to me to be wrong in principle and likely to be counterproductive in practice. Foreign policy should not in my view be equated with the single market. It is inherently different. To attempt to grab foreign policy for the European Commission would have courted humiliating rebuffs from the ministers in the council. If they were obliged to choose between backing Javier Solana or me, there was only one possible outcome. In any event, playing entirely within the rules, the commission was in an extremely strong position. We were "associated" with the conduct and formation of the common policy, and we managed many of the instruments that sustained it and gave it teeth. The more sensibly and competently we did these jobs, the more influence we would have in making policy: we were responsible for trade and economic cooperation as well as for environment policy; we managed large development programs both for the poorest countries and for those where Europe had big political interests, for instance, in the Balkans and Middle East. Increasingly, the European Union was trying to act jointly to deter organized crime, drug trafficking, and illegal immigration; we managed complex relationships with other countries covering regulatory convergence, transport, customs cooperation, research and education agreements, health, and consumer safety rules. All these matters represent the detailed and sometimes prosaic but important business that makes up relations around the globe today. It was not always very sexy. But at least in the back office, the levers were connected to machinery; pull them and something normally happened, if sometimes too slowly.

There were inevitably tensions between the institutions that served the front and back offices. The secretariats that worked for the Council of Ministers and its high representative resented the European Commission's access to useful things—like money. Some of its members would have liked to take over bits of the commission's responsibilities whenever it suited them—money here, the negotiation of an agreement there—and move on as the world's headlines changed, leaving bureaucratic confusion and policy discontinuity in their wake. Early in my time as a commissioner, I produced a note for my colleagues in the commission on the difficulties we faced playing our part in foreign and security policy. The note was distinguished by the elegant and witty clarity of my chef de cabinet's prose style. Elegance, wit, and clarity were not usually the hallmarks of commission documents. The result was foreseeable. The document was leaked and gave offense for correctly noting, among other things, that foreign policy was about more than photo opportunities, and that the commission was always likely to be treated like a maid, expected to serve the meal and clear up the dirty dishes when the guests had departed.

The institutional architecture for the CFSP was plainly, to use Brussels language, suboptimal. To make it work required that the high representative and the relevant European commissioner get on well together. Javier Solana and I were not totally lacking in amour propre, though I suspect that the fires of political ambition in both our breasts had burned low by the time that we were thrown together. We genuinely liked each other—Spanish Socialist and British Tory—and simply made things work, despite the advice and attentions of some of the institutional warriors in both camps. In over five years, and thousands of media reports, no one was ever able to point to an occasion when one of us had contradicted the other, a tribute, I believe, to our common sense. It did sometimes require saintly behavior from both of us, for which I hope that our reward will one day come, if not in this world then perhaps in the CFSP-free next. Solana is ubiquitous and charming, an intelligent and well-read networker of prodigious energy.

The now-rejected constitutional treaty, however, proposed dealing with the structural disjuncture by merging the jobs of high representative and commissioner for external relations. This is called double-hatting; to sound a little theological, it was proposed that two functions should reside in one person. The high representative would also serve as the vice president of the commission. He would stand at the confluence of two streams of activity: the political and security-minded functions that would remain in the hands of the member states and those functions that the member states had already assigned to the commission. This even higher representative would be extremely busy, though presumably he would be provided with deputies. It is not a perfect piece of institutional engineering, as befits an uneasy compromise among the small group in the convention that drew up the draft constitutional treaty, the minority of member states that wanted to go further in giving foreign policy a distinctively European personality and management, and the majority who were keen to preserve the previous independence (and division) in responsibilities. Despite the dumping of the draft treaty, some arrangement like this is likely one day to emerge.

How would a double-hatted foreign policy chief—the word *bipetassic* has not yet been used, but it can only be a matter of time—relate to and deal with foreign ministers, bolster Europe, and strengthen its power? This is the most problematic area of all. The imagined representative would preside over the council that actually makes policy. I am not sure this is wise; to be responsible both for chairing meetings and for providing their main input would create some scratchiness. Looking around the table at twenty-five other foreign ministers, would the high representative consider himself their boss—or just their representative? We know what the answer will be in the British, French, and virtually every other European foreign ministry. Many years ago, Henry Kissinger asked his famous question, "If I want to find out what Europe thinks, whose telephone number do I call?" Ironically, there have been plenty of times in recent years when Europeans could have asked the same question about America. Should we telephone the State Department, the Pentagon, or the National Security Council in the White House? And when we get through, will anyone know the answer? During the first Bush administration, for example, Kremlinology had been replaced by Washingtonology. Who owned this or that piece of policy turf? As far as Europe is concerned, will the number to ring in the future be the high representative's or will there still be a string of calls to the German, British, and French foreign ministers? Take the European negotiations with Iran over constraining any nuclear ambitions it might have. The earliest European overtures to Iran were made by Solana, myself, and successive foreign ministers in the presidency of the European Council.

We visited Tehran only to have Machiavelli quoted approvingly at us by the president, and to be asked by the Iranian foreign minister whether we would like to conduct meetings with him and his colleagues in English or French. When the issue got bigger and more significant, the three "big country" foreign ministers took over—"the three tenors," we called them—not even bothering to take Solana or a representative of the country holding the presidency of the council with them (though Solana is now fully involved in the policy). An American secretary of state will surely continue to have to make several telephone calls, no matter what happens. What matters most is not whether there are several telephone numbers, but whether there is a similar response or message from whoever is on the line.

This goes to the heart of the question of the effectiveness of European efforts to make foreign and security policy. I mean no disrespect to the twenty-two other member states, but there is no European policy on a big issue unless France, Germany, and Britain are on its side. Unless *they* work together, nothing else will work. It is as clear and simple as that. Of course, others can and will make important contributions, and the addition of new members constantly adds to Europe's insight about far-reaching parts of the world with which other member states may be unfamiliar. But without the "big three," there is no European policy.

That was most evident over Iraq, which also exposed some of the weaknesses of the present system of trying to make a common European foreign policy. The subject of Iraq was scarcely debated in the council: as the arguments heated up elsewhere—at the United Nations in New York, on the telephone lines between London, Paris, and Berlin—we pretended in Brussels that there was nothing amiss. The great Iraqi elephant sat in the corner of the room, and we edged nervously past it pretending it was not there. "Elephant? There's no elephant." There was a sort of code that was usually observed, which dictated that no foreign minister should say anything too direct or blunt that might embarrass a colleague. To their credit, one or two ministers, including Finland's and Ireland's, occasionally broke the unwritten rule and raised a contentious issue. It was a little like committing some physical indecorum in a great-aunt's drawing room—maybe excusable but not very nice. But after all, the European Union was in a sense created as an alternative to foreign policy. Our policy for years had been to biff our neighbors; now we were in bed with them. And maybe—the biggest "maybe" of all—making foreign policy with fifteen or twenty-five is such a public activity that it is bound to involve more genteel playacting than real life, kitchen-sink drama.

Meetings of the council were certainly large. The ministers, usually accompanied by a senior adviser, sat at the table; the ranks of Tuscany milled behind, not raising a cheer but conducting their own diplomatic activities directly with one another—amending a text here, negotiating a compromise there—or by mobile telephone. Over the years, the number present was gradually cut down so that instead of having, say, 150 or more in the room, there were only fifty or sixty. The size of the gathering meant that the most sensitive business was usually done at lunch, at which only the ministers themselves were present. Their diplomatic advisers hung about in the corridor outside, hoping that their minister was keeping close note of the wrangling. I recall a colleague from the 1980s whose transcription of one such meeting simply read, "Mr. X spoke well for Britain." Meetings restricted to ministers only can lead to bizarre ruses. At the Maastricht meeting, with a session at which only presidents and prime ministers were in the room, John Kerr (then Britain's ambassador to the European Union) managed to position himself at one crucial moment under Prime Minister Major's table. The nearest thing I saw to this occurred at a meeting between European and Asian ministers. On that occasion, ministers were dining at an inner table, with one official per delegation seated behind. At one point, the Japanese minister— a feisty woman—began reading from a script that bore no relationship to the subject under discussion. Her official crept across the carpet from his place to hers, holding the appropriate brief (not admittedly Labrador-like in his teeth) and, having arrived under his minister's table, placed the relevant speaking note on top of the one she was reading before reversing on all fours to his seat.

One result of having so much of the sensitive and interesting business occur at council lunches was that some ministers were barely present for any other part of the proceedings. They would arrive in the late morning and depart in early afternoon. This meant in effect that some foreign ministers, perhaps inadvertently, gave up control of the overall coordination of the European agenda. In the 1980s, foreign ministers had been given the responsibility for resolving single-market blockages because only they had the clout to do it. By the 2000s, they had lost that clout, and had even lost the primitive urge to fight for it. This reflects the extent to which traditional high "foreign policy" has been sucked into the offices of presidents and prime ministers, while inter-European policy is no longer regarded as foreign.

Consistency and continuity in foreign policy are difficult when a new calamity can always knock you off course; another day's headline can impose short-term decisions that threaten long-term objectives. The imminence of high-level meetings can also drive decision making in an unhelpful or precipitate way. As a manifestation of its arrival on the world stage, the European Union had put in place a calendar of summits and bilateral meetings at the senior level. We had summits with America, Canada, China, India, Russia, Japan—sometimes twice a year. There were regular meetings with our Mediterranean Arab and Israeli friends, Latin Americans, the Gulf Cooperation Council, the African Union, Australia, New Zealand, the lot. The more senior the level of the meeting, the greater the pressure that we should take some gift to the table to confirm the pretense that we were having a good and useful meeting. Russia was particularly adept at understanding how to play this game against our own interests.

Summits, meetings, visits—much of the routine for foreign policy practitioners involves a stately progress from one airport VIP lounge to another. The issues covered by a minister's brief can be fascinating, and when you get the occasional opportunity to do a real negotiation it pumps up the adrenaline. But too often, the interesting business has been done before the arrival of the so-called principals. Officials have conjured "deliverables" from the mush of unresolved business between the parties—something for you, something for me—to advertise success and a further "thickening up" of the relationship. There will probably also have been days and nights of haggling over a communiqué, so that nothing contentious has to be resolved when ministers arrive with their entourages of advisers, secretaries, and spokesmen. The infinitives are already split; the qualifying clauses appended; the clichés added to taste. Meetings can easily degenerate into the reading of speaking notes to people who are not listening, with occasional, allegedly informal exchanges of view that turn too easily into *café de commerce*, a slightly superior cab driver's worldview marked by a string of ". . . and another thing." But traveling the world, albeit at a frenetic pace, seeing at least something of other places from the window of a speeding car, is a more inherently interesting and privileged activity for a politician (though not necessarily more valuable) than trying to manage social security or immigration policy. And you find yourself sitting on the sofa with more celebrities, famous and infamous, than can be claimed by even the usual run of chat-show hosts.

My first experience of this came when, as Britain's development minister, I made my first visit to Islamabad. Pakistan's then military dictator, General Muhammad Zia-ul-Haq, gave me an hour of his time a couple of years before his airplane was mysteriously blown out of the sky. The general, whose moustache and gap-toothed smile bore an uncanny resemblance to the British actor Terry Thomas, was seeking to make a point to me about Pakistan politics. He began his comment, "As I said to the late Mr. Bhutto." With a chill down the back of my neck, I recalled that the general had not long before hanged Bhutto, the prime minister he had overthrown. Fascinating as many one-to-one meetings have been, nothing since has given me the same frisson as that first outing.

How do you get any consistency when policy is made by twenty-five ministers all busy flying around the world? I tried to approach the question crab-wise by encouraging Europe's foreign ministers to discuss our budget—the resources that we had to support our policy—and to check whether our spending priorities matched our political ones. Britain's Robin Cook was keen on the idea, but otherwise I did not make much progress; foreign ministers are not very interested in budgets, which is one reason why they get pushed around so much by their finance ministers, who see foreign ministry resources as an easy target for cost-cutting. We were consistent about one thing at least in Brussels. When we did not have a policy, we would go on a visit, or send High Representative Javier Solana, or both him and me, or the so-called troika of the foreign minister currently presiding (for six months) over the council, his predecessor, and his successor. Later, the troika came to mean the presiding foreign minister, Solana, and myself, with perhaps one or two others thrown in, and I once spent an interesting week flying around the

Congo and its neighboring states with the Belgian and Spanish foreign ministers, the EU's special representative for the African Great Lakes, and Solana. So the number was flexible, but the purpose usually the same. An act of presence on the ground was too often a substitute for having anything very useful to say or do once we had got there. This is what I had meant when I eschewed foreign policy by photo opportunity. If we succeeded in getting as far as the conference table, it seemed, the European interest was sufficiently served.

Despite all these problems, the positive aspects of our attempts to launch a European policy far outweighed the negative, especially when one considered the complexity of the whole business. We were trying to make policy with, and for, fifteen and later twenty-five member states. What is surprising is not how much we did not achieve, but how much we did—though in my judgment there was one big failure, on Israel and Palestine, and one less justifiable missed opportunity, on Russia. The overall balance sheet is positive, an outcome that was not inevitable and owes much to a growing sense that Europe does have a distinctive contribution to make in international affairs.

This was especially true in the part of Europe that had produced our terrible shame only a few years before, the Balkans. By 1999, we had developed a clear strategy for the region and by and large we managed to stick to it. Taking as our model the way we had related to the newly liberated countries of Central and Eastern Europe a few years before, the European Union offered the countries of the former Yugoslavia, plus Albania, the prospect of becoming EU members. If they started to put their countries in order, politically and economically, we would enter into agreements with them (similar to the "Europe Agreements" that had performed the same function in our ten new member states), whose successful conclusion would unlock the door to the commencement of negotiations for membership in the Union. We would assist their post-conflict stabilization by associating them with Europe, and the more closely their governance and economy resembled our own, the faster we would move to bring them into the European Union.

We embarked on this policy in the wake of the death of the nationalist leader in Croatia, Franjo Tudjman, even with Slobodan Milošević still presiding over his gang of criminals and hard-line generals in Belgrade.

The Kosovo war had just ended and our first task, partly in order to show that the campaign had been justified, was to begin the task of reconstruction there, working with and through the UN mission that was charged with administering the territory.

My first visit to the capital, Pristina, in the autumn of 1999, revealed the scale of the task. Kosovo had been badly knocked about by the fighting; everywhere there were burned-out houses and farm buildings, bombed churches and mosques, wrecked military vehicles. On top of the war damage, there was overwhelming evidence of years of neglect and underinvestment. Kosovo might have been regarded by the Serbs as the Albanian jewel in their crown, but clearly they had not cared very much about how well it was governed and cared for. One of our earliest tasks was to attempt to provide a few hours of electricity every day. I have toured all too many power stations during my career, from Khartoum to Central India. Most of them appear much the same to a history graduate such as myself, but not Kosovo's two plants. They looked as though they had been assembled using the larger bits from a car trunk sale. The blackened boilers grunted and squealed in grimy cavernous halls. We were shown around by a regiment of electricity workers, plainly a recently recruited cash nexus of Albanians replacing Serbs on a welfare payroll. Outside the power station's main buildings, in between piles of junk, a few end-of-season Iceberg roses struggled to remind us that there were nicer and better things in the world than clapped-out power plants. (A couple of years later, I saw a similar contrast in the shadow of the grim nuclear plants at Chernobyl in Ukraine. A wild bitch played with nine beautiful puppies in the brambles and scrub surrounding that dreadful, murderous place.)

The European Union was the main donor in Kosovo, and we faced an early problem. How could we spend our assistance rapidly and reasonably well? Not a week passed without Madeleine Albright, then the American secretary of state, or her Balkans front man, Jim Dobbins, telephoning to find out how we were translating promises into contracts, plans, and real-time spending. Our past performance did not give them much confidence. This was the first big test of Europe's ability to run things competently and we passed it, speeding up delivery by cutting corners where we could, setting up a special reconstruction agency, and

giving the excellent officials sent out to manage it the necessary authority and political cover. We did about as much as we could to restore
infrastructure, rebuild homes, and provide a skeleton government. But
the unresolved question of Kosovo's long-term status, the tensions
between the majority Albanian and minority Serbian communities, and
the hold of organized criminals over much of what there was of commercial life deterred the inward investment that the territory needed,
and continues to need, if it is to have any chance of picking itself up.

Kosovo provided a paradigm of the problems Europe will face elsewhere in trying to rebuild a failed state after conflict or internal breakdown. First, how do you turn donors' pledges of support into real and
useful investment? The end of a war these days (Kosovo, Afghanistan,
Iraq) or the launch of a peace process (Palestine, Sri Lanka) is always followed by a donor's conference, at which well-wishers flap checkbooks at
one another in rival displays of generosity. Unpicking the offers is the
first problem—grants are mixed up with loans, old money with new,
multiyear promises with single-year ones. The objective of these conferences is never to get an accurate figure for real donor commitments but
to tot up the largest figure possible. Then comes the task of turning that
figure into spending on the ground. In the time lag between pledge,
contract, and expenditure, history packs its bags and moves on to the
next political disaster and the next pledging conference. The United
Nations—particularly through its Development Program—should be
enlisted, as the only possible "neutral" observer, to keep a close, public
tally on what is really promised and when it is spent. Those who regularly promise but do not spend must be identified.

When this first wall of spending hits a decrepit economy, it can have a
hugely distorting effect, not least as local employees are recruited to work
for well-meaning, incoming agencies at external salaries. Schoolteachers
suddenly discover that it pays better to drive the car for an aid official than
teach children. This problem is exacerbated by the swarm of new nongovernmental organizations that arrive in the wake of conflict to join
those brave ones already on the scene. I have always been a great supporter
of nongovernmental organizations; when I was a development minister, I
switched part of Britain's aid budget into their programs. They can be
brave groundbreakers and represent part of the core of civil society. But

they are not beyond criticism, and some of their lobbying can be extremely damaging, as Sebastian Mallaby has pointed out in his recent book on the World Bank. Given the numbers that pour into post-conflict zones, they can be a menace as much as a benefit. Moreover, as military planners have come to appreciate more clearly the relationship between security and reconstruction, they have fudged the distinction between the work of soldiers and the work of NGOs. This puts aid workers at risk.

Successful reconstruction in a place like Kosovo requires security, and Europe is not yet at all good at managing the transition from decisive military intervention to heavy-duty policing. We do not seem to have much of a model from America, either. As we have seen more recently in Afghanistan and Iraq, it is much easier to put military personnel into the field than paramilitary or regular police officers, judges, prosecutors, and prison wardens. Europe is trying to remedy this deficiency; it is uphill work. You do not require a degree in criminology to know what is necessary to clean up a place like Kosovo. First, you need to be able to identify and catch criminals; then to hold them securely; then to protect witnesses; then to organize a proper trial; then to have an honest judge, paid enough or independent enough to hand down a correct verdict; then to be able to hold the guilty in secure prisons. Putting in place the various stages in this chain is very difficult, as Paddy Ashdown has found in his heroic efforts to forge one in Bosnia and Herzegovina.

Kosovo also showed the importance of building up governing institutions at the local level; democracy takes root there better than at the top. Functioning and responsible local democracy (alongside security and job prospects) is crucial to dealing with one particular problem throughout former Yugoslavia—refugee returns. The international community established a right of return in the Balkans that Britain would never have attempted in Northern Ireland. There, a Protestant family hounded out of a house in Catholic West Belfast would have been resettled in a Protestant community. In the Balkans, from Croatia to Macedonia, we have insisted that Catholic Croats, Orthodox Serbs, and Moslem Albanians or Bosnians should be able to return to homes from which they were driven. It is an admirable policy, showing up Europe's opposition to ethnic cleansing and ethnic clearance, but putting it into practice is tough work. Governments in Balkan countries promise their support for the policy; it only works satisfactorily if local communities are committed to it as well. It is gratifying that, while the task of returning refugees to their homes has not been completed by any means, so many refugees have already gone home to houses and villages from which they fled in fear not long ago.

My saddest experience in Kosovo was returning in the spring of 2004, just after Albanian Kosovo gangs had turned on their Serbian neighbors in a brief orgy of burning and killing. There was a nasty Balkan symmetry to this violence. We had intervened in Kosovo to protect Albanians from Serbs, and now Serbs were being persecuted in their turn. It was not only apologists for the Albanians who argued that the violence was the result of frustration at the failure to resolve the question of Kosovo's final status and to confirm that Kosovo was liberated from any prospect of return to Belgrade's rule. The violence certainly cast doubt on Europe's previous policy of insisting that Kosovo would have to show that it lived up to civilized standards before we could consider its status for EU association. We cannot walk away from our insistence that decent standards should be observed there, above all the protection of minority rights, but we shall need to deal with the status question at the same time we insist on higher standards, not afterward. Whatever happens, we cannot allow Kosovo to turn into a barbarous bandits' haven on the edge of the European Union.

The fall of Milošević gave the people of Serbia the chance to escape their history, an opportunity that they have had some difficulty seizing in recent years. I like to think the European Union contributed to the dramatic events that toppled Milošević. We gave financial support to NGOs in Serbia and, more important, to the independent media. We arranged for exemptions to the oil regime in force against Milošević's government and ran oil into the democratically controlled municipalities in Serbia, to which Milošević had denied oil supplies for homes and public buildings. This project—named "Energy for Democracy"—strained Europe's rules of financial accountability, but we managed somehow to stay within them and got the fuel to the parts of Serbia that comprised the heartland of opposition to the old regime. It was a bold but imaginative policy, the brainchild of the current Serbian deputy prime minister Miroljub Labus and his group of opposition economists. Milošević tried to stop the deliveries, but they got through, to the delight of people in Nis and other cities, and helped the opposition—literally—to keep the homefires burning through a harsh Balkan winter. The following autumn in 2000, Milošević was overthrown.

No policy in the Balkans will be wholly successful unless we can persuade Serbia to embrace wholeheartedly the need for political and economic change. It is the largest piece in the old Yugoslavian jigsaw, previously the center of economic life there. The assassination of the post-Milošević prime minister, Zoran Djindic, a complicated, smart, sinuous young man, showed that the tentacles of organized crime were still wrapped around some of the institutions of the state. There were plenty of good, competent political managers in Serbia—the economic ministries were usually in professional hands—but progress was held back by a refusal to shake off the past. The main nationalist leader, Vojislav Kostunica, a decent enough man, exemplifies the problem, resisting a policy of full cooperation with the War Crimes Tribunal in The Hague (although in 2005 a number of high-profile indictees were at last sent to the tribunal) and giving sustenance to wholly unrealistic aspirations to take back Kosovo, or at least play the main part in determining its destiny. The cause of reform in Serbia may well have been retarded as well by Europe's insistence that Serbia and its sibling republic, Montenegro, should try to make a success of their existence as two parts of the same federal state. Montenegro is a small country, running down from the mountains where its capital, Podgorica (a monument to the worst of 1960s brutalist Socialist architecture), sits, to a beautiful coastline. In Milošević's closing years, we gave Montenegro supporters an outpost of opposition to his regime. Montenegro has one industry—an aluminium plant bought by the Russians—and another rather more lucrative activity, smuggling: mostly duty-free cigarettes. Alarmingly, Russian investors have started to show an interest in Montenegro. I doubt whether they are the sort of investors who would get a seal of approval from Transparency International.

We insisted on the Serbian-Montenegro marriage for defensible reasons, worrying that without it Kosovo's status might be raised prematurely and that other territorial boundaries in the region would come under scrutiny. I now doubt whether allowing Montenegro to go its own way will have much effect elsewhere. It may, however, free Serbian politicians to concentrate on the reform agenda that really matters for their European destiny and enable Europe to focus rather more energy on pushing reforms in Montenegro, whose future should consist of more than boosting European morbidity figures by lowering the price of smoking to the continent's nicotine addicts.

The organized crime that corrupted political life in Serbia is probably—apart from the need to escape from history—the greatest problem facing the whole region. The Balkan countries pretend to us that they are tackling it energetically; and we sometimes pretend that we believe them. We don't. The problem is particularly bad in Albania, where criminal gangs seem to have evolved naturally out of the old clan system. The years of Stone Age Communist isolation have been followed by an explosion of entrepreneurial activity in international crime. Albanian gangs are the most feared in Europe and, now, in America. They run the drugs, illegal immigration, and prostitution rackets in a number of European countries and have taken over the crime in several American cities. They are a threat to the stability as well as the prosperity of their own country and of some of its neighbors. Europe has had only partial success in building the capacity in Albania to fight these criminal elements. I recall a dinner with one Albanian prime minister in Tirana at which he tried to persuade me that he and his government were doing everything they could to crack down on crime, a point I found difficult to accept given that every time good and conscientious officials were appointed to jobs like the head of the customs service they were, soon afterward, removed. While we were having dinner together in a private room of the hotel, one of my officials was in the hotel's bar observing the prime minister's bodyguards negotiating his gambling debts with a bunch of dark-glassed heavies from Greece.

The fallacy that distorts much diplomatic discussion about the Balkans holds that, if only we could change a few of the national boundaries in the region, all would be well—swap the area north of Mitrovica in Kosovo for the south of the Presevo valley in Serbia, tinker with the northern reaches of Macedonia around Tetovo, carve up Bosnia and Herzegovina again, and so on. I said earlier that it might have been possible before Yugoslavia was dismembered by force to arrive at a neat solution, straight out of nineteenth-century Great Power diplomacy, to the Eastern Question. But it would have been a long shot. Today, it is difficult to see how boundary tinkering could lead to anything except calamity.

Bosnia and Herzegovina is the best example of the sort of trouble that would be likely to explode. This country, whose geographical and political identity was carefully crafted under hands-on American tutelage at Dayton, Ohio, in 1995, is an uneasy amalgam of Bosnians, Croats, and Serbs. If it were to break apart, the fallout for the whole region would be catastrophic. Bosnia and Herzegovina was the stage for the worst atrocities of the Balkan Wars, above all the massacre at Srebrenica, where some eight thousand Bosnians were slaughtered by Serb forces. Sarajevo itself, scene of the assassination by a Bosnian Serb of the Archduke Franz Ferdinand and his beloved wife, Sophie, on St. Vitus's Day in June 1914, still bears the many scars of its siege and bombardment by later Serb killers. Europe is committed to making Bosnia and Herzegovina work as a country, even while its two highly autonomous entities shy away from the creation of the national institutions (in policing, defense, the tax system, or the customs service, for example) that are required. The slowness of the progress is only bearable when one recalls the bloody pit out of which the journey began. Paddy Ashdown now presides over Europe's and the international community's efforts to nudge and shove the country in the right direction. He is a natural for such a task. It is a pity that we do not still have an empire for someone with his decent instincts and extraordinary, youthful energy to help run. There is a paradox when someone with this sort of flair takes on such a job. It is desirable to develop local political talent with the courageous determination to take and own the most awkward political decisions. Ashdown inevitably fills most of the available political space. Which local leaders will come after him? Nevertheless, under his overlordship Bosnia and Herzegovina has made real progress, not least in seeing the return of refugees to their original communities and the establishment of a working system of law and order, a major achievement. The European Union has mounted its first major military operation there, which may be a model for future European security activities outside NATO.

We came closest to a return to ethnic conflict in Macedonia, or—as we had to call it to massage Greek sensitivities—the Former Yugoslav

Republic of Macedonia, FYROM for short. Tensions between the majority community and the Albanian minority boiled over in 2000–01, as the government went halfheartedly through the motions of addressing minority grievances. There was fighting in and around the main Albanian town in Macedonia, Tetevo, and the government (led by a politician devious even by Balkan standards) began buying weapons it could not afford from Ukraine, which of course assured us that it was not selling them. The secretary general of NATO, George Robertson, High Representative Javier Solana, and I flew back and forth to Skopje, nagging, coaxing, and bullying those political leaders prepared to listen into calming the atmosphere, accepting a small NATO security presence, and reaching a wide-ranging agreement (named after Lake Ohrid, where it was signed) that dealt with Albanian grievances over issues such as language, public sector employment, and university education. We were helped by a decent president with a lot of courage if little political power. President Boris Trajkovski was, rather improbably, a Macedonian Methodist and frequent attendee of prayer breakfasts worldwide. He was a great bear of a man, much given to hugging and tears. I remember one particularly stressful night during which Solana and I encouraged him to act as boldly as his instincts told him was required, as a mob of extremists bayed outside the small presidential palace for our blood. Occasional sounds of gunfire were not terribly good for morale. Trajkovski, alas, died in an aircraft accident after the crisis was ended, in great part thanks to his own courage. The combination of NATO muscle and Europe's political influence and money helped to avert disaster. Fittingly, Macedonia has now lodged its own application to join the EU, though its journey will be quite a long one.

That should not be the case in Croatia, in many ways the star pupil of the region. Part of that expression would not find favor with the Croatians themselves: they do not like to think of themselves as Balkan at all, and when you read their history, visit Zagreb or Dubrovnik, or look at their per capita GDP figures, you can understand their point. The Croats played their own, often discreditable part in the violent breakup of Yugoslavia, and though a Catholic, I cannot say I much admired the role of the church both in Croatia itself and in the surrounding countries. It became a focus for and protector of intransigent nationalism, cultural identity, and irredentism. In the town of Mostar in Bosnia and Herze-govina, where the shelling of the fifteenth-century Turkish bridge by Croat forces became a symbol of the communal animosities that launched the Balkan Wars, the divisions between Catholic and Moslem citizens are advertised by the huge crucifix raised on the Catholic side of the city, looming in a show of less than Christian triumphalism over the ruined streets below. I wonder whether the bishop and his local clergy have ever asked themselves what Jesus would have thought of the raising up of this giant representation of His torture and death. He died for the salvation of *all* mankind, including Bosnian Moslems. After President Tudjman's death, the Croats moved fast to install an open democracy. They have held fair elections, at which power has been transferred from one party to another. They have a good and professional civil service that has implemented the reforms pressed on them by the European Union both rapidly and well. Successive governments have faced down extrem-ist opponents. But the government still has to demonstrate its unremit-ting commitment to the work of the Hague Tribunal, and the pace of refugee returns, though much improved, has been slower than would be desirable. Croatia works as a country. It is determined to gain EU mem-bership, and as soon as it complies fully with the Hague Tribunal, it will begin negotiations. They should not take too long.

In the Balkans, Europe's "pull me, push me" policy has impelled countries along the path to reform, with a lot of financial support and the prospect of one day joining the European Union. It has worked pretty well. I will deal in the next chapter with the two areas where I think European policies have been less successful. As for other countries and continents, it would be wearisome to tour the world, describing visits here, there, and everywhere, recounting small victories and whitewash-ing small defeats. When I was a party speechwriter, there was a particu-lar sort of speech that I always tried to avoid drafting—the *tour d'horizon* of domestic or international policy. Any paragraph that began, "And now I turn to agriculture . . ." or "Moving on to the Ivory Coast . . ." was plainly part of a speech that no one should want to deliver and no one would want to hear. The senior Labour politician Denis Healey had his own phrase for orations like this, a "tour de gloss." I will therefore avoid trying to spin a rambling tale that would seek to incorporate Singapore,

Wellington, São Paulo, and a cross-section of all the other places to which I traveled on behalf of Europe, and which deserved my and Europe's attention during my five years as a commissioner.

However, there was one bizarre visit to Pyongyang to see the North Korean leader Kim Jong Il that taught me that the European Union should not get too big for its boots. Europe is not a significant political player on the Korean peninsula, though we have delivered in less than a decade more than 500 million euros in humanitarian assistance and support for the development of alternative power supplies to their planned nuclear plants. Our European team went to North Korea largely as a political favor to President Kim Dae Jung of South Korea. He had made a visit to Washington in the early days of the Bush administration to confirm that America would continue to support his "sunshine" policy of reconciliation with the North. Despite reassuring noises from Colin Powell and the State Department, he was cold-shouldered at the White House. His policy seemed to be in ruins and he turned to Europe for a gesture of support. The Swedish government (then holding the EU presidency) was rightly happy to see if there was anything we could do to give some more encouragement to the reconciliation policy. It was agreed that Prime Minister Goran Persson, Javier Solana, and I should fly to Pyongyang to try to persuade Kim Jong Il to resume the dialogue and contacts he had begun to make with Seoul.

We flew into Pyongyang to an airport with the longest and largest number of runways I have ever seen, presumably because their principal purpose was not civil, and were greeted by a crowd in traditional costumes waving what looked like gaudy-colored feather dusters. We were driven to the despot-sized state guesthouse (it had huge bedrooms and bathrooms and miniscule bars of soap), where we awaited the "Dear Leader." Over two days we saw him for more than six hours. Each meeting was a surprise. We would get a sudden order to be on parade in a salon or corridor, and Kim would suddenly appear through a door or from behind a wall hanging like a character in pantomime or a Feydeau farce: now he's nowhere, now he's here; now you see him, now you don't. I half expected him to appear at any moment through a trapdoor in the floor, but perhaps that is what he was doing. He looked extraordinary— a bouffant hairstyle all his own, in which each hair seemed to have been individually seeded in his scalp; built-up Cuban heels; shiny gabardine boiler suits. He would usually see us with just an interpreter and one other official. He struck us all as highly intelligent and generally spoke without any briefing notes. Kim's tyranny is unfathomable to the outsider, and presumably to most insiders as well. Pyongyang itself looked like a gloomy stage set; it was impossible to know what went on behind the facades of the buildings we passed in our motorcade. Unlike every other city I have ever visited, there was no sign of any commercial activity whatsoever. We banqueted with Kim and a group of grumpy old men, with faces like Christmas walnuts, in heavily bemedaled uniforms. We were served much better Burgundy than we would have drunk in Brussels. Outside the people starved.

Since then, the nuclear crisis in North Korea has turned into a front-page story. Others may be able to help to solve it, especially the Chinese, South Koreans, and Japanese. But it is only the Americans who really matter, a point we rapidly came to understand on our own visit. There we were, visiting peacemakers from Europe, and all that this tiny tyrant wanted to talk about was . . . America. Why did policy seem to have changed from Clinton to Bush? Why were the Americans so rude about him, calling him awful names? Why were the Americans able to manipulate the South Koreans? Who did they think they were, threatening his poor country? Why did they have so many weapons threatening him from the South? Apart from that, all he wished to raise was whether he might be able to make an official visit to Sweden, a point on which Mr. Persson ducked and weaved with consummate political skill. Anyway, there it was. We went as European peace emissaries, accomplished nothing despite our best efforts and intentions, and spent all our time discussing what American policy might be.

America is a superpower, partly because it is the only country whose will and intentions matter everywhere and are everywhere decisive to the settlement of the world's biggest problems. Europe can help to solve those problems, but there are only some parts of the world—like the Balkans—where our role (while not necessarily crucial) is as important as, or more important than, that of, say, China in the case of North Korea. I turn at the beginning of the next chapter to one of the places on Europe's doorstep where that is true.

8

NEIGHBORHOOD WATCH

Neighbours, everybody needs good neighbours,
But here's a friendly word of warning
Just be careful what you say . . .
Neighbours, you pick your friends
But not your neighbours
Just a slight misunderstanding
And the mayhem never ends,
Neighbours, interfering with each other
Be sure that that's where the friendship ends.

—Theme song for a British TV soap, *Neighbours*

All politics, we are told, is local; diplomacy, too, starts close to home. Foreign ministers sensibly give priority to securing a stable neighborhood for their countries. Since the United States is the only global superpower, it has an interest in the stability not only of its own neighborhood (forcefully expressed ever since the Monroe Doctrine) but in what happens in everyone else's neighborhood, too. So the promise of EU membership for the liberated countries of the Soviet empire in Central and Eastern Europe, a promise that helped to secure their peaceful transition to democracy and capitalism, fulfilled an American strategic interest as well as a European one, although in the case of Europe the challenge was closer to home. But enlargement of the European Union, as I remarked in the last chapter, is not a process that can go on indefinitely. Moreover, not every neighbor will want to become an EU member state, so other policies are required. Framing these approaches is not easy, especially given that Europe's immediate neighborhood poses large and varied problems, but America has a stake in our success.

To the east, the Russian Federation gripes about its loss of empire and watches suspiciously as its onetime colonies join the European Union and NATO (or aspire to do so). Putting its faith, as before in its history, in a strongman rather than in strong institutions, it resiles from any serious commitment to establishing a pluralist democracy. Europe should work for a comprehensive partnership with Russia. We have a long border with the country. We are Russia's biggest trade partner. Russian problems can easily spill over into our own territories. Europe does not inherit today the job of containing Russia and its satellites that was performed by the United States in the years spanning from the Second World War to the fall of the Berlin Wall, but we do have the task of trying to sustain Russian reform and deter Russian backsliding. At the moment, it is alas nonsense to suggest that Europe's important (not yet "special") relationship with Russia is based on shared values. Later in this chapter, I will come back to Europe's difficulties in putting together a consistent and coherent policy on Russia and some of the results of this failure.

To the south, beyond Shelley's "blue Mediterranean," lie the troubled lands from the Maghreb to the Mashraq of some of the Arab League states, countries that share the southern littoral of the sea that has both brought us—Europe and the Islamic world—together and kept us apart. Here, in our region, are some of the most intractable problems facing the world today: poverty, protectionism, political alienation, religious extremism, authoritarianism, abuse of human rights, gender discrimination, violence. In some countries, democracy begins to stir; in all of them, the remnants of ancient cultures remind us of better and happier days. Across the whole region, the dispute between Israel and Palestine poisons politics, aborts progress, and nurtures conspiracy and suicide bombing.

These are countries with which most European nations have ties of history, culture, politics, and commerce. We have colonized them, killed their inhabitants and been killed by them, stolen their wealth, bought their products, borrowed from their civilization, suppressed their aspirations, corrupted their systems of government, and recently and fitfully tried to show them better ways of governing themselves. We know one another well, and now many of their former citizens dwell in our own countries. Many more will do so—the majority perhaps illegally—if we mishandle our relationship with them in the future. This is part of the intimacy of our relationship. For America, these countries comprise an immensely important geostrategic relationship, given a particular depth by America's emotional ties to Israel and its concerns about energy supply. For Europe, it is rather different; this is our "next door."

Nothing matters more to Europe than the way we handle our relations with this sharp edge of the Islamic world. Get them wrong, politically and economically, and our borders will be subjected to unmanageable migratory pressures; the tensions in Arab countries will spill over into our own societies; and our tolerance will be tested to the breaking point. We are seeing this already, as civil liberties in some European countries are curbed because of fears about the violent problems we may import. As I shall argue, I do not believe that there is a "war" on terrorism in any conventional sense, nor that we can realistically look forward to a day when the threat of terrorism has been totally eliminated. But I do think that a successful partnership between Europe and the Arab world could go far to limit terrorism's threat around the globe.

The relationship between the Arab lands and Europe will either bring closer the future predicted by the American political scientist Samuel Huntington or else consign him to the university library shelves. Huntington's influential 1993 essay in *Foreign Affairs*, subsequently lengthened into a book, foresaw a "clash of civilizations" that in recent years we sometimes seem to have been sedulously promoting. Some of the global problems that we will face in this century—for example, whether China can make a smooth accommodation between economic license and political authority—are probably matters for a circumscribed few, in this case a small cadre of bureaucratic politicians in Beijing. Others—like environmental disasters—have already been set in train by greed and ecological pillage, and the West (and particularly America) appears reluctant to try to mitigate the consequences. But a clash between the world that likes to think of itself as being primarily made in the mold of the New Testament and the Islamic world of another book raises issues for all of us, though we could still avoid it. Yet there is a real danger that we will trigger catastrophe through acts both of omission and commission. How can things have come to this?

Let us for a moment revisit the Huntington thesis. Hot on the heels of liberalism's triumph in the 1980s and '90s—the breaching of the Berlin Wall, the fall of Europe's last empire, the opening of markets by technology and international agreement—Huntington warned against the easy assumption that we could relax with the Cold War won, without the use of those engines of death stockpiled in silos from Utah to the Ukraine. "Conflict" was not, after all, a subject for the history books. "The most important conflicts of the future," he wrote, "will occur along cultural fault lines separating civilizations from each other." The differences between civilizations were more fundamental than those between political ideologies, and the more the world was shrunk by technology, the more we became aware of them. Globalization weakened local and national identities, and the gap was filled by religion, with non-Western civilizations returning to their roots, re-Islamizing, for instance, in the Middle East. Moreover, cultural—or as he largely argues it, religious— characteristics are less likely to change than those that are political or economic. "Conflict," he notes, "along the fault line between Western and Islamic civilizations has been going on for 1,300 years," and "on both sides the interaction between Islam and the West is seen as a clash of civilizations." Popular in some academic circles in the West, his theories are also extensively quoted on jihadist Web sites in the Arab world.

There were other civilization clashes to which Huntington drew attention. Yet his arguments never convinced me. I spent a good deal of time during my years in Hong Kong pointing out that there was not some cultural divide between the so-called Confucian world ("so-called" usually by those who have never read Confucius and tend to confuse him with Singapore's Lee Kuan Yew) and the West, which seems comfortable with Asians being stripped of civil liberties and denied democracy. It was fashionable to argue before the 1997–99 Asian financial crisis that suppression of civil liberties was the reasonable price that the countries of Southeast Asia had paid for spectacular development. There was deemed to be some umbilical relationship between GDP growth and locking up trade union leaders, political opponents, and inquisitive journalists. Singapore's mix of bland authoritarianism and social engineering was thought, for example, to reflect some deep Asian cultural preferences. The history of the region and the variety of its political developments were ignored. China's republican revolutionary Sun Yat-sen had apparently never existed. Many of us argued that human rights were universally valid, and that democracy under the rule of law was the best system of government anywhere. With the Asian financial crash and the discrediting of the Asian model of crony capitalism and authoritarian politics, the controversy seemed over. The clash of civilizations might have been regarded as the stuff of provocative academic seminars. Then the planes slammed into the Twin Towers, and the way the West viewed the world changed.

Well, of course, it is not quite that simple. The pretexts, the causes, the narrative of atrocity began much earlier than 2001. And we had scholarly guides to point us down the right exploratory tracks. Oh, to have been the publisher of Professor Bernard Lewis, sage of Princeton and scholar-almost-in-residence to Washington's tough guys, led en masse by Vice President Dick Cheney. I admit to a personal debt to Lewis's scholarship. I have enjoyed, and I hope learned from, a number of his books. But I started to worry, as I read on from *What Went Wrong?* to *The Crisis of Islam* that I was being carefully pointed in a particular direction, lined up before the fingerprints, the cosh, the swag bag, and the rest of the evidence. "Most Muslims," he tells us in *The Crisis of Islam*, "are not fundamentalists, and most fundamentalists are not terrorists, but most present-day terrorists are Muslims and proudly identify themselves as such." Well, yes—and that sentence resonates (loudly) in parts of the policy-making community in Washington. But what if I had tried a similar formulation on some of these same policymakers just after the IRA bombed Harrods in London: "Most Catholics are not extremist Irish republicans, and most extreme republicans are not terrorists, but most terrorists in Britain today are Catholic and proudly identify themselves as such." I suspect that it is not a sentence that would have increased my circle of admirers in America, not because it is wrong but because it is so loaded with an agenda. Anyway, what we have been taught is that there is a rage in the Islamic world—in part, the result of history and humiliation—that fuels hostility to America and to Europe, too, home of past crusaders and present infidel feudatories of the Great Satan. Clash go the civilizations.

However we address the Islamic world, it is important to avoid sounding like those politicians and church leaders who suggest that the West dwells on a higher moral plane, custodians of a superior set of moral values and attitudes. In particular, in Europe we sometimes appear to have filed and forgotten the gas chambers, gulags, and our Christian heritage of flagrant or more discreet anti-Semitism and Islamaphobia. European prejudices may be rock solid, but our pulpits are made of straw. What of this Islamic world that allegedly confronts our own civilization? Sometimes we forget that three-quarters of its 1.2 billion citizens live beyond the countries of the Arab League, in, for example, the democracies of Malaysia, Indonesia, the Philippines, and India. Asian Muslim societies have their share of problems, not least dealing with pockets of extremism, but it makes no sense to generalize about an Islamic anger allegedly engulfing countries from the Atlantic seaboard to the Pacific shores.

If we focus on a narrower range of Arab countries—North Africa, Egypt, the Levant, the Gulf, the countries in the cockpit of current struggle and dissent—what do we find? In 2002, the Arab Thought Foundation commissioned a survey by Zogby International of attitudes in eight countries: Egypt, Israel, Jordan, Lebanon, Kuwait, Morocco, the United Arab Emirates, and Saudi Arabia. Their results confirmed other similar if not identical surveys by the Pew Research Center and others. From the survey it is clear that Arabs, like Americans or Europeans, are most concerned about matters of personal security, fulfillment, and satisfaction. Perhaps it is a surprise that they do not appear to hate our Western values and their cultural emanations: democracy, freedom, education, movies, television. Sad to say, the favorite program on Arab television is *Who Wants to Be a Millionaire?* Other survey evidence underlines this point. The UN's Second Arab Human Development Report, published in 2003, quotes the World Values Survey findings that Arabs top the world in believing that democracy is the best form of government. They are way ahead of Europeans and Americans, and three times as likely to hold this view as East Asians.

There is not much sign of a clash of values here. The problem seems to be rather simpler. The Arab world does not mind (what began as) American and European values, but it cannot stand American policies and by extension the same policies when embraced or tolerated by Europeans. As the American national intelligence director, John Negroponte, said explicitly in hearings in the Senate in early 2005, "Our policies in the Middle East feed Islamic resentment." So the Arab world holds very negative opinions of the United States and the United Kingdom (even while holding, according to the same survey, positive views about American freedom and democracy). Why is the United Kingdom in this pit of unpopularity alongside the United States? Partly, I suppose, because of what we are seen to do and partly because of what we are silent about. Who knows how widely Saint Thomas More is read in Arab lands? But his tag *"qui tacet consentire videtur"* (silence is seen as agreement) is true everywhere. Perhaps it can cheer us in Britain to discover that France comes out best in these surveys, scoring very positive ratings, as do Japan, Germany, and Canada.

What sort of policies feed Islamic resentment, and particularly the hostility in Arab countries? The invasion of Iraq obviously features high on the list. But in 2002 the issue that stood out from the Zogby survey was hardly surprising, given the absence of peace in the Middle East. The survey's authors write that "after more than three generations of conflicts, and the betrayal and denial of Palestinian rights, this issue appears to have become a defining one of general Arab concern. It is not a foreign policy issue. . . . Rather . . . the situation of the Palestinians appears to have become a personal matter." As the recent work of, for example, Richard Perle and David Frum has shown, this apparently incontestable point is, for a particular school of American thought, a deliberate and alarming blind spot.

Terrorism has given a savage twist to the debates about values in the Middle East and the best way to abate hostility to America and to some European countries. American attitudes to terrorism were inevitably shaped by the terrible events of September 11, 2001. Initially, the atrocities drew Europe and America more closely together. I flew straightaway to America with High Representative Javier Solana and the Belgian foreign minister (who was then holding the EU presidency) to discuss immediate assistance for America in the counterterrorism campaign. Among the issues we discussed with Secretary of State Colin Powell was the provision of support for Pakistan to encourage it to fight terrorism itself. We continued on within days to Islamabad. But as the months passed and the war on Iraq was advocated and planned, America and Europe drew apart, with Europe not always fully appreciating the extent of the U.S. trauma—the sense of violation, the shock at discovering that to be invincible was not the same as to be invulnerable. The subsequent "war on terrorism" has been understood in Europe as a metaphor: a phrase to describe the myriad responses required of the civilized world to address problems that do not admit of definitive solutions, let alone of military ones. America, by contrast, has really felt itself to be (if not domestically conducted itself as though it were) at war; it is a war that ratchets up patriotic sentiments to unparalleled potency. The election in November 2004 was won by a war president with Kabul and Baghdad under his belt, and more citadels to storm, more heights to seize.

Terrorism is abhorred in Europe. We have every reason to hate it from Spain to Ireland, from the United Kingdom to Italy, from Germany to Greece. The Spanish have demonstrated extraordinary resolve in standing up to the Basque separatists, ETA, and, as I said before, it was deplorable to characterize the electoral returns after the Atocha bombings as a sign of national cowardice. I have already noted my own long-standing resentment at past indulgence by some Americans of the champions of Irish terrorism and its paymasters on the other side of the Atlantic, and the 2005 bombings of London by Islamic extremists served only to expand the awful range of terrorism within Britain's borders. So Europeans hate terrorism. But we are also uncomfortable with the one-dimensional nature of the debate in some quarters, the unwillingness to accept that terrorists might on occasion be using abhorrent means to pursue ends that we may or may not agree with, but which are susceptible to reason and whose causes can be addressed without a war. It is as if any discussion of the causes of alienation and hatred (for example, on the part of the British-born-and–raised suicide bombers who attacked London) was evidence of appeasement. The idea of a world divided between good and evil—between us and them—sits uncomfortably with most Europeans. Throughout recorded time, asymmetric threats have been the weapon of the weak against the strong. We find them sanctioned by history when the cause is just, the means proportionate, and the outcome good. The morality is not always very clear. History, after all, is written by, or largely about, the victors, including England's national hero of the fifteenth century, Henry V, who murdered his prisoners before his triumph at Agincourt. As Sir John Harington wrote in the early seventeenth century:

> Treason doth never prosper: what's the reason?
> For if it prosper, none dare call it treason.

Britain's history from Kenya to Israel to Ireland to South Africa is peppered with examples of terrorism, events that have elided into politics. Terrorism sometimes has precise political causes and objectives—the Mau Mau, the Stern gang, the IRA, the ANC. Sometimes it has had less focused aims—for instance, Errico Malatesta's "propaganda of the deed," which tried to draw attention to injustice and destroy the nerve of ruling elites by murdering presidents and princes, czars and kings. Today's terrorism by Islamic groups, able through the advance of technology to shatter civilized order through terrible acts of destruction, seems closer to the anarchists than to the gun-toting politicians like the Irish ones I myself know best, who were notorious for their ability to carry both a ballot box and an Armalite. The ideas that sustain Osama Bin Laden and those who think like him (who are not all members of a spectacularly sophisticated network of evil, but nonetheless fellow believers in a loose confederation of dark prejudices) can hardly be dignified with the description of a polished political manifesto. They do not travel far beyond the old graffiti, "Yankee, Go Home." But they do represent a form of political, social, and cultural alienation, which we should seek to comprehend. Joseph Conrad investigated these dark corners in his novel *The Secret Agent* and described one of his fictional terrorists:

> He was no man of action; he was not even an orator of torrential eloquence, sweeping the masses along in the rushing noise and foam of a great enthusiasm. With a more subtle intention, he took the part of an

insolent and venomous evoker of sinister impulses which lurk in the blind envy and misery of poverty, in all the hopeful and noble illusions of righteous anger, pity and revolt. . . . The way of even the most justifiable revolutions is prepared by personal impulses disguised into creeds.

It is not normal for men and women to want to get up in the morning and strap bombs to themselves or to their children and set out to kill and maim. How does a sense of injustice, which so often inspires surrender to religious simplicity, come to trigger evil? Further, why does the West's notion of spreading freedom, capitalism, and democracy look to some others like licentiousness, greed, and a new colonialism? We should surely try to fathom the answer to these questions, and understand that we can make them either more or less soluble.

No one should seek to excuse or explain away the outrages of September 11. The cause was horribly unjust; the means abominable. But it is not a surrender to organized evil to assert that there are some policies that would demobilize the recruiting sergeants of terrorism. The reasons for what happened cannot be placed outside rational discussion. Nor, in my view, can terrorism ever be eradicated from the face of the earth. Complete elimination of the threat could only be achieved in a global Orwellian police state that denied freedom to everyone. That would negate the values for which America and Europe stand. Paradoxically, it would also demand of good men the sort of just resistance—and potentially violent resistance—that it was seeking to stamp out.

Americans and Europeans are now agreed on a positive agenda (as well as a fist of security options) for combating terrorism and its causes. Americans have come rather late to the issue, albeit with muscular enthusiasm. But their credentials are suspect and their application of principles is prone to a pretty blatant display of double standards. Europeans have been laboring in the vineyards for a decade but with too little conviction, energy, and tough-mindedness. Indeed, so low-key have been our efforts that most Americans (including many otherwise well-informed policymakers, academics, and journalists) had no idea that we were doing anything. If there were only one area of policy where we really need to try to make the Atlantic alliance work more successfully, this is it. We have the ideas, the money, and the need. There will be no excuse if we turn these ideas into a shambles.

In 2002, the UN Development Program (UNDP) produced a report (the predecessor to the one I mentioned earlier) on the Arab League countries. *Time* magazine called it the most important publication of the year. It unleashed a tidal wave of debate across Arab countries about the reasons for the region's comparative backwardness and inadequate performance. Well over a million copies of the report were downloaded from the Internet, many from Arab countries. Why did a scholarly survey have such an impact?

The first reason is that its authorship caused surprise and endowed credibility. It was written by Arab scholars and policymakers, not well-meaning outsiders. Second, its analysis was captivatingly honest and politically bold—too bold for some. When I raised its conclusions with a group of Arab League foreign ministers, there was a lot of averting of eyes and shuffling of papers. They were anxious to move on to the next agenda item. How could it be that, in terms of economic performance in the last quarter of the twentieth century, the only region that did worse than the Arab countries was sub-Saharan Africa? Why had personal incomes stagnated through these years? Why had per capita wealth in the region fallen from one-fifth of the Organization for Economic Cooperation and Development's average to one-seventh? Why were productivity, investment efficiency, and foreign direct investment so low? How could the combined GDP of all Arab countries be lower than that of a single European country, Spain?

The answer came in the prescriptions summarized by the UNDP's Arab regional director. In the director's view, Arab countries needed to embark on rebuilding their societies on the basis of:

1. Full respect for human rights and human freedoms as the cornerstones of good governance, leading to human development
2. The complete empowerment of Arab women, taking advantage of all opportunities to build their capabilities and to enable them to exercise those capabilities to the fullest
3. The consolidation of knowledge acquisition and its effective utilization

Governance, gender, education—this is the Arab world's own formula for improvement and modernization, and a formula, too, which European partners on the other side of the Mediterranean have been trying gently, too gently, to promote. We have been attempting to establish a free-trade area around our shared sea by 2010, to encourage more trade between Arab countries and to assist those, like Morocco and Jordan, who are themselves committed to modernization, democratic reform, and the nurturing of a more lively civil society. But the more I worked on this policy with its ambitious objective, the more I began to fear that Europe was more concerned about a free-trade *area* than about free *trade*, at least in the sort of agricultural products grown in southern European countries.

There is a strong link between better government and better economic performance, and between the accomplishment of both those objectives and greater stability. Authoritarian governments are less likely to be good economic managers; they shelter corruption and suppress the sorts of pluralism—a free press, for instance—which bring transparency to economic governance. The result of authoritarianism in the Arab region is twofold. First, lower economic growth fails to create the jobs that demographic pressures constantly demand in the Arab world. Young men without jobs, without the dignity of work, and without cash in their pockets are easily attracted to other causes than the relatively innocent occupation of making money. Second, the denial of civil liberties itself causes resentment, driving debate off the street and out of the coffee shops and into the cellars. Bad economic performance, especially when associated with large wealth and income differences, combines with the suppression of dissent to breed trouble—big trouble.

How should the Arab world's European neighbors support the process of modernization that is so greatly in our own interest, with the relief of pressures from illegal immigration, the opening of new and expanding markets, and the exporting of stability to our near neighborhood in the mix? And I do not for a moment accept that it is none of our business, since successful and stable neighbors are very much in our own interest. Nor do I buy the argument that encouraging democracy in the Arab world only creates trouble, with the risk that we will replace more or less compliant authoritarian friends with rabid fundamentalist regimes, established on the basis of one man, one vote, once. I have never been convinced by the argument that free politics is inherently more unstable than command politics. Is Saudi Arabia more stable because it knows only the first fragile green shoots of democracy? Has it in the past inadvertently exported young terrorists, and not always so inadvertently financed extremist activity, because it is too free? What offers the best prospect of stability in Egypt—continuing the past policies of President Hosni Mubarak or allowing the political openings cautiously advocated by his son? Does oil wealth across the region bring democracy-lite stability or simply postpone a violent democratic shock? The West would already have done much to promote modernization, better economic management, and improved government if we had been more committed to reducing our dependence on environmentally deadly fossil fuels. Cash-rich oil producers have been able to buy off the need for reform. Every gas-guzzling sports utility vehicle, lumbering through urban traffic on the school run, is a symbol of some of the worst environmental and economic practices sustaining some of the worst of the political ones.

There are some clear ground rules that outside well-wishers should follow. We are talking about other peoples' lives and countries, not our own. "Better," as T. E. Lawrence argued, "to let them do it imperfectly than to do it perfectly yourself, for it is their country, their way and your time is short." It is imperative that the agenda of modernization—in education, in the rule of law, in participatory government, in opportunities for women, in nourishing civil society—should be owned by Arab countries themselves. Recognition that this will all take time, and that you need to prepare for the long haul, is not code for procrastination. It is not enough, for example, for Arab intellectuals to say what they want and then hunt for excuses for not doing anything more about it. Authoritarian governments in the Middle East have been adept at using the Israeli-Palestine issue to legitimate their rule and to provide an excuse for avoiding reform, and too many Arab modernizers have gone along, burying the democratic cause in the wider issue of a struggle for Arab dignity. We also have to be careful in supporting better government and democracy, neither to preach nor to offer—as we have in such grotesque profusion—evidence of double standards. We should expect the same of everyone, regardless of how pliable some authoritarian countries may be when our transient strategic interests throw up new short-term imperatives. If democratic modernization looks like a Western tactic for securing our own interests, we risk discrediting the ideas in which we believe and turning our Arab friends who share the same ideas into seeming stooges. Above all, as we have very painfully discovered, it is difficult to impose a free society through invasion and military might, spreading democracy through the region in the tracks, as it were, of Jeffersonian tanks. Some suggest that the elections in Iraq (which were held at Iraqi insistence despite American efforts to shelve or dilute them) administered a sharp democratic jolt to the region. This may be in part true, and the bravery and determination of those who voted in Iraq were certainly impressive. But the jolt came at a very high cost, for the Iraqis themselves and for the reputation of America and its allies.

The argument for democracy in the Arab region began well before the Iraq invasion. Moreover, the invasion was not justified on the neoconservative, revisionist grounds that after thousands of innocent casualties we would be able to hold an election and thereby demonstrate to others in the region the benefits of democracy. The allies stumbled on the case for democracy only when their earlier jumble of justifications for the war crumbled in their hands. That we now have to make the best of what has happened (forgetting the costs and focusing on the removal of Saddam Hussein and his murderous cronies), while abundantly true, is not the same as saying that the war—its pretexts, conduct, and aftermath—was warranted all along. The invasion certainly emboldened and recruited terrorists, and may well have caused some of the modernizers among Iraq's neighbors, including Iran, to question whether the price paid for democracy in terms of death, injury, instability, and societal breakdown was too high; and for conservatives in those countries the sight of democracy being, as it were, imposed by force would have confirmed their view that it is an assault, a secular, Western abomination. In addition, you cannot make war on another country every time you want to give democracy a boost. So, we want to see democracy in Syria next: Does the Pentagon have the battle plan ready yet? Whatever else we may have learned in Iraq, the lesson spelled out by Winston Churchill in *My Early Life* comes bleakly to mind: "Never, never, never believe any war will be smooth or easy, or that anyone who embarks on the strange voyage can measure the tides and hurricanes he will encounter. The statesman who yields to war fever must realize that once the signal is given, he is no longer the master of policy but the slave of unforeseeable and uncontrollable events."

There are better ways than war of spreading democracy and the rule of law. The strategy that Europe has pursued, though with insufficient ardor, is our Mediterranean partnership. It is based on a series of trade and cooperation agreements between the European Union and individual countries. They have taken a long time to negotiate and almost as long, on the European side, to ratify. It was sometimes difficult to explain to our Arab co-negotiators how it was that agreements, to which we allegedly gave so much priority, spent years rambling up and down the legislative corridors of Europe's parliamentary democracy. When I became European Commissioner in 1999, we had already negotiated agreements with Tunisia, Morocco, Israel, and the Palestinian Authority. During my tenure, we completed negotiations with Algeria, Egypt, Lebanon, and Syria. We opened our markets a bit to our southern neighbors—with the promise of more progress on sensitive agricultural products and services—and they opened their markets a bit to us. We committed about one billion euros a year in grants to support Arab development, and about twice that in loans from the European Investment Bank.

The agreements were supposed to encourage economic and political liberalization, so that the creation of a free market would be accompanied by a growing approximation of systems of governance, laws, and regulations. The European Union also wished to promote greater cooperation with the Arab world in areas such as policing and immigration control. Any ambitions to promote security cooperation were thwarted by the Israel-Palestine strife. The performance of our partners varied enormously. Jordan and Morocco won most of our gold stars, combining some political modernization with sensible economic management. The Tunisians were good economic performers and were progressive on gender issues but had a human rights record that was the source of frequent angry debate in the European Parliament. The Egyptians were subtle, charming, and difficult to help, with one or two ministerial holdovers from the days of Nasserite socialism slowing down our development programs. (It is instructive that Egyptians seem to be so successful entrepreneurially everywhere but in Egypt.) The most difficult of our partners were the Syrians. Dealing with them made the task of Sisyphus with his boulder seem straightforward. No one can visit Damascus without seeing what a formidable country Syria could be—culturally and intellectually. (I remember a passionate discussion about Margaret Atwood's novels with the president's and foreign minister's hard-line female interpreter and adviser.) But Syria is caged by history, corruption, and authoritarianism, with its young president unable to move the country out of the shadow of his late father and his father's brutal cronies. At my first meeting with Bashar Assad—a young ophthalmologist who had studied in London—I thought him an open, rather geekish young man. He said most of the right things. Unhappily, delivering on them proved more difficult. Syria has been bogged down in its colonial adventure in luckless Lebanon and ensnared in a not wholly paranoid fear of Israel. Our economic negotiations threatened the cartels operated by the military and Ba'athist lackeys, and it was clear that the successful conclusion of this part of our talks represented a hard-won success for the president and his young advisers. With its security services almost certainly out of control, Syria will need tough but constructive handling.

Late in the day in the Syrian talks, we were obliged to insert into the text of the proposed agreement a clause on the proliferation of weapons of mass destruction as well as a clause on terrorism. Unfortunately, importing other policy objectives into the drafting of agreements, a process that began with the attachment of human rights clauses to all EU agreements, has grown into a regular feature of EU diplomacy that hobbles our negotiating and reduces our flexibility. It would be a laudable strategy if the agreements were then policed fairly rigorously. They are not. In one of the more unsavory twists of Western diplomacy, we Europeans were concluding negotiations that included requirements on human rights with countries to whom our American allies were shipping terrorist suspects to be tortured as part of the ill-considered practice known as "extraordinary rendition." This was taking outsourcing to unimagined lengths. A human rights clause was one of the more difficult nuts to crack in our trade negotiations with Saudi Arabia and the other

Gulf countries. I remember a long night's discussion in Brussels on human rights with a group of foreign ministers from the region, after which I felt that all of us on the European side of the table might be expected to show that we understood the error of our ways by driving down to the Gran' Place to search out a few adulteresses to stone. There are two better options that the European Union should adopt that are both honest and practical. First, any conditions applied to an agreement should be made positive rather than negative; we should reward good behavior, not threaten to penalize bad. Second, if an issue is sufficiently important—say, terrorism or weapons proliferation—Europe should not even start to negotiate an agreement with a country that is not equally serious about the matter. It devalues the currency of international cooperation to draft clauses with painstaking solicitude that everyone acknowledges are likely to be honored mainly in the breach. Winking at electrodes, as it were, makes for wretched diplomacy. Few authoritarian governments go weak at the knees at the prospect of a European démarche.

Europe is now trying to turn its existing Mediterranean agreements into a tighter and more generous neighborhood policy, and this will obviously be the main vehicle for our contribution to the drive for reform and modernization in the region. There are three problems. First, the offers we make to our partners are insufficiently generous. We are still far too cautious about agricultural liberalization. The southern European countries that are most insistent on the political importance of the Mediterranean are usually the most resistant to concessions on importing products from Arab countries—olives, tomatoes, fish, cut flowers, soft fruit, and so on. There is a simple trade-off. If we do not take their tomatoes, we will be on the receiving end of shiploads of their illegal migrants and, moreover, we will reduce employment prospects for the young in the region, making it all the more likely that some of them will be radicalized. We also need to help speed up the harmonization of standards—including those of good safety and public health—between the countries of Europe and our neighbors to deal with one of the main non-tariff barriers to increased trade. In addition to being more generous on trade, we should offer more development assistance. This is where my argument about positive discrimination bites. If we want to help drive reform, we should set aside a larger share of our budget to support those who commit themselves to it. We were starting to try this at the margins with the programs run by the European Commission; I hope these efforts will survive. In my experience it is very unusual for European governments to agree to cut back aid programs because of, say, bad human rights performance in a particular country. There will always be a European president or a prime minister, with a particular client or friend in the region, prepared to intervene on the client's behalf—even when that partner's government has been reneging on its promises of economic reform or hanging dissidents from the rafters by their thumbs. President Chirac, for instance, had a soft spot for the Tunisian regime. So a more effective European contribution to better governance in the region should combine greater generosity with more tough-mindedness about its recipients.

Third, we need to be much more active in promoting trade and investment within the region. The countries of the southern Mediterranean want to trade more with Europe and America, but they hardly trade with one another. Perhaps 5 percent of their trade is with their Arab neighbors. In too many countries there is still an autarchic reflex and a belief in economic self-sufficiency. But they are too backward and usually too socialist to manage on their own. They lose out on all the economies of scale, all the opportunities for shared investment and manufacturing that regional integration would provide. Outsiders put their money elsewhere, farther afield. With all the arguments about outsourcing in Europe, and all the debate about off-shore manufacturing, no one ever points a finger of blame at the Arab world. The money stays away; it goes to Asia; so the unemployment grows. There have been belated efforts by some Arab countries, including Tunisia, Morocco, Jordan, and Egypt, to create something closer to a common market through what is called the Agadir process. When it was finally launched after years of discussion, one of the foreign ministers responsible for it said to me, "We have saddled the camel." Maybe, but it plods rather slowly up the first dune. America and Europe should bend their efforts to promote free trade around the Mediterranean and between the Mediterranean countries and those Arab countries to the east, the members of the Gulf Cooperation Council, Iraq and Yemen. Trade, investment, growth, jobs:

that is a large part of the answer to the growth of extremism and the spawning of terrorism.

In previous years, we in Europe have not spent very much time discussing these issues, on which we could make a considerable difference, preferring instead to wring our hands and rend our garments over Palestine and Israel. It was a tribute to the resilience of our work to build a network of agreements with countries around the Mediterranean's southern and eastern shores that the process survived with Israel, rightly, a full participating member. Indeed, the Barcelona Process meetings provided the only forum where Israelis and Arabs regularly met, debating political as well as economic issues. But so long as the bloody dispute over the future of a Palestinian state persists, it will be impossible to incorporate regional security in the partnership.

It would not be an exaggeration to say that European foreign ministers discussed Palestine and Israel virtually every month, both at the lunch meetings I described earlier and at occasional larger informal meetings as well. Sometimes a minister had just been to the region and had something interesting to report back; sometimes a representative was sent on the usual round of visits; sometimes a formal meeting of Barcelona Partners or the Quartet powers of the United States, the United Nations, the Russian Federation, and the European Union had just occurred or loomed on the horizon. Nothing ever changed very much, certainly not for the better. After the first relatively hopeful period, in 2000–01, when the outlook was buoyed by talks at Camp David and then later at Taba, everything went downhill, faster and more disastrously than anyone had anticipated. Starting with Ariel Sharon's walk on the Temple Mount, Ehud Barak's political destruction, and then Yasser Arafat's at best ambiguous attitude to the employment of the most horrendous violence against Israeli targets, the massacres of the innocent, the reprisals, the house demolitions, the blockades, and the building of the security barrier clocked up ever more dreadful statistics of hopeless horror. We all meant well and worked hard. Javier Solana in particular worked himself into the ground. But what did we achieve? Maybe we could never have achieved anything on our own. What was certain was that a Pavlovian rejection of any course of action that might distance Europe from the Americans was the main determinant of

Europe's political behavior. It was in a way absurd. We had, at least in theory, the same objectives as the Americans. But declaring those aims too strongly, along with proposals for trying to achieve them, risked opening up some clear water between us and Washington. While we were prepared to do this from time to time—for example, over the Israeli fence—on the whole we preferred to delude ourselves that Washington was as committed to an end to settlements and to an agreement based on the 1967 borders as we were ourselves. It may be that with the 2004 presidential election safely and soundly in the bag, the Bush administration's policy and Europe's will coalesce. It would be helpful if they did.

What is clear is that unless we make better progress in resolving the Israeli-Palestinian conflict, it will continue to embitter the West's relations with the whole Islamic world. Washington's engagement is certainly essential to a solution, but Europe could legitimately be more independent in setting out its own views. This would raise the political cost of America hanging back from active engagement. In any case, I spent five years talking, visiting, and drafting communiqués on behalf of the European Commission, all while Israel and Palestine were locked into a downward spiral of death and destruction, each seemingly intent on causing pain to the other, with one side plotting revenge and the other exacting a terrible retribution against the last ghoulish act of vengeance.

I should stand back for a moment and offer a confession that will attract criticism by the bucket load. I believe that, in the Middle East, there *are* two legitimate howls of rage, two storylines, not one. I also share with the wise and intelligent former foreign minister of Israel Shlomo Ben-Ami the view that, in his words, "the Holocaust . . . should not give the Jews and Israel any moral immunity from criticism, nor is it proper for Israelis to conveniently dismiss all and every attack against their reproachable policies as anti-Semitism." I regard the anti-Semitism that was part and parcel of Christianity for centuries as a dark stain on my religion. The behavior of the leadership of my own Catholic Church in the terrible Holocaust years was deplorable. Anti-Semitism is a malevolent sentiment that I find difficult to comprehend, and it is deeply offensive when *any* criticism of Sharon or the policies of the Likud Party is ascribed wholesale to anti-Semitism. Hostility to Sharon's policies and the practices of the Israel Defense Forces can at times drift into anti-Semitism, but it is unfair always to conflate the two.

On one of my early visits to Washington as a European commissioner, a senator said to me, "You'd better understand. We are all members of the Likud Party now." Well, I was not. Nor, I believe, were most Europeans. The people I most admired were those like Yossi Beilin and the other leaders of the peace movement, whose activities demonstrated that however great the security problems in Israel, Israel remained a free society. There was far more debate in Israel's media about its strengths and weaknesses, about the successes and failures of its policy, than is evident in the way the American press and television cover these issues. Betselem and other human rights organizations point out the human and civil liberties costs of the occupation of Palestinian lands. Judges rule against the government, insisting that even in dealing with security issues there is a price that a free society has to pay to retain its moral core. Israel is a plural, free society, and it should not be treated like an illegitimate pariah.

Ending the bloodshed does not await the discovery of a hitherto secret diplomatic formula. The ingredients of a peace settlement are well-known and sat at the heart of the discussions at Camp David and Taba. The Mitchell Commission covered them in 2001. The Quartet's road map gave the international community's endorsement to a political gazetteer for putting them in place in 2002. The Geneva initiative in 2003 demonstrated that there were still courageous men and women in Israel and Palestine who could find the path to peace and to a way in which the two states could live harmoniously side by side in what, with shame if not irony, we still call the Holy Land. We know that a two-state solution will require cast-iron guarantees to Israel about its security; the normalization of its relations with its Arab neighbors; borders between the two states based on those that existed in 1967 with negotiated territorial swaps; the sharing of Jerusalem as the capital of the two states; the end of Jewish settlement activity; and an agreed curtailment of the right of Palestinian refugees to return to what is now Israel. We know how the violence should end, but will it?

The international community's policy in the last few years has been based on three propositions: first, that Ariel Sharon and his government genuinely believe in the creation of a viable Palestinian state; second, that the Palestinian political leaders will be able, and have the will, to convince their community that that goal will only be achieved if they give up violence, even against what they see as an illegal and aggressive occupation of their own land; and third, that Sharon and his government will take action—for example, on the dismantling of settlements—that will help the Palestinian leaders to accomplish the leadership tasks assigned to them. It has taken gymnastic leaps of faith to believe over the last few years that these propositions remain true. Now we have the real test in circumstances made more propitious by the arrival in 2004 of time's winged chariot, and its departure with Mr. Arafat on board.

Throughout the first Bush administration, we were told in Europe that Arafat himself was *the* problem. I heard Condoleezza Rice say it over and over again. She would brook no disagreement. Most of us found no difficulty in recognizing that he was *a* problem, and a very big, bad one indeed. But *the* problem? Anyway, whether with a definite or an indefinite article, the problem is no longer there, so progress should be a lot easier, and in a second Bush term there will presumably be fewer political constraints on heavier involvement in the Middle East—if, that is, there were any at all before! Sharon's decision to quit Gaza is welcome, provided it is a step on the road to creating a viable Palestinian state and not a collection of different scraps of territory, divided by concrete, soldiers, and barbed wire. No state that resembles a Swiss cheese can be regarded as viable. No sustainable solution can be found in establishing a mixed bag of Palestinian Bantustans with the symbols of sovereign statehood but the reality of fragmented and impoverished dependence. Should the rest of us have any doubts at all about the outcome envisioned by Sharon and those in Washington who support, unquestioningly, this "man of peace"? If the building and expansion of settlements is a guide, skepticism is, alas, justified. While the Oslo Peace process rolled on, building confidence it was said, Israelis continued to build settlements around Jerusalem and on the hillsides of the West Bank. Settlement activity—creating new facts on the ground—continues to this day. Settlements housing a few are closed down in Gaza; settlements housing many are constructed on the West Bank. Tear down here, build up there. When Sharon's senior adviser Dov Weisglass said in late 2004 that the plan to disengage from Gaza in effect froze the peace process, that it was just so much "formaldehyde," and that the Americans agreed that large settlements should be retained on the West Bank with many only being addressed at some date when "the Palestinians turn into Finns," his remarks had a pretty authentic ring. Europeans should be tough with the Palestinians over security, much tougher than we were able to be when Arafat still survived in the rubble of his office, his baleful influence far greater than his governing authority. We should press for far tighter monitoring of Palestinian security activities. The help we give the Palestinian authority should continue to be dependent on Palestinian fulfillment of strict conditions. (The institutional arrangements in Palestine that everyone now accepts as a suitable channel for assisting the would-be state are largely the result of the pressure we in Europe exerted in recent years.) However, we will not secure the long-term changes necessary in Palestine unless there is clear evidence of an equivalent Israeli response, and the dismantling of settlements is the best measure of Israel's commitment to a sustainable solution.

A peace settlement between Israel and Palestine would help transform the prospects for the relationship between the West and the Arab Near East, and indeed between the West and the whole of the Islamic world. It would be absurd to suggest that Islamic terrorism has been driven above all by compassion for the Palestinian people, whose condition does indeed deserve the greatest sympathy. But the terrorists exploit the Palestinian issue and, conversely, it fertilizes terrorism's breeding grounds. Television footage of Israel Defense Force helicopter gunships rocketing Palestinian refugee camps alongside similar pictures of American assaults on Iraqi Sunni heartlands inevitably result in more or less complete identification in Arab minds of the Israeli and American causes. This does not help America, Europe, or the moderates and reformers in the Arab world. Nothing matters more in President Bush's second term than peace between Israel and Palestine.

Sharon has exploited very cleverly the American fear of terrorism and the understandable determination of the American people and administration to root it out in his handling of the Palestinian intifada. Similarly, Vladimir Putin has sought to identify his own war in Chechnya with the global campaign against terrorism. This is not a wholly unreasonable point. The Chechen rebels are wicked and brutal. If one were, however, to take the comparison entirely on the Russian president's terms, the conclusions would be pretty depressing. The Chechnya war grinds horribly on, contaminating the northern and southern Caucasus, an indictment of Russian incompetence and corruption. If the overall effort to contain and reduce terrorism goes as badly elsewhere, then we all face a miserable and very dangerous future.

It is easy to twig how we in Europe could find it so difficult to put together an effective and coherent position on the Middle East and on Iraq. But it is more puzzling to fathom why we had so much of a problem in managing sensibly our relations with Russia. It should be an important aim of European policy to promote the growth of prosperity, stability, and freedom in Russia as in our other neighbors. Indeed, the task in Russia should be given priority because Russia is so large and carries a history of superpower status, a hugely influential cultural heritage, and substantial energy supplies that Europe needs. You do not have to warm to the angst-ridden Russian soul or enthuse about all those dripping birch forests to recognize how much Western Europe owes culturally to our great Slavic neighbor, how much we created problems for ourselves by cutting Lenin's Russia off from the rest of Europe (which, admittedly, it wanted to consume in the flames of revolution), and how much the resistance to the postwar threat of nuclear-armed Communist tyranny helped to define the nature of West European democracy. Europe should sympathize with Russia's efforts to recover from the crude early effort to embrace democracy and capitalism without property rights, the enforcement of contracts, and the rule of law, which, not surprisingly, produced chaos, robbery, inequality, and lawlessness. I guess we should also be understanding about the bruised Russian sensitivities caused by its loss of empire. Many of us have experienced that. But sympathy and understanding can only stretch so far. When I hear some Russian spokesmen on this theme, I wonder how much partners of Britain would have commiserated with us in the 1940s and '50s if our worldview had sounded like the self-pitying rant of a member of the League of Empire Loyalists.

After seventy years of isolation, the Russian economy remains small—perhaps 1 percent of world output—with low investment, a decaying infrastructure, large and distorting subsidies to housing and electricity, little by way of a small business sector, and doubts about private property rights. The economy floats on the success of the energy sector—oil and gas—and has benefited over the past five years from cautious management and institutional and legal reforms, some of which have even been properly implemented. Yet when Russia becomes a member of the World Trade Organization, I doubt whether we should expect the profile of Russian exports to Europe and the rest of the world to change much. Energy and commodities predominate; it will be a long time before "Made in Russia" is a label that attracts customers. Russia receives little foreign direct investment given its size, and the Yukos affair—the looting of a private company whose owner's political ambitions riled President Putin—will reduce the flow even further. Capital flight from Russia and the laundering of cash through Cyprus and other off-shore banking centers suggest that many of the Russian entrepreneurial class (within and outside the law) see better prospects of earning a fast ruble abroad than at home.

The demographic prospects in Russia are grim. The population shrunk in the decade after the collapse of the Soviet Union by five million; it has the highest mortality rate in Europe and one of the lowest birth rates. Russia's own estimates suggest that the population will contract by over 30 percent to 101 million by the middle of the twenty-first century, but statisticians concede that it could be lower; at the moment the death rate exceeds the birthrate by 70 percent. There is an epidemic of public health problems—drugs, alcohol, tobacco, and sexually transmitted infections—and the war in Chechnya has helped to spread TB. While Russia has a skilled and educated workforce, and a strong community of scientists, public health and demographic problems will affect the size and quality of the workforce and, if Putin is to be believed, national security as well. In his first state of the union address in July 2000, Putin warned, "We are facing the serious threat of turning into a decaying nation."

I imagine that it is often tough in Russia to distinguish between legitimate business and organized crime. A friend of mine tells the story of a next-door neighbor in his apartment block—quiet, from the North Caucasus, kept to himself. Once a week a large car stopped outside the block;

two bodyguards got out, covering the street with concealed weapons; one then entered the building ahead of a third man carrying a bag full of money. The neighbor took delivery. It was all very matter of fact— *Neighbours*, Russian-style. The consequences of corruption are equally evident. Where the Yeltsin family and their hangers-on blazed the trail, the former secret policemen who now surround Putin follow close behind. When we were negotiating WTO access with the Russians, the last two sticking points were awkward precisely because they touched on corrupt private interests: the overflight charges that European airlines have to pay to fly over Siberia and the liberalization of telecommunications.

President Putin's regime rests on pillars that would have been familiar to the last czar before the revolution—the army, the secret service, the Kremlin bureaucracy, and nationalism. "Our partner" and "our friend," as President Chirac and Chancellor Schröder call him, has tightened the grip of his security apparatchiks over political life in Russia. Taking the wicked massacre of children by terrorists at the Belsan School in 2004 as an excuse, Putin has continued the squeeze on such Russian pluralism as had begun to flower. The government now controls the audiovisual news media; print journalists are browbeaten and even poisoned; provincial governors are handpicked by the Kremlin rather than elected; and the security services have greater powers to silence opposition. For all those who have seen strong signs of nascent Russian pluralism—as I did at the so-called Moscow School (a training course for democratic activists)— the Kremlin's reversal of policy on modernization and reform is doubly depressing.

I first met Putin in late 1999. We were in Helsinki for the EU-Russia Summit. At the last moment, President Boris Yeltsin was indisposed, not a rare occurrence during his presidency. He sent his acting prime minister, Putin, to represent him. He is a slight, fit-looking man, sharp-witted, very cold-eyed. He has a good line in rather hectoring argument, seizing on alleged double standards to deflect criticism, and is well briefed with particularly strong opinions about Moslems (at a press conference he turned away questions from one journalist about Chechnya with an unsavory reference to the brotherhood of the circumcised), terrorism, the Baltic States and their attitude to their Russian-speaking minority, and the strategic importance of oil and gas. That first encounter was on a day when the news agencies were reporting explosions and great loss of life at a market in Grozny. We asked him about the reports. He claimed to be uninformed but said he would check on them. He came back to us to say that it was what counterterrorist experts call an "own goal." The Chechen rebels ran a weapons bazaar and some of their own explosives had detonated. At lunch he sat between Javier Solana and myself. We quizzed him about this response. He looked us in the eye and repeated the story. It was odd. I had never been so blatantly lied to at a meeting like this before. Normally, mendacity comes in better disguise. The damage had, of course, been done by Russian forces, which were soon to reduce Grozny to a ruin like Beirut or Kabul. We knew that Putin was lying. He knew that we knew he was lying. He did not give a damn, and we all let him get away with it—on that occasion, and again and again.

At first we used to raise Chechnya at meetings. At the heads of government meeting a few weeks after that first encounter in Helsinki, with the media in a frenzy of concern about Russian abuse of human rights in Chechnya and the disproportionate use of force against the rebels there, Gerhard Schröder, supported by Jacques Chirac, suggested that the European Union should put on hold the provisions of our long-standing cooperation agreement with the Russians. This was a meaningless gesture, and I said so, questioning exactly how I was to describe the results of our decision if pressed by the media or even by our own officials. Chirac loftily responded that this was a matter of bureaucratic detail, and that the European Commission should leave the big political issues to leaders. This was the high-water mark of President Chirac's insignificant stand for human rights in Russia. Within weeks he was cozying up to Putin and he never looked back. And within weeks as well, my officials and I at the European Commission were being hectored for being uncooperative with Russia.

The whole Chechnya story continued to be depressing. Critics of Russian policy could not fool themselves that there was an easy way out of the murderous crisis. The state that was created after the first Chechnya war in the mid-1990s was a terrorist haven. It was never going to be easy to find a political accommodation, and while Russia exaggerated the threat that Chechnya posed to its territorial integrity, it could legitimately expect the international community to give this integrity unqualified support. We could also have provided more practical support for fighting terrorism in Chechnya and to reconstructing the economy of the territory. But there was never a realistic Russian political strategy; the Russian armed forces were brutal, corrupt, and incompetent; and our efforts to help—for example through the provision of humanitarian assistance—were treated with derision. Russian officials—the president, prime ministers, foreign ministers—obfuscated and lied. They ignored our letters. They denied that we had raised concerns about specific issues with them—for example, access for humanitarian workers to the UN's secure radio network. Naturally, they got away with it.

As I said, in the early years we at the commission would raise Chechnya with Russia at our meetings. This usually happened when the presidency was in the hands of the smaller northern member states—Denmark, Ireland, Sweden. But increasingly Chechnya was regarded as the European Commission's rather tiresome obsession. At a summit in Moscow that took place under the Spanish presidency, José María Aznar—who had flown to Moscow in President Putin's private jet—brushed the issue aside as being of little consequence. Prime Minister Berlusconi went a step further and acted, in his own words, as Putin's defense attorney at a toe-curlingly embarrassing press conference, giving him extravagant cover on Chechnya, the Yukos affair, and media freedom. Meanwhile Russian and Chechen casualties in the North Caucasus mounted. Some estimates suggest that in the wars fought by Presidents Yeltsin and Putin, 250,000 Chechens have died and the population of the territory has fallen from 1.25 million to 500,000 at the most. Our ally, friend, and partner in the fight against terrorist barbarity does not appear at first blush to have much to teach us.

The effect of our feebleness in handling Russia is as bad for Russia as it is for us. Negotiations are endless and do not get very far. In every discussion the Russians try to "cherry-pick," focusing on the issues that concern them and ignoring the ones that bother Europe. Because we are not consistent and firm, we do less business than we would like, and so do the Russians. In five and a half years, we did three significant deals with Russia. We had a more or less satisfactory negotiation on WTO access, despite the efforts of some member states to push us into unnecessary and disadvantageous concessions. We also concluded a difficult agreement with Russia about Kaliningrad and a third in 2004 that extended the trade and cooperation agreement negotiated with Russia by the original fifteen EU member states to the ten new members. I had responsibility for these two latter sets of talks. Negotiations on Kaliningrad were particularly troublesome because Mrs. Putin herself came from Kaliningrad, and because the key issue of access through Lithuania to this part of Russia (now girdled by the EU) meant that all the president's and the Duma's dislike of the Baltic states, once part of the Soviet Union, bubbled to the surface. Despite the renegade behavior of some of the EU member states, we settled an agreement on Kaliningrad through the leadership of the tough, no-nonsense Danish prime minister, Anders Fogh Rasmussen, who held the chair on our side of the table. In the case of the extension of our Russian agreement to the new members of the European Union, we were helped above all by the members themselves. The arrival in the European Union of the former Soviet satrapies, now proud and independent states with a certain experience in dealing with Moscow, firmed up our policy. An ounce of their experience was worth several tons of humbug from Paris, London, Berlin, and Rome.

Why did the bigger EU member states—France and Germany, in particular—find it so difficult to develop a sensible, principled strategy on Russia? In Germany's case, maybe Chancellor Schröder was affected by President Putin's fluency in German, though it is odd to like someone for an attribute acquired in order to function as a spy in your own country. I imagine there were three main reasons for the Chirac-Schröder approach. First, Putin was seen as a useful and occasional ally against the United States (not least during the run-up to the Iraq war), and the notion of Europe as a counterpoise to Washington might have been given a little more credibility if Russia were to be added to the European mix. Second, President Chirac in particular sees diplomacy in terms of great men, the leaders of great countries, talking together in mirrored, marbled halls. Cast detail to the winds; history is made by those who understand the grander picture and can summarize its most salient features in a portentous platitude. Third, some Europeans assume that Russia's energy resources give Moscow a hold over us. In truth, Russia needs our market just as much as we need Russia's product, and if we were smarter we would strengthen our negotiating hand by doing more to increase the flow of oil and gas to Europe from the rich fields of Central Asia and Azerbaijan.

The main victims of our failure to develop a better and more balanced relationship with Russia are its neighbors. Again, here we fool ourselves. I began this chapter by saying that Europe wants stable, well-off neighbors. This is not Russia's aim. Russia wants weak neighbors and a sphere of influence inhabited by dependent supplicants. So we make no progress in solving the disputes that enfeeble Russia's neighbors: Moldova's problems with the breakaway bandit territory of Transdnistria; the dispute between Armenia and Azerbaijan over Nagorno-Karabakh; the weakening of Georgia through Russian support of South Ossetia and Abkhazia. "Where can you still see the Soviet Union these days?" I once asked. "In the Russian Foreign Ministry," was the reply. Actually, the ministry's DNA has older origins. Russian foreign policy around its borders is czarist in intent: post-imperialism as practiced, in Georgia's and Moldova's case, under the protection of corrupt Russian troops involved in the smuggling of drugs, weapons, fuel, and alcohol. As Professor William Wallace has observed, there is something dangerously absurd about a policy that bitterly resists any autonomy in Chechnya in the North Caucasus while supporting the secession of nonviable parts of Georgia in the South Caucasus.

Perhaps we should take some recent comfort from Russia's decision not to intervene in the last triumphant stages of the "Orange Revolution" in Ukraine, whatever they had been conspiring to do earlier. It will take vigilance to ensure that Ukraine is not now bullied off the democratic path it has chosen by political threats or by Russia's manipulation of Ukraine's energy requirements. But the survival of a democratic prospect in Kiev does not tell us much about what will happen in its bigger, encircling neighbor. Russia has been one of the great survivors of history. With luck it will resume its erratic journey toward democracy and pluralism. Europe is not, however, doing much to encourage this process, conniving rather at policies and attitudes that will create a more dangerous neighborhood for us all. Russia needs a strong and outspoken partner in Europe, not a mealy-mouthed pushover. If we want Russia to share our values, a good place to start standing up for them is in Russia itself.

9

INVINCIBLE BUT VULNERABLE

At some point we may be the only ones left. That's okay with me. We are America.

—President George W. Bush, 2002

European governments spent the first months of George W. Bush's administration trying to get a fix on the new team. We had known more or less where we stood with the Clinton administration. They were familiar faces, pursuing familiar policies, embroiling us from time to time in familiar rows. They were heavily involved in the Middle East. They were pursuing a strategy of tough engagement with North Korea. Following initial hesitation, they had settled for a cooperative policy with China. After India went nuclear, they had slowly rebuilt a relationship with Delhi. They worked closely with us in the Balkans. They seemed to understand what we were becoming in Europe. They argued with us on trade but seemed to share our sentiments on development assistance. They disagreed with us on the outcome of a variety of multilateral negotiations—banning land mines, binding the international community to combat climate change—but differences of opinion rarely degenerated into sterile slanging matches. Secretary of State Madeleine Albright was regularly on the telephone inducing us to deliver what we had promised and complimenting us when we did. When you went to see her or Sandy Berger, the national security adviser, you had the impression that they were genuinely interested in what Europeans had to say. I remember a visit that Albright and I paid to Bosnia, during which the two of us established a timetable for the changes that local politicians needed to make. We met political leaders in Sarajevo together and took turns banging the table. The French made a mild and silly fuss about it in Brussels. What was all this hobnobbing with the Americans? At the European Commission, we took no notice.

Not everything in those days was sweetness and light in the commission's relations with Washington. There had been serious quarrels, for example, about the conduct of the war in Kosovo, and we might recall Ambassador Ray Seitz's feeling at an even earlier stage that the two Atlantic partners were slowly drifting apart. But no one then was talking about marital breakdown; the focus—when our relationship was discussed at all—was on mediation or counseling.

Whatever else we anticipated from the Bush presidency, we certainly did not expect that everything would continue as before. There were rumors that the acronym chosen to describe Bush policy was ABC— Anything But Clinton. Yet any changes that might be taking place (and I will come shortly to three of them) were delivered to us wrapped in soothing words by a new secretary of state, who initially calmed incipient anxiety just as later on he aroused puzzled sympathy. Colin Powell is a marvelously reassuring figure, knowledgeable, articulate, and charming. It is, I imagine, a coincidence that the three public officials I have met who best combine natural grace and authority are all black: Nelson Mandela, Kofi Annan, and Powell. Powell was as calming an influence on Europeans as other members of the administration and some of its hangers-on were irritants. If America wanted to look like Gary Cooper in *High Noon*, send in Colin Powell; if it wanted to appear like Charles Bronson in *Death Wish*, then deploy the public talents of Vice President Dick Cheney or Secretary of Defense Donald Rumsfeld. I had personal reason to be grateful to Powell. Once or twice when I expressed concerns about the drift of American policy—on, for example, the "axis of evil" speech and Guantánamo Bay—his public responses were pretty friendly and gentle by the standards that were to become all too common. On a trip to Washington on one occasion, I was outraged by two columns, by Charles Krauthammer and George F. Will, in the *Washington Post* denouncing Europeans as anti-Semites and suggesting that, having failed to complete the "final solution" in Europe, we were now trying to make good that failure by promoting it in the Middle East. I wrote an angry rebuttal, denouncing anti-Semitism but distinguishing between that hateful prejudice and the criticism of Ariel Sharon and the Likud Party's policies. A couple of days later, in Madrid for a meeting, I had a call on my mobile from Washington. It was Colin Powell to congratulate me on the article.

The three policies that made us a little nervous were first, the Middle East; second, the Korean Peninsula; and third, the abrogation of the 1972 Anti-Ballistic Missile (ABM) Treaty, which had sought to forestall the development of long-range nuclear missiles through limiting the defensive systems against them. The Bush team plainly did not intend to continue the Clinton administration's level of engagement with Israel and Palestine. The reason given was simple: Clinton had tried so hard at Camp David and Taba in 2000–01, but because of Yasser Arafat he had failed. It had been a humiliating rebuff and even Clinton could not have gone on like that. Progress was extremely unlikely so long as Arafat was in business. Thus the Bush team stood aside, the politics drifted, and the violence grew. On Korea, even before North Korean breaches of its past promises on nuclear weapons became public, President Bush appeared to turn his back on the reconciliation policy pursued by the government in Seoul, even though Colin Powell had initially endorsed it. (Hence, the surreal visit we paid to Pyongyang.) As for the ABM Treaty, the Bush administration made it clear that this was a matter between the Americans and the Russians; and if the Russians could be pushed into accepting what was in effect a fait accompli, then there was no place for the rest of us to grumble around the table. The ABM Treaty had to go so that America could resurrect the "Star Wars" defensive shield so beloved of President Reagan, his protégés, and so many defense industry manufacturers. With Anna Lindh, Sweden's foreign minister, boldly in the lead, we raised the issue at a meeting with Condoleezza Rice, then the national security adviser, in her cramped White House office. We got a sharp dressing down. It was not for us to question America's identification of threats to its security and its assessment of the best way of tackling them. If Washington perceived a security threat then the administration would be derelict in its duty if it did not deal with it. The ABM Treaty was scrapped; "Star Wars" tests were conducted, without providing much positive evidence of the effectiveness of the system; tragically, a few months later America was attacked with less sophisticated technology but devastating effect.

There was one issue, above all, that went well beyond the usual foreign policy agenda and that really turned off European opinion and underlined that things had changed. It was President Bush's brutally direct rubbishing of the Kyoto Protocol on Global Warming in 2001. We were not stupid. We knew that any American administration would have great difficulty getting binding commitments to the reduction of greenhouse gas emissions through Congress. But the president's rejection of the treaty—it was "flawed" and "unrealistic," he said—went well beyond a statement of the prevailing political reality in Washington. It was like the Pope denouncing Galileo. This is Washington here, ex cathedra, and we tell you that the sun goes around the earth. World, get stuffed. Even Secretary of State Powell could not sell this one, try though he might and indeed always did, rarely allowing even a hint of body language to indicate disagreement with the ill-judged orders he often had to follow.

As the months passed, a political grouping with members both inside the administration and among the ranks of its cheerleaders outside began to make itself and its opinions increasingly known. The assault on America in September 2001 gave these ideologues greater prominence and their ideas more resonance. I am obviously referring to the neoconservatives, who gave a spurious intellectual dressing to the muscular, assertive nationalism that guided Washington's policy in the wake of Al Qaeda's murderous assault. I am not convinced that it makes much sense in practice to attempt an elaborate dissection of the differences between, say, Donald Rumsfeld and his former deputy, Paul Wolfowitz, just as there would be little useful distinction to be made between a Marxist-Leninist who conforms to a belief system that explains everything and a Stalinist who simply wishes to exercise power without constraint. (The views of nationalists and neoconservatives are, of course, neither Marxist nor Stalinist.) Neoconservatives certainly possess a body of received opinion as well as an unhealthy enthusiasm for conspiracy that betrays perhaps how many of them have journeyed from the Far Left to their present political home. Assertive nationalists, on the other hand, simply want to do whatever they believe to be in America's immediate interest, with no hand-wringing appeal to allies or debate with Nervous Nellies and Doubting Thomases.

As a conservative, I assert that the one thing that *neoconservative* does not mean is conservative. As is often the case, *neo* means not "new" but simply "not." Neoliberals are not usually liberals; neointellectuals rarely open books; neoconservatives are definitely not conservatives. After all, conservatives want to conserve things, especially if they are working pretty well, recognizing, as the prince in Lampedusa's great novel *The Leopard* did, that things must occasionally change in order to stay the same. But a world made by America, largely in America's image, in which America has done so well, is not, in the neoconservative opinion, to be preserved, with change coming only where necessary to maintain order and stability. The present world order must not merely be changed; it must be overthrown and overturned, with Afghanistan and Iraq becoming the Normandy Beaches in the next world war. What is required in this neo-world is permanent revolution, or at least permanent war. This is Mao, not Madison. A prominent neoconservative, Max Boot, told readers of the *Wall Street Journal* that he looked forward to "a new era where America, like the British Empire, will always be fighting some war, somewhere, against someone."

Many of the neoconservatives cut their teeth thirty years ago with the late Senator Henry "Scoop" Jackson of Washington State. Socially a liberal and a strong environmentalist, Jackson opposed détente with the Soviet Union and supported the Vietnam War. He championed Soviet Jewry and gave strong backing to Israel's policies in the Middle East. Some of his acolytes went on to serve in the elder Bush's administration, where they were eventually frustrated. They considered George H. W. Bush's policies, particularly his failure to topple Saddam Hussein, anemic and deficient in chutzpah. During the Clinton administration, they strongly supported Benjamin Netanyahu and the Likud Party, opposed the Middle East confidence-building process created at Oslo, and pressed a return to the first President Bush's unfinished business in Iraq. For neoconservatives like Wolfowitz, the September 11 attacks provided a justification for war on Iraq. For all the relevance this had to stamping hard on Al Qaeda, it could presumably just as well have been war on Egypt, Saudi Arabia, or Syria.

It is a characteristic of neoconservatives that the world is divided into good and evil; the faithful judge political character according to the willingness to use force and believe that the main factor in determining the relationship between one nation and another is military power. Islam is seen as a threat to America's interests and in many of its guises plainly belongs to the Manichaean dark regions. Israel and its history appear to be seen literally through the chapters of the Old Testament's books of Joshua and Judges, where Jericho and Ai are torched—the latter "an heap forever, even a desolation unto this day"; where the kings of the Amorites are hanged from five trees; where the children of Israel are delivered into the hands of the Philistines for forty years, and the blind Samson is avenged of the Philistines and the loss of his eyes as he pulls down the pillars and buries his enemies in the rubble. I find this biblical approach to politics as chilling as the plaque at Hyde Park Corner in London commemorating the First World War role of the Machine Gun Corps, which reads, "Saul has slain his thousands, and David his ten thousands," a memorial tribute to the technology of mass killing. Fire and sword, shock and awe: this is the world of the neoconservatives, dangerous to us all because, in Edmund Burke's famous phrase, "a great Empire and little minds go ill together."

Yet as I have argued, the world against which American neoconservatives and nationalists rail and roar was largely made by their own countrymen. The draper from Missouri, President Harry S. Truman, helped by an extraordinary generation of public servants, used the might of America to remake the world in the spirit of Woodrow Wilson's dream after the First World War. Their undertaking in the 1940s was extraordinary. "The enormity of the task," Dean Acheson later wrote, ". . . only slowly revealed itself. As it did so, it began to appear just a bit less formidable than that described in the first chapter of Genesis. That was to create a world out of chaos; ours, to create half a world, a free half, out of the same material without blowing the whole to bits in the process."

Truman, his secretary of state George C. Marshall, and their colleagues created the institutions of global governance—political and economic—that shaped and arbitrated our times. They actively promoted the winding up of Europe's empires through self-determination. They created the military alliance that contained the last "evil" empire—Russia's colonization of Central and Eastern Europe. They encouraged the opening of markets and invested hugely to help put continents back on their feet. The formula worked in Europe and in East Asia.

This is the world in which I grew up. It was not a time when everything went right. Vietnam demonstrated the limits of rationalism and metaphor in the conduct of foreign affairs—a point to remember whenever dominoes are called into evidence in discussing some alleged security imperative. We also discovered in the jungles and paddy fields of Southeast Asia that technology and wealth are insufficient to fight and defeat an idea. In addition, the West's tendency throughout the Cold War, to divide the world between good countries that supported us and bad ones that flirted with the Soviet bloc, distorted policy, often laid up problems for the future, and from time to time corrupted our values. You could be very bad indeed, but provided you were on "our" side—taking our money, our weapons, and our parlimentary "whip"—your sins would be forgiven.

Overall, the American postwar settlement was a spectacular triumph. By the century's end, America's president was able to claim, and did so regularly, that for the first time in history more people lived in democracies than in tyrannies. Moreover, in fifty years we saw a sixfold increase in world output accompanied by a twenty-fold increase in trade in goods; we were producing the same amount of goods and services every three years that it had taken the whole of the previous century to produce. Pax Americana was good for the world.

You can pick up the threads of America's strategy in Marshall's speeches, not least his famous Harvard commencement address in 1947, which announced his aid plan for Europe. "Our policy," Marshall argued at Harvard, "is directed not against any country or doctrine but against hunger, poverty, desperation and chaos. . . . Its purpose should be the survival of a working economy in the world so as to permit the emergence of political and social conditions in which free institutions can exist." Elsewhere he took this point further. "Democratic principles," he said, "don't flourish on empty stomachs. . . . people turn to false promises of dictators because they are hopeless and anything promises something better than the miserable existence that they endure." All of which convinced the soldier-statesman that he should vigorously oppose—again in his words—"the tragic misunderstanding that a security policy is a war policy." It was on the basis of this philosophy that America helped to create a world richer and more stable than any would have imagined possible at the outset of the enterprise. But however fabulous American power, the United States still had to work with others, by and large legitimizing its leadership through its acceptance of the rules that America more than any other country had created. Another soldier turned politician, President Dwight D. Eisenhower, made the point, "No nation's security and well-being can be lastingly achieved in isolation but only in effective cooperation with fellow nations."

The world has changed, partly because of some of our successes. But there is never a moment when the task of keeping the peace is finished, when liberal democracy is secured forever. The first volume of Karl Popper's thrilling defense of the open society ends with a reminder that we have to go on carrying our cross, fighting for humaneness, reason, and responsibility, planning for both security and freedom. The struggle never ends. The beginning of a new century has brought new dangers. But in my judgment there is no better way of tackling them than the cooperative, consensus-building, example-rich approach taken over most of the last sixty years with America in the lead.

The threats come from many directions. The first group of threats that confronts us today emerges from, and survives among, the detritus of empires. They sweep from the Balkans to the Persian Gulf, much of Africa, the Central Asia republics, Kashmir, and even in a sense to the Korean Peninsula. Add to these other flash points, such as Taiwan, which have been left behind as history has rolled forward. In several of these cases, the prevention of conflict is made both more necessary and more difficult by weaknesses in the international agreements we have negotiated to prevent the manufacture and proliferation of nuclear, chemical, and biological weapons.

Second, on every continent, failed or failing states spawn problems. In the past, developed countries perhaps kidded themselves that they could be insulated from the problems of the world. If a country collapsed into penury and civil war, that was sad for its people. We might offer them loans and assistance. We might lecture them about the benefits of open trade, good government, and so on. But ultimately it was their problem if they could not dig themselves out of their hole. Today we see that we cannot wall ourselves off from the misery around us. There is, for a start, the so-called CNN effect. It is harder to inure ourselves to starvation and genocide when we witness it in our homes. But even if we could, there is the problem that failed states become the breeding ground for terror. Once our concern was with state-sponsored terrorism. Today we are equally concerned by terrorist-sponsored states of the kind that existed in Afghanistan. A U.S. official rightly remarked, when America's "National Security Strategy" was published in 2002, that the threats in today's world are more often from failing states than from conquering ones.

Then there are three horizontal groups of problems, all in some ways connected. There is the revolt of the alienated, to which I have referred already. Traditional communities and cultures are undermined by urbanization and modern science, which constitute a challenge to existing beliefs. Literal interpretations of the Book of Genesis are challenged by Darwin; ancestral orthodoxies about gender are confronted by social, economic, and political changes; television invades domestic lives where even books were hitherto only seen rarely. Reversion to religious fundamentalism is a very human reaction to what is seen in many societies as not the best of Western culture and values but as brash imperialism. The issue is not just a question of Islamic fundamentalism. It occurs in other religious traditions as well. And it exists within cultures as much as between them: just look at the messages spelled out on some of the Christian fundamentalist Web sites. It is not easy to adapt to new ideas, new science, and new influences that challenge traditional authority and received opinion. This resistance to the new and the global does not necessarily turn into a threat. But religious fundamentalism does sometimes find expression in political radicalism and hatred of alien, often Western and specifically American influences. Radicalism may be eminently justified by the brutality, greed, and inefficiency of a great many governments in the world. The current, widely prevalent hatred of America is *not* justified, whatever mistakes it makes. Nor will this hatred be eliminated by dropping bombs on the haters (and their neighbors).

Closely allied to the revolt of the alienated is the revolt of the dispossessed. The simple fact is that much of the world is desperately poor. And with modern communications and the aggressive marketing of Western culture, the poor are now much better informed about how the other half lives. It is hardly surprising that there is widespread hostility to globalization as a Western conspiracy designed to benefit primarily its aggressive advocates. I have little doubt that globalization—the combination of technology, capitalism, and the opening of markets—has made most people better off. Yet over a billion people have been left behind to subsist on less than a dollar a day, creating a risk that globalization will choke on its own inequities. That argues strongly for more generous and better-managed flows of development assistance. While we should not exaggerate the past failures of development aid, nor delude ourselves about the extent of our generosity (a particular problem among Americans), we have too often—to borrow from the title of a book on the subject—found the quest for growth in poorer countries elusive. How *can* we better convert good intentions and large checks into less global inequity, especially in those countries where the concept of the nation has carried little force, and where development has had less impact among elites as a governing philosophy than as a means for staying in power and amassing wealth?

I was a development minister in the 1980s, spending a good deal of time in Africa. I lived for five years in Asia in the 1990s and then began visiting Africa again in the last few years in my job as European Commissioner for External Relations. The comparison was a depressing experience. There is still much poverty in Asia, but there is also rising prosperity, greater stability, and hope. The greatest development problems accumulate in Africa, where in too many countries violence, tyranny, and corruption incubate misery and disease. We have frequently aided and abetted turning bad polities into kleptocracies by ill-directed development assistance, instead of providing the right incentives for recipients. It is all very well hunting for excuses, and admittedly there are plenty: in some cases (though not by any means all) the long-term consequences of colonialism; the impact of geography that, while not destiny, can give rise to prodigious natural difficulties in the belt of countries on either side of the equator; and unfair global commercial arrangements and inadequate external support. All this explains some of the problems faced by Africa, but we are perhaps too prissy, too nervous about political correctness, in pointing to some equally pertinent reasons for endemic failure—wickedness, greed, murder, bad government, pillage. A great American journalist, Keith Richburg, spent years as the *Washington Post*'s Africa correspondent in the era of genocide in Rwanda and civil war in Somalia. Richburg is black. He wrote a brave book about his pride in identifying himself as an American, and his inability to feel a similar sense of identity with what he witnessed in Africa. So for him the description *African*-American was not a bit how he felt.

I have too many memories of the horrors of African decline, not least a long visit in 2001 to the shambles of the Democratic Republic of Congo and its neighboring states, which have spent the last few years robbing Congo of its natural resources (blood diamonds, for example) and fighting their proxy civil and tribal wars across its vast impoverished spaces. The capital, Kinshasa, is a wreck of a city. The poor Congolese, to have endured (read Conrad) the worst of colonialist exploitation and then the worst of postcolonial misrule. I visited Harare, Zimbabwe, on the same trip, for an awful encounter with President Robert Mugabe whose army, doubtless commanded by some of the best officers that Sandhurst, Britain's foremost military academy much used by commonwealth armed forces, could train, has been the worst of the looters in Congo. I had visited Mugabe last in the mid-1980s, when he was frequently cited as a model of African magnanimity. No more. He had turned into a crackpot tyrant, who, with a gang of thuggish cronies, has ruined this beautiful country. The two-hour discussion with him largely focused on Western mendacity, wicked colonialism, the pleasures of doing business with the wise Margaret Thatcher, and the serpentine behavior of Tony Blair's allegedly homosexual clique. I am quite sure that neither prime minister would have recognized the picture that he painted.

Mugabe looked and sounded deranged. When Lord Carrington was doing business with him, negotiating the relegitimizing of Rhodesia in the early 1980s, he used to muse on the pleasant Lancastrian ring to the pronunciation of Mugabe's name backward, "E-ba-gum." Just over twenty years on, Mugabe has moved far beyond humor. Yet when he addressed the UN General Assembly in 2001 in the wake of explicit evidence of vote-rigging, the use of violence against his opponents, and the growing impoverishment and starvation of his people, he was cheered to the rafters by most of the African delegates present. For me, this said all too much about what is wrong with Africa. Until the African Union, and the continent's regional organizations—led by South Africa and Nigeria above all—are prepared to take a tougher line on bad government, corruption, and the preservation of democracy, Western donors are not likely to be able to make much difference in tackling the continent's woes, even if we spend more money (as we should) on development assistance. Countries can recover from disaster, as Mozambique (once riven by colonial and civil wars) has recently shown. But without political stability, too many problems fester and deteriorate with results from which we in the West cannot insulate ourselves.

Throughout my years as a European commissioner, we were intermittently involved in efforts to bring peace to Sudan, where one conflict succeeded another. As the West witnessed the latest killing in Darfur, I had a grisly sense of déja vu. War in that country seemed without end. Back in late 1988, I had made my third visit in a year to Ethiopia, this time to visit the camps on the Nile River plain in the southwest of the country, which were accommodating refugees from the brutal war between the government in Khartoum and the Sudanese People's Liberation Army in the south. I had long discussions with some of the younger Sudanese inhabitants in the camps about their experiences. Most of them had similar stories. They had spent three or four months escaping from Sudan, trekking back and forth across the country to get away from marauding gangs of hostile tribesmen or detachments of the Sudanese army. About half of those who started off on the journey actually got through. One group of young boys—led by teenagers about the same age as my older daughters—told me of their long march; seventy began the journey; forty eventually completed the march, sustained over three months by a diet of berries, roots, and leaves. I asked one of the sixteen-year-old leaders how they had found their way to the Ethiopian border.

He replied matter-of-factly that it was very easy; they had simply followed the trail of corpses.

At the end of my visit, I was asked if I would address the school that had been set up for the 12,500 camp children, 60 percent of whom were, in the euphemism of the aid workers there, "unaccompanied," by which they meant orphaned. After I had spoken, they asked if they could sing to me. They sang the Lord's Prayer in their language, Dinka, and then a text from Isaiah which I assumed to be the verses about beating swords into plowshares. I was wrong. Lying in my bed that night in the British ambassador's comfortable bungalow on the hillside above Addis Ababa, as the old fan whirred above my head, I spotted a Gideon Bible on the table and looked up the reference they had given me. What they had actually been singing was a text familiar from carol services at home: "The people that walk in darkness have seen a great light: those that dwell in the land of the shadow of death upon them hath the light shined." Too many in Africa still dwell in that land of the shadow of death, with little prospect of the light shining on them unless we can combine better government with more generous assistance.

There are other lessons about poverty and development. An earlier period of globalization, almost as remarkable as today's in its effects, occurred at the end of the nineteenth and the beginning of the twentieth centuries. The results were memorably described in Keynes's *Economic Consequences of the Peace*. In those years, the gates were opened to trade in agricultural products as well as in goods, to the movement of people as well as that of money. At the very least, America and Europe have to ensure that the international trade talks that began in 2001 at Doha, Qatar, result in fairer rules and greater access to Western markets for the things that poor countries produce, especially food. It is indefensible for the rich countries of the West to spend almost seven times as much on subsidizing our agriculture as we do on aid.

Finally, there are the problems thrown up by increasing globalization that require a coordinated international policy response. Globalization offers tremendous opportunities; look today at Asia's advances in the fall in the number living in poverty in China and India. But Dr. Jekyll is stalked by Mr. Hyde. Modern science, machines, and communications may unleash benefits and free trade may produce prosperity, yet globalization has also given birth to environmental degradation, the drug trade, terrorism, the proliferation of weapons, transnational crime, and the swift spread of communicable diseases like AIDS, SARS, and the imminently threatening Avian flu. What does it require for us to move from an intellectual understanding of these problems to a more determined attempt to turn comprehension into policy and effective agreements? Perhaps the threat of Avian flu hanging over Asia and the rest of us will do the educational trick, though I fear that we may find ourselves dealing with its dreadful consequences rather than preventing it from turning into a pandemic. All these problems should remind us that stability and prosperity—a goal of foreign policy in each separate nation—can only be achieved if nation-states can act together in pursuit of interests that transcend their boundaries.

Put all these horrors together—failed states, alienation, poverty, the global reach of terrorist violence—and what do you get? One consequence undoubtedly was the atrocity of September 11. America's horrified surprise at its own vulnerability confirmed neoconservatives in their view that their country should not allow itself to be a buried piece on the global chess board, a queen hemmed in by pawns. As the preeminent world power, America has the strength—it believes—to exercise power unencumbered, free from the entanglements of international law or the demands of allies. And it is not just a question of whether America *can* behave like this. There is a persuasive, sometimes dominant, school of thought in America that argues that it *should*. One American sovereigntist, Jeremy Rabkin, has described recognizing that your first duty is to protect your own democracy and the rights of your people as a "dictate of the law of nature." Another prominent neoconservative, John Bolton, was promoted in 2005 to be U.S. ambassador to the United Nations in a gesture that indicated the Bush administration was not without a rather macabre sense of humor. Bolton has indicated on a number of occasions how the "America only" rule should work in practice. For example, at a UN conference to discuss controls over the deadly trade in small arms in 2001, when he was under secretary of state for international security and arms control, Bolton asserted frankly, "The United States will not join consensus on a final document that contains measures contrary to our constitutional right to keep and bear arms." Armed thugs in Sierra Leone and Sudan, dependent on the small arms trade for their killing power, could take comfort from the mantle of protection thrown over their activities by the American Constitution.

Bolton can be considered the Pavarotti of neoconservatism; his views have taken the roof off chancelleries around the globe. For Bolton there is no *United* Nations, there is only the one nation that counts, America. Cooperation is for sissies. Some apologists in Europe for the Bush administration claim that Bolton's appointment to the United Nations did not represent a blow to multilateralism, but was a shrewd way of advancing support in America for a reformed United Nations while also removing him from policy making (if not heated debate) in Washington. But representing the world's only superpower at the United Nations is not like hiding your lantern under a bushel. We will assuredly hear more from Bolton. The last time I saw him, I opined that we needed to use sticks and carrots to deal with Iran. "I don't do carrots," he replied. No, indeed, but the rest of the world may soon do a good line in raspberries.

For neoconservatives like John Bolton, unilateralism is not just a reflection of U.S. power, but a positive virtue. America's hegemony is benevolent, and such is the primacy of American values and institutions that it is no bad thing if others must adapt themselves to U.S. preferences. I can see why that view is so attractive. There is something dismally repellent about philanthropy and international do-goodery divorced from real human relations: well-meaning and well-dressed peripatetic internationalists talking interminably about poverty in a variety of the world's more expensive capitals; the endless fudge; the dreary, unreadable declarations; the maelstrom of self-interested humbug masquerading as high principle. At one such meeting, I happened to be reading Charles Dickens's *Bleak House* and wondered whether Mrs. Jellyby might have slipped unnoticed into the conference hall with her concern about the "cultivation of the coffee berry—and the natives of Borrioboola-Gha on the left bank of the Niger." Better, surely, the honest pursuit of profit and national interest. Did we learn nothing from Adam Smith?

While understanding this point of view, I cannot share it. On the contrary, the instinct to return to a narrow definition of the national interest—to assert the primacy of U.S. concerns, and especially economic interests, over any outside authority—constitutes a threat not just to the developing international order, but to the United States itself. As I have argued, for the best part of fifty years the United States, almost above all other nations, has been internationalist—and a tremendous force for good in the world. Has the system of global governance created after the Second World War now outlived its usefulness? Is conventional multilateralism now outdated because of the imbalance between American power and that of all others? Has technology unleashed forces that overwhelm the borders and conventional governing institutions of nation-states, so that traditional modes of cooperation between them inevitably fail? Has the liberal dream of an international community been shown up for a sham by the selfishness of rich and powerful countries ruthlessly focused on the protection and enhancement of their own interests? Answer "yes" to all those questions and you are left with a pretty bleak outlook, a Hobbesian world in which capitalist democracy defends its wealth and values from the random violence of the angry and the poor in the "gated communities" of rich suburbs. Is that how the world has to be?

It is not obvious to me that the Taliban and Al Qaeda, Palestine and Pyongyang, heroin and AIDS, the Pentagon's precision-guided munitions and the spasmodic acceptance of the UN's authority—to name a few salient features of our times—demonstrate that the Truman-Marshall approach no longer works. On the contrary, it seems clear that we need more of it, not less. But it is equally clear that unless the United States is prepared to lead a rejuvenation of multilateralism, it is not going to happen. So how do we persuade Washington of this?

First, it is important to recognize that the task is not impossible. Opinion surveys (for example, those undertaken by the Chicago Council on Foreign Relations and the German Marshall Fund) demonstrate that Main Street America still views international affairs much the same way it did two generations ago, whatever the mood within Washington's Beltway and whatever the growth in conservative and Christian fundamentalist sentiment. American voters still believe strongly in international cooperation; indeed, large majorities even appear to favor signing the Kyoto Protocol and supporting the International Criminal Court. They also, rather sensibly, believe that America should try to share its global role with Europe, even when Washington disagrees with European governments. Why should a sensible American citizen want his or her own country to bear the heaviest burden in defending civilized countries against all the potential threats to security and well-being?

The biggest doubt is not whether most Americans would like Europe to help carry the world, but whether they think Europe really will. In Europe, we huff and we puff—how much breath does that leave to do anything serious? We know the nature of the task of advocacy that we have to perform. We need to persuade Americans that the concept of a nation whole unto itself is anachronistic; that the "national interest" must involve *inter*national cooperation and *inter*national obligations; that the things Americans want—jobs, prosperity, peace—can only be secured if the United States works with others; that the dark side of globalization can only be tackled by unprecedented levels of international cooperation; that the threat or use of military might is not always the only or the right way to keep the world safe. But in order to perform this last task, we in Europe must be prepared to face the question that force *is* sometimes required to uphold the international rule of law, and to be able to provide some of that force ourselves. To make Americans believe in multilateralism, Europe has to do more to sustain it.

Neither the task of persuasion nor the demonstration of increased European capacity to make multilateralism work will be easy. Today there is a much more aggressive strain of nationalism in America's attitude toward the rest of the world. Watch Fox News to get a taste of this, piping hot. Explaining the difference between American and international news coverage of the buildup to the war in Iraq, one of the channel's stars, Bill O'Reilly, asserted, "Well, everywhere else in the world lies." America can set its own course, ignoring the doubters and the liars, because if it needs to do so, it can destroy any enemy, just like that. And this military certainty comes appareled in moral conviction. Anatol Lieven reminds us, in *America Right or Wrong* (2005), that the vice president's wife, Lynne Cheney, in her A-to-Z *Patriotic Primer* for schoolchildren, writes that "Z is the end of the alphabet, but not of America's story. Strong and free, we will continue to be an inspiration to the world." I hope this becomes true again. But the book brings rather alarmingly to mind the Victorian alphabet reader *Babes of the Empire*, which included this classic quatrain:

D for the Dervish in sunny Sudan.
Oh see him perform his eccentric can-can!
But now he has joined us—the pride of our nation;
He dances from frenzy to civilisation.

Perhaps no one was listening when Tony Blair, in his fine speech to both houses of Congress in 2003, said (greatly daring), "All predominant power seems for a time invincible, but, in fact, it is transient."

The notion of belligerent self-sufficiency infused the Republicans' presidential campaign in 2004. Admittedly, no one expects election campaigns to have much in common with a Socratic dialogue. Hyperbole rules with the assistance of a smidgeon of mendacity. Nevertheless, even by the customary standards, the outpouring of hostility against foreigners and their multilateral entanglements came as a surprise. To suggest the need to consult allies was apparently to advocate the outsourcing of foreign policy to Paris and Berlin. All seemed to take their lead from President Bush himself, who had said in his State of the Union address in 2004, "The course of this nation does not depend on the decisions of others." A successful election campaign behind him, and with his former national security adviser, Condoleezza Rice, installed as secretary of state, the president set out to mend fences with the treacherous Europeans. But was he using real planks and nails? Had there been a conversion, on the flight to Brussels, about the need for allies, who might be expected to have their own opinions and to wish to express them occasionally?

There will be several difficult tests of whether there have been any significant second-term shifts. But since a current and perhaps understandable strand in European thinking to avoid, if we can, any impression of damage to or change in the transatlantic relationship, there will be a reluctance to ask any of the questions that may produce the wrong answers. So no one, for example, will raise the issue of one of the central tenets in the Bush administration's national security strategy, namely the new doctrine of preemption of threats, which, roughly translated into Rumsfeldian, means this: since we in Washington don't know a lot of things that we don't know, we should reserve the right (being bigger and more powerful than anyone else) to attack others before we are attacked ourselves. Two of the greatest living historians in Europe and America have given their verdict on this assertion of *droit de grand seigneur.* Sir Michael Howard regards it as "one of the most important documents in the history of America," which "seemed to be demolishing the whole structure of international law as it had developed since the seventeenth century." He could have cited President Eisenhower's view: "We cannot consider that the armed invasion and occupation of another country are peaceful means or proper means to achieve justice and conformity with international law." For Arthur M. Schlesinger, Jr., the strategy represented a fundamental shift from a foreign policy based on containment and deterrence through multilateral agencies to hitting your enemy (if necessary on your own) first. As the strategy asserts, "the best defense is a good offense." Successive presidents, he has noted, have rejected this approach, which he believes dwells on the very edge of legality. In the most controversial application of this principle in Iraq, Schlesinger argued that the Americans went beyond preemption and that the president chose to fight a preventive war. In *War and the American Presidency* (2004), he wrote, "The entire case for preventive war rests on the assumption that we have accurate and reliable intelligence about the enemy's intentions and military capability—accurate and reliable enough to send our young men and women to kill and die." We now know that the information on Iraq—and this is the mildest criticism one can make—was neither accurate nor reliable. So what price prevention, preemption, and wars of choice today? What is the status of a strategy that reminds us of Truman's dictum, "You don't prevent anything by war, except peace."

Our best bet in Europe is probably to act in ways that make it less likely that the strategy will be tried out again, and more likely that the United States will return to more familiar, popular, and successful ways of dealing with the world and of exercising global leadership. This requires that we should define more clearly what Europe wants to do and can do in international affairs and then narrow the gap between aspiration and delivery. There should be, first, no question of Europe trying to be another superpower. We cannot be and we should not try. There is presently only one superpower, and it is our task to live alongside it and help it to carry its responsibilities effectively. Second, there is nothing to be said for Europe in effect assuming a role as unfriendly neutrals, captious critics of what America does but incapable of doing much ourselves to make the world more as we would like it to be. Third, I am not attracted by the idea of aspiring to be America's global adjutant, obedient acolytes who do more or less what we are told, like it or lump it. The sensible role that Europe should want to play is as a capable partner, respected for its advice and its ability to act on its own when necessary, defining ourselves not in contradistinction to America but as allies with minds of our own.

This requires of Europe at least four things. First, Europe needs to make greater progress in developing and upholding common positions on foreign and security policy. The problems in doing this are overwhelmingly political rather than institutional. Does Prime Minister Blair want to carry other Europeans with him when seeking to play the part of friend at court in Washington? Does Chancellor Gerhard Schröder have any clear idea of how to develop Germany's role, balancing its Atlanticist sympathies against its traditional position of helping to define and lead the European debate? Unfortunately, he always gives the impression that the very short term is for him very long indeed. Does it matter much what Prime Ministers Silvio Berlusconi or Jan Peter Balkenende think outside Italy and the Netherlands? Is there any consistency or meaning to President Jacques Chirac's practice of French exceptionalism? Even when they are right, the French can be infuriatingly perverse or incomprehensible. Having scolded the Americans for bullying the world in 2002–03, President Chirac then tried to bully Europe's new member states for having the cheek to disagree with him. There was more than a hint of Napoleon, and more than a wisp of inherited glory about his biographer, the silky smooth and amiable French foreign minister Dominique de Villepin (who has since become the country's prime minister) when he spoke in the UN Security Council against America's Iraq policy. "France," he said, "has always stood upright in the face of history before mankind." Does this mean anything at all? Obviously it sounds much better in French. It echoes General de Gaulle's words, carved on the pedestal of his statue on the Champs Elysées, "There exists an immemorial covenant between the grandeur of France and the freedom of the world." Change the name of the country and an American Republican neo-con could not put it any better.

Second, Europeans have to do more to shake off the reputation that we are nonpaying passengers in America's chariot. We are too inclined to criticize America while depending on its security shield; too prone to advocate multilateralism while knowing that if a multilateral solution requires force nothing much is likely to happen unless America is involved. We are now starting to develop the capacity to act with and even without NATO support in peacekeeping roles, as can be seen in the Balkans and in Africa. Whenever there is heavy work to do, as in the air war over Kosovo in 1999, we still have no other option but to call on American firepower. This does not add to Europe's credibility as a serious partner to the United States, and Americans should scold us for not yet having this capacity and for dragging our feet so long in developing it.

It is depressing that most surveys of public opinion suggest that Europeans want their countries to do more together on the world stage, provided it does not cost taxpayers more money. This disingenuous self-deception should be challenged by those political leaders who bang the European drum. France and Britain both spend about the same proportion of their GDP on defense—2.6 percent and 2.4 percent respectively—making them the most serious military powers in the European Union. In comparison, Italy spends 1.9 percent, the Netherlands 1.6 percent, Germany 1.4 percent, and Spain 1.2 percent. Procurement and research budgets are correspondingly low. The story might not be quite so gloomy if Europeans spent their existing budgets better with improved standardization and interoperability of equipment. We regularly set goals for improving these capabilities that we subsequently miss. It should not be as bad as this. Even though Europe spends much less than America, we still have in aggregate the second-largest defense budget in the world and have on paper 1.5 million troops. *On paper.* In fact, we have difficulty meeting the target of a force of 60,000 for rapid deployment, which requires 180,000 troops in three rotations a year and the ability to move them a long way at short notice. We can just about manage that deployment, provided, that is, we can lease transport aircraft from Ukraine, Russia, or America. Plans to construct our own military transport began in 1984 and stretch ahead to 2020—that's if we're lucky.

Europe faces other deficiencies that reflect the simple fact that we were moderately well prepared to fight a war against a Soviet threat across the central German plain thirty years ago but rather less capable of dealing with today's security problems. For example, our experience in the Balkans demonstrated that we had not invested enough to protect our communications against modern interception. Serbian and Croatian intelligence were able to monitor our electronic communications during operations in Bosnia in the last few years. To be fair, Europe has done slightly better at developing the capacity to undertake the sort of civilian jobs that are required during and after military deployments—the provision of police, lawyers, judges, prosecutors, experts in civil administration, and civil protection teams. But the overall picture is far from good enough to satisfy inquisitive American friends. Even a modest improvement would enhance Europe's credibility as a partner.

"Military power by itself is never enough to sustain your predominance," Donald Rumsfeld was told by a panel he set up to consider the global pressures on America's military machine. This brings us to the third task for Europe, to show that we understand the relationship that the visionary George C. Marshall highlighted between security and economic development. We have to do more to reduce poverty, promote sustainable development, and build governing institutions in poor countries. I have already noted some of the difficulties here, and also stressed the importance of the work. It is work where the European contribution outstrips the American; we should not crow but, since it is easier to persuade European taxpayers to give more for development assistance than for defense, we should further increase the work we are prepared to do here.

Joseph Roth, who chronicled the last days of the Austro-Hungarian Empire, wrote in one of his short stories, "Towards the end of the nineteenth century, the people of my native place were of two sorts: they were either very poor or very rich. To put it another way, there were masters and servants." That empire did not last. Extremes of affluence and poverty threaten today's global stability for similar reasons. The international community is committed to reducing these huge disparities with the target of meeting a series of so-called Millennium Development Goals, set out by the United Nations in 2000 and endorsed at the Monterey Conference in 2002. The targets include halving the proportion of people whose income is less than one dollar a day, reducing by two-thirds the mortality rate for children under the age of five, and meeting a host of other objectives in health, education (including raising literacy levels), and the environment (for example, providing more clean water and air). To achieve these goals there will need to be a big increase in aid from developed countries, whose performance in this respect worsened through the 1990s. In the late 1980s total development assistance from the rich countries as a percentage of their income was about 0.33 percent; today it stands at 0.25 percent. There is still a target, accepted by most donors and by the European Union as a whole, to increase this figure to 0.7 percent. Few countries, all of them European (Norway, Denmark, Luxembourg, the Netherlands, and Sweden), keep this pledge. To put these percentages into absolute figures, the rich countries have pledged to double the amount they were spending in 2002 to about $100 billion per year in 2010. Another $50 billion per year would be required to meet the goals they have accepted. These figures are not outlandishly high when set against the $900 billion per year that the world spends on armaments and the figure of more than $300 billion per year that we spend on subsidies to farmers in rich countries.

The European Union has helped countries meet these targets in a way that is far more effective than our past attempts, when everyone endorsed the 0.7 percent figure and then most countries forgot about it. We have agreed that over a succession of set periods those EU member states which spend less than the average percentage of gross national income allocated by the whole of the Union should raise their budgets to at least that figure. Each time that happens, the average will rise, the target will increase, and aid budgets will be ratcheted up toward the UN figure, at least for the better-off, longer-standing member states. All of the fifteen older EU member states have now pledged to get to 0.7 percent by 2015. Europe's performance is not great, but it is getting better.

America's contribution to development has become a fraction larger in recent years, starting from a much lower base. Jeffrey Sachs has pointed out that since 2001 defense spending in America has gone up by 1.7 percent of gross national income, tax resources have declined by 3.3 percent, and development aid has grown by 0.04 percent. Surveys suggest that Americans think they give about thirty times more in development aid than is in fact the case. Nor is it true that private giving by Americans makes up for public parsimony. The figures given to make this point erroneously include as development assistance private workers' remittances to their families back home. Despite President Bush's admirable commitment to global programs for combating AIDS, America's contribution to poor countries is at the bottom of the OECD's league table: even Italy's miserable 0.17 percent beats America's 0.15 percent. The gap between America and the rest of us looks set to continue to grow. That may well be part of the price we pay in Europe for demonstrating that when it comes to meeting broader multilateral targets, we are not paper tigers.

The fourth task for Europe is to do all we can to persuade Americans that the best way of applying what the United Nations has called "the glue of common interest" is by working to strengthen that global institution in whose creation the United States played the decisive role. For Europeans to prevail upon Americans to love the United Nations may be as tough an assignment as for Americans to induce the British to love the European Commission. Both institutions play the role of symbolic bad guy in national debates, partly because of the things they get wrong (exaggerated though these failings may sometimes be), partly because of the way (inevitably perhaps because of the behavior of their members) they come to personify the gap between human aspiration and all-too-human delivery. A day at the United Nations does bring into especially sharp focus the lavish dollops of fudge to which I referred earlier in this chapter. But for every hypocrite and scoundrel at the United Nations, there are dozens of men and women working for it in miserable places around the world, putting their lives on the line and often losing them— more UN civilian workers have been killed in recent years than peacekeeping soldiers. The United Nations represents what we should want the world to be, and the fact that it falls so far short of the ideal is our fault, not that of the ideal itself or of those who try to serve it.

Scandal and mismanagement eat away at confidence in the institution and we are more merciless about it because it is an international body, staffed by people with "diplomatic corps" license plates, than we would be about the same failures at home in national institutions. While American critics hammered away at the UN's serious mishandling of the oil for food program in Iraq—much the fault of the member states themselves— the surprising and expensive role played by Halliburton in Iraq's redevelopment seemed to pass by without equivalent public scrutiny and attack. In the spring of 2005, Kofi Annan put on the table a comprehensive set of proposals for better management of the United Nations, with an eye to restoring its moral authority, improving its effectiveness in dealing with threats like terrorism, reasserting its functions in legitimizing the use of force in international disputes, enhancing its ability to build democratic institutions in countries torn apart by strife, preserving human rights everywhere, and gaining greater clout in tackling economic, social, and environmental dangers. It is no good picking and choosing the bits of these proposals that one likes and leaving the rest on one side; no good refusing to grant the secretary general greater responsibilities to make him more effective on the grounds that the United Nations is inherently unreformable. The United Nations is only unreformable if we choose not to reform it.

Reform is in the interest of small and weak states. But it is even more in the interest of the large and the powerful, and above all it is in the interest of the United States. America needs a strong and credible United Nations. It needs it to do some of the dirty work to prevent conflict and to clear up afterward, as in East Timor, Kosovo, and Afghanistan. It needs the United Nations to shield its might from the world's resentment and to communicate its purposes to the rest of the world. It does not diminish itself by accepting the UN's authority, something it should and often wants others to do. American power requires an agent of legitimization in order to ensure that America does not lose the authority it has gained through its historic commitment to the rule of law. Machiavelli was wrong: it is not better to be feared than loved. It is even worse to be neither feared nor loved.

European governments have to say these things politely but firmly to our American partners. Europe should accept the UN reform proposals and campaign for them aggressively together as one and singly as twenty-five member states. We should tell the United States that we want it to be what it was when it helped rescue Europe from the dark: the world's leader, acting through working institutions of global governance, the world's moral and political exemplar at home and abroad. America can continue to change the world for the better—not simply because of what it can do to other countries, but because of what it can persuade those other countries to become.

10

MEANWHILE, ASIA RISES

Two separate reports from the *Wall Street Journal*, June 13, 2005:

China may win the sprint, but India will win the marathon.

—Kamal Nath, India's minister of commerce

Chinese people have a saying; "If you respect me by an inch, I'll respect you by a foot."

—Bo Xilai, China's minister of commerce

Once upon a time the "Muzak" of China, blaring out in railway stations and from the megaphones on government buildings and street corners, was the old Communist Party anthem, "The East Is Red." It isn't red anymore. In China, Maoist command economics has given way to . . . what exactly? Let's call it for the moment "market Leninism," as coined by Nicholas D. Kristof and Sheryl Wu Dunn in their book *China Wakes*. In the Asian continent's second greatest land power, India, a gentler, more benign but not much more successful brand of socialism is gradually, too gradually, being replaced by more open and liberal economic management. The result? The number living in poverty in both countries has plummeted; two great countries are beginning to retake their places as world leaders; and the rest of the world ignores what is happening— or nervously ponders the consequences for all our futures.

I have seen close-up the changes in both countries. My initial sighting of China was in 1979. I had gone to Hong Kong with a small group of MPs during my first summer vacation at Westminster. During our week in the colony (or "territory," as it was usually euphemistically called), we were taken up to see the border with China at a spot between the main crossing at Lo Wu and the next crossing to the east at Wen Jindu. From police posts, we peered over the barbed wire at the village of Shenzhen, the meadows, the paddy fields, and the slow-moving sailing barges on the waterways. This was where several Hong Kong policemen had been killed just over a decade earlier by Red Guards during the Cultural Revolution, atrocities that spilled over into bombings and violent demonstrations in Hong Kong. But the scene we saw that day in 1979 had the timeless and gentle innocence of the pictures on blue and white porcelain. This was willow-pattern China, stretching unknown and unknowable back into a history from which it could not break free, and away to the distant mountains, deserts, and mighty rivers that crisscross its vast spaces.

As governor of Hong Kong, I returned to this border frequently to show visitors what now lay on the other side of the boundary fence, and to inspect the work of the police patrols who attempted to prevent immigrants from crossing illegally into Hong Kong to find out for themselves whether its roads really were paved with gold. The village of Shenzhen has become these days a bustling Special Economic Zone, transformed into a sort of suburb of Hong Kong by China's embrace of capitalism. The porcelain pictures have been shattered. Now there are skyscrapers, shopping malls, discotheques, businessmen, crooks, factory workers, and prostitutes—and traffic jams, too. I remember one midnight inspection at the border, looking across at the blazing headlights of the traffic in Shenzhen's busy streets. It was raw, frontier capitalism—Adam Smith stir-fried by Gradgrind and Fagin.

For many China watchers, it is the transformation of Shanghai that provides the yardstick for measuring change. This is hardly a rigorous test. Periodic visits to Shanghai tell even less of China's overall development than occasional snapshots of New York or Los Angeles would tell of America's. Nevertheless, Shanghai provides dramatic evidence of China's emerging force. When I first used to visit the city in the 1980s it was difficult to recognize in the drab urban surroundings the louche, glitzy, international city of the pre–World War II years. It would be an exaggeration, but not much of one, to say that after 8 or 9 P.M. you could count one by one the dim electric lights in the streets. On the famous *bund*, Shanghai's waterside esplanade, only the Peace Hotel and its aging jazz band recalled the vivid past; and it was never clear how these vintage musicians, along with the elderly quick-steppers, the dusty worn carpets, and the cut-glass whiskey tumblers had survived Jiang Qing—Madame Mao—and her gang of four partners in the Cultural Revolution who had made Shanghai the stronghold of their political madness. Today, the city has recaptured the razzle-dazzle of the past. On a recent visit to make a program for the BBC, we sat after dinner, Australian Cabernet Sauvignon in hand, on the roof-level terrace of our restaurant on that same *bund* bathed in neon, looking across at the skyscrapers on the other side of the river in the area called the Pu-dong. Shanghai has elbowed its confident way into the new century.

Where Shanghai blazed ahead, others now follow. Today, gazing out of your hotel room in other Chinese cities, you cannot escape a sight familiar from Shanghai or my old home, Hong Kong: everywhere you look, there are cranes. On an official visit in 2001 to Xian, the city that stands at the gateway to the poor western provinces, we finished our banquet with the deputy governor of the province and went for a walk in the old Moslem quarter of the city. We strolled along the broad medieval city walls, and hearing the sound of dance music from a park below, climbed down to see what was going on. In a corner of the park, with fairy-lights in the trees, there was a large public dance floor, and two or three hundred Chinese kids line-dancing. The clothing labels were the same, regardless of whether the garments were pirated copies, as they would have been from Tokyo to Toronto: Nike trainers, Ralph Lauren polo shirts, Pepe jeans. It's less than half a lifetime since Mao suits and disciplined drudgery. At least today, even if you cannot practice politics freely in China, you have the liberty—up to a point—to escape from politics. As Deng Xiao-Ping might have said, it is indeed glorious to get rich, and far, far better to line-dance than starve.

And China *is* getting rich, though not with the inevitable accumulation of rewards assumed by so many foreigners, and by Chinese investors like my interpreter in Xian. I noticed as we drove from meeting to meeting (and, to be honest, from terra-cotta warriors to museums of magnificent Han Dynasty artifacts) that he spent most of his time making calls on his mobile phone. "What are you doing?" I asked. "Talking to my stock-brokers," he replied—using the plural. "I make more money playing the market than working for the government." "But what happens," I asked, "when the market falls and you lose money?" "You never lose money," he replied confidently, "investing on the stock market in China." I hope the day never comes when he discovers this is not true. China, with its present political structure, would have great difficulty coping with a "feel-good" factor that turned suddenly and nastily sour.

But so far, so good for most Chinese. The number living in extreme poverty fell by 220 million in the last two decades of the twentieth century. This is substantial progress from what amounted to a ground-zero start. Less than forty years ago, 38 million Chinese died in Mao's great famine; hundreds of millions struggled to survive on a daily calorie count (itself probably exaggerated by Mao propagandists like Han Suyin) that was below that deemed just about sufficient to sustain human life in Auschwitz. While the people starved, grain and other foodstuffs were sold abroad to buy armaments and the equipment for Mao's heavy-industry crackpot projects. Resources were misallocated in what were horrendously large quantities for a poor country in order, for example, to shift industries from their original locations to what were deemed by Mao to be more strategically defensible inland sites. He wished as much as possible of China's industrial infrastructure to survive the nuclear war that he coolly contemplated. *"Mercacciones innumeras"* (an incalculable amount of trade), Christopher Columbus had noted in the margins of his copy of Marco Polo's *Travels*. This has always been China's condition. It took the malign genius of Mao Tse-tung, who was probably responsible, according to the brilliant biography of him by Jung Chang and Jon Holliday, *Mao: The Untold Story*, for over 70 million deaths, to add yet more impoverishing ruin to all that caused by the civil wars of the 1930s and '40s and by the Sino-Japanese War. The full measure of Mao's wicked years of power is the speed and scale of the recovery since his own death and the beginning of the reforms boldly launched by Deng Xiao-ping. When you bounce back from hell, the recovery looks all the more impressive. For some economists, the big question is not why

China has done so well in the last quarter century, but why it has not done even better.

For eighteen of the last twenty centuries, China's economy has been—so far as one can make these measurements—the biggest in the world. Later in the twenty-first century, it will be again, which should not come as too great a surprise given that its population is about one-fifth of the world's. China's growth is admirable; it has been managed without regional or global disruption; it does not look as though it is about to end. But most important, this growth is manifestly good for China and the rest of us, and is not something to fear but something we should all hope can be sustained. In the winter and spring of 2004–05, as I was writing this book, it appeared that China and the United States alone were responsible for about half the world's recent growth—China as a result of making and selling things, the United States largely as a result of borrowing (particularly from China) to buy the things that others (again particularly the Chinese) manufactured. One stunning example: Wal-Mart had become a larger trade partner of China than Russia or Australia. China makes two-thirds of all the world's photo-copiers, microwave ovens, DVD players, and shoes; half of our digital cameras; and two-fifths of our personal computers. As the new workshop of the world, China has become the third-largest exporter, and within a decade is likely to be the world's largest exporter—and importer, too. When I became governor of Hong Kong in 1992, China's average tariffs stood at 41 percent; after China joined the World Trade Organization in 2001, they fell to 6 percent, the lowest level for any developing country. And China's own market is increasingly important for its neighbors—many of its factories assemble the components it imports from other Asian countries—as well as for the rest of the world. China's economy is surging ahead, leaving a clutter of superlatives in its wake, with even the starchy economists in the International Monetary Fund predicting that it will be able to continue growing at a "scaled-back" 7.5 percent a year into the indefinite future, drawing on an almost unlimited supply of cheap labor and the benefits of a gradual shift in investment from the inefficient public sector to the far more dynamic private. Too good to be true? As usual there are those who tumble over the dividing line from rational to irrational exuberance.

This has always been the case. The potential riches of trading with China have invariably unhinged Westerners. They have been seduced by statistics that would have been impressive even without the old Chinese tradition of exaggerating them. In their book on the Sino-Japanese conflict in the 1930s, *Journey to a War*, W. H. Auden and Christopher Isherwood recorded that "the daily news bulletin was read by Mr. T. T. Li: 'Of seven planes brought down by Chinese ground forces, fifteen were destroyed by infantry.'" The tradition lives on. But when it comes to economic discussion, it is no longer really necessary because the story is sufficiently impressive without hype. Nevertheless, the Chinese dream is always oversold and comes smothered in snake oil. I do not particularly blame the Chinese for this. A Chinese official once explained to the distinguished American journalist and Sinologist Jonathan Mirsky why Mao's China in the 1970s was so enthusiastically and so incorrectly misreported in the West: "We wanted to deceive you," he said, "but you wanted to be deceived."

The best account of the results of mindless China frenzy is *The China Dream* by Joe Studwell, the editor of the *China Economic Quarterly*. He notes how many of the great warlords of Western capitalism made fools of themselves—and sometimes lost the collars and sleeves of their shirts—by leaving their usual commercial criteria and common sense at home when they set out, great corporate visionaries, to take China by storm. McDonnell Douglas, General Motors, Daimler-Benz, General Electric, Deutsche Bank, and AT&T are a few of the giants who bear the scars associated with being a Sino-visionary. Studwell is particularly good at picking apart the meager commercial results of the tours to China made by Western political leaders with ever-growing regiments of businessmen. I used to see their entry to or exit from China in Hong Kong. I counted them out and counted them in along with the huge figures of claimed new business. Germans, French, Canadians, British, Americans—they came and went with presidents, prime ministers, and trade ministers leading the pack. Very few people—a few tiresome journalists on the Asian *Wall Street Journal* and commentators like Studwell—ever asked what happened to all these alleged deals. The answer was—not much. Studwell concludes, "Even with state-supported exports at fire sale prices, it is unlikely that a quarter of the $40 billion of deals signed on government to government trade missions in the mid-1990s ever went ahead." The most significant sales on a commercial basis were for aircraft, which the Chinese bought because they needed them, not because they were doing political favors for anyone. But that did not stop them from playing off Boeing purchases against those of the European Airbus. (The Chinese were quick to learn the game and to repeat a winning tactic.) None of the major deals allegedly agreed in $12 billion of memoranda signed by American missions to China ever came to anything. On his first "showbiz" trip to China, the late American secretary of commerce Ron Brown claimed to have netted $6 billion of business. An official at the American embassy in China told Studwell that the actual business resulting from the visit added up to about $10 million.

Will the China boom continue? There are plenty of reasons for caution. Corruption exacts its own tax, consuming—some think—between 10 and 20 percent of the country's GDP. Misgovernment is widespread, with environmental degradation (for example, desertification) and public protests over municipal housing, the loss of jobs, and arbitrary local taxes. Failed and failing state enterprises gobble up investment, leading to the politicization of credit and an incipient banking crisis. There is a huge overhang of bad debts. Regulation is nonexistent or haphazard, with rampant fraud, counterfeiting, and smuggling. How in these circumstances can e-commerce or credit cards be developed? There is widespread tax evasion and capital flight. Overseas investors, who pour their money into China, extract only the same returns from these huge commitments as they receive in aggregate from much smaller investments in South Korea and Taiwan. Investing in China is not like winning the lottery. And for all the spectacular growth figures, China remains much poorer than the West in terms of per capita income, even when you base the calculations on the lower costs of the services that people sell one another domestically, like haircuts, transport fares, or restaurant meals.

Despite all this, the Chinese economy keeps thundering away, and there is plenty of good news on the other side of the balance sheet. With 60 percent of the population still living in the countryside, China has access to much more cheap labor. As the state sector shrinks, the private sector, which grows about twice as fast as the rest of the economy, will be able to attract more of the resources available for investment. The more efficient allocation of capital should boost productivity. China's economy is more open to trade and investment than most others, with exports and imports making up 75 percent of the GDP against an average of 30 percent for comparable countries. *The Economist* magazine calculates that if China grows at a scaled-down 8 percent a year, and income distribution remains as it stands today, by 2020 the top 100 million households in the country will have an average income equivalent to the current average in Europe. It will be nothing less than the birth of a huge middle-class market, most likely hankering for the sort of consumer goods that Europe and America have pioneered, but that Asians increasingly design, make, and sell. In Singapore I recently saw a brand of Asian malt whiskey called "Matisse." Whiskey, not cognac? Branding in this case clearly demonstrates the sort of cross-cultural myopia that would encourage Samuel Huntington to reach for his laptop.

At the end of his book on Western advisers in China, *The China Helpers*, which profiles everyone from the Jesuit missionaries of the seventeenth century to the Soviet military advisers who gave early support to China's nuclear ambitions, Jonathan Spence argued that for China the time for turning to outsiders for help was over. He concluded, "Chinese advisers have begun to compete in many areas with advisers from the West, seeking to provide the validity of a Chinese worldview through the sophistication of Chinese expertise. The battle has been joined. China, which once surpassed the West, then almost succumbed to it, now offers to the world her own solutions." The book was first published in 1969, and it did look to some observers then as if China, even in the middle of the Cultural Revolution, had a new model of austere socialism to offer the world. We now know, however, the suffering and hardship this model produced. So what happened? For all the talk about Chinese characteristics and socialist trappings, China bought into capitalism—into all its virtues and all its vices—both so that the Communist regime could survive and (to be fair) so that the people could prosper and make the most of their formidable energies and aptitudes. A Confucian society that had espoused one Western ideology, dreamed up by a German Jew in Europe, now turned to another that we in the West like to claim as our own, even though its principles are everywhere valid and its practices everywhere more benign than any known alternative. How should we now react to China's capitalist conversion and its results?

There is a Chinese saying for every eventuality. As I left my post as Hong Kong's governor in 1997, in the midst of the pouring rain, I heard my smartest diplomatic adviser telling a group of Western journalists that there was an old Chinese adage, "When a great man leaves, the heavens weep." When I challenged him to admit that he had made it up, he stood his ground, but looked sheepish about it. My own preferred approach in present circumstances would go far beyond another—real—Chinese saying, "What you can't avoid, welcome."

China's economic progress helps rather than hurts America, Europe, and the rest of the world. Its growth has lowered the price we pay for many of the goods we buy (a 30 percent reduction in real terms over the past ten years in the cost of clothing and shoes in the United States); created a bigger market for the West's own goods; and provided a motor for regional and global growth. The only economic threat China poses is to low-paid uncompetitive jobs in the West. Why do so many Western politicians seek to preserve these badly paid jobs rather than vote for the funds to retrain workers for much better paid jobs? No politician I have ever met wants to work in a badly paid job himself.

At the beginning of 2005, with the end of the global quota regimes on textiles, protectionist squawks have been directed at China's forward rush in exports, and these protests have been linked to grumbles about the unfair advantages Chinese exports enjoy because of the country's undervalued currency. We always knew that the end of quotas would lead to a surge in Chinese clothing exports; we prepared gingerly for this outcome, dismantling protection too late and too slowly, and providing China with a shoddy lesson in the virtues of free trade. We are in danger of giving China a lesson that we only really believe in following international economic rules when it suits us to do so. As for the currency, it is worth recalling that during the East Asian financial crisis of 1997–98, China's maintenance of its currency stability helped to abate the effects of the crash and boosted the recovery from it. I doubt whether the cautious revaluations of China's currency started in mid-2005 will make much difference to the economy's competitiveness in global markets.

Overall, China's economic emergence has not disrupted the world's economic progress but enhanced it. Would we have preferred it if China had continued to be poor and backward? Think of the costs to America, Britain, and Europe of supporting a country of that size. But where problems arise in how we meet this large, unwieldy newcomer, they should be dealt with not by trying to contain or harry China, but by seeking to involve its public and private sectors in constructive global economic management. Russia—which did not have to qualify on economic grounds—was added to the rich countries' G7 as a sop for wounded nationalist pride and as a reward for abandoning totalitarianism in favor of an abbreviated form of democracy; Russia will even chair the G8 in 2006. Frankly, Russia—despite its energy riches—is not going to make much difference to our economic futures. But China will. Even if we insist on retaining the hurdle of democratic credentials as a barrier to membership in the G8 club, we must look for ways to involve China (and perhaps India, Brazil, and South Africa) more formally in these economic discussions.

Some of China's neighbors regard its rise nervously as a real or at best a potential threat. They worry that, like nineteenth-century Germany, China may be just too big and powerful for its own continent. Japan has watched the Chinese economy grow from one-twentieth of its own size in 1980 to a quarter of its size today, and observes with apprehension the development of China's navy and China's ambitions to explore for increasingly necessary oil in seas where Japan, too, feels it has proprietary interests. For its part, Russia notes that while its own Far East territories lose people and industry, neighboring Chinese regions boom and prosper. Given these worries, how can China not be considered a threat to its neighbors, and to its only potential rival in the future, the United States?

Nothing will prevent China from having a huge impact on the coming century. Whether or not that is for good or ill will partly depend on how the rest of us respond and help shape China's global role. We will have to do a lot better than the superpowers of the past. Russia manipulated Chinese politics and conflicts with the primary intention of containing Japan and installing a puppet regime in China; the puppet outgrew and outlasted the string-pullers in Moscow. The United States followed a messy involvement in China's civil war with containment, keeping at bay the howls of the McCarthyites who blamed American leaders for losing China for the Free World. Nixon and Kissinger wisely restored relations, although the degree of their infatuation with Mao Tse-tung and his subaltern in tyranny, Chou En-lai, was as unnecessary as it was abject.

China's politics continue to loom darkly—unlike their embrace of capitalism. An unhealthy growth of belligerent nationalism—seen most notably in the tolerated, and even encouraged, anti-Japanese riots in 2005—is probably the main reason for us to be concerned about China. This nationalism is partly a result of the historic distrust and animosity between China and Japan. China's criticism of Japan is understandable, as anyone who has visited the memorial in Nanjing to the Chinese civilians slaughtered by Japan in 1937 would surely agree. Japan's apology for its war record in Asia has never been as generous and wholehearted as Germany's in Europe, and some Japanese diplomats still question whether criticism of their behavior in China is wholly justified. For the record, it is. But China should beware allowing the growth of the sort of aggressive nationalism that set Japan on its own militaristic path seventy years ago. Nationalist sentiment also endangers cool thinking in China about how to handle Taiwan. America and Europe must continue to discourage domestic factions in Taiwan from provoking the mainland by flirting with the symbols of sovereign independence. But we must also persuade China that while it may not be a point that can be explicitly conceded, Taiwan's political reunion with the mainland will have to await political change in China, no matter how close the two become on the economic front. Chinese leaders should not fool themselves that better-equipped armed forces and (by 2020) the possession of more than one hundred long-range missiles will force the happy fulfillment of their national dream.

The best way of encouraging China to behave responsibly, and of discouraging the deliberate stoking of nationalist sentiment as an alternative to the sort of quasi-moral fervor that Communism used to inspire, is to treat China as a responsible partner. And by that I mean a full and functioning partnership with the United States, Great Britain, and Europe, not simply diplomatic grandstanding. China should be drawn into meaningful multilateral relationships with the West and be a party to the creation and enforcement of the growing network of international rules and regulations. The precedent was laid with the negotiation of Chinese accession to the WTO, and we should encourage more of the same. We need China if, as I shall argue in the final chapter, we are to defuse one of the continent's greatest security challenges—North Korea, and the broader issues of which Pyonyang's behavior on the world stage is merely the most strident example—and tackle other global problems as well.

My own relationship with China and Chinese officials when I was governor of Hong Kong was the subject of much comment, and indeed some amusement, as a result of the imaginative and rich use of the Chinese language to denounce me. As governor, I had interpreted the promises made to the people of Hong Kong concerning the transition to Chinese sovereignty—promises of a modest and truncated development of democracy and safeguards for the rule of law and civil liberties—as they read in the official documents. I imagine that most democratic parliamentarians would have done the same. The Chinese view, on the other hand, was that these promises should be interpreted through the prism of a Chinese veto on any political change whatsoever in the decade before 1997. Much of the invective was presumably motivated by the old Chinese stratagem of killing the chicken to frighten the monkeys. But the chicken was neither killed nor spit-roasted, and emerged two years after my departure from Hong Kong as the European Commissioner responsible for External Relations—including those with China. From that moment on, Chinese officials behaved impeccably toward me, giving me considerable "face" as they would say, rolling out red carpets and generally showing their most generous and genial side. I have inevitably mused about the reasons for this, trying not to kid myself that there had been an instantaneous conversion to my virtues nor believing—since I went on saying much the same things—that Chinese courtesy had bought me off when it came to talking about democracy or human rights. First, Chinese behavior was very professional; their senior officials are invariably much more sensible than the advice they get, for instance, from business supporters. They understood that they were more likely to serve their own interests by trying to get along with me than by ostracizing me. The Chinese take a long and practiced view. In Hong Kong I had been doing my job. They knew exactly where they stood with me, even if they did not like what I did and the way I did it. On the other hand, I suspect that when I left they concluded that they had not been very well advised on what I was up to and on how to handle me. Hong Kong was stable and rich. We had not looted the colony before our departure nor sailed off in *Britannia* with the silver teaspoons. They assumed sovereignty over a splendidly successful city. Second, I think they recognized that whatever my views on democracy and human rights (which they knew well and were to get to know even better) I had an almost obsessive interest in their country, believed it would shape all our futures, and wanted my own country and Europe to have the best possible relationship with China. The first time I met a senior Chinese official after I became a European commissioner, he said to me in English, "Pang Ting-hong" (my Cantonese name) "this time we should cooperate." "Agreed," I replied, "but that is what I would like to have been able to do last time!"

A few months after I arrived in Brussels, the then Chinese foreign minister, Tang Jiaxuan, came to see me. Like his successor, Li Zhaoxing, he was a cheerful and experienced diplomat. He sat down at the large table in my office and looked up at a line of photographs of my daughters on the wall. "How come," he inquired, "such beautiful daughters have such an ugly father?" "The minister is telling a joke," the Chinese ambassador said quickly. Minister Tang went on from his opening crack to tell me that senior leaders—he read this sentence out carefully from his brief—had concluded that I was "an element of concord not of discord." So there it was: not just remission but a pardon for past crimes. While I was a commissioner, I saw President Jiang Zemin several times (after one of these meetings, his interpreter asked if I would sign a copy of my book *East and West* for him) and met his successor, Hu Jintao, whose rapid rise to the top suggests that he must be a pretty formidable bureaucratic politician.

I was lucky to be dealing with China at a time when Europe's relationship with the country was developing strongly. This partly reflected the fact that continuing European integration—the launch of the single currency, the broadening of the single market, enlargement of the

European Union—fit China's worldview, in which there are several poles of influence, not simply one hegemon: not a very surprising idea if you represent over a fifth of humanity. I sometimes felt when I met Chinese visitors that they seemed to believe more strongly in Europe's world role than we did ourselves. They certainly took resolutions from the European Parliament almost as seriously as the European Parliament did. We produced two sensible strategy documents during my years as a commissioner, both of which drew cordial and thoughtful responses from the Chinese side. We became increasingly important trade and investment partners, and developed close working contacts in many other areas—the environment, education, research, economic regulation, transport, satellite development, combating illegal immigration, and so on. We worked assiduously—particularly our Trade Commissioner, Pascal Lamy—to secure China's entry into the WTO. An annual summit with Chinese leaders kept an eye on the progress of this burgeoning relationship. I recall a state guesthouse meeting in Beijing with Jiang Zemin that had been planned for rather too close to the hour at which my colleagues arrived on an overnight flight. (I was fortunate to have flown in the day before.) We sat in the usual horseshoe-shaped arrangement of white antimacassar-covered chairs, the lidded mugs of tea on the small tables beside each of us constantly replenished from large vacuum flasks. The room was hot; the night flight had been long; and I suddenly realized that I was the only member of the European party who was awake. Jiang Zemin and I had an interesting discussion about Shakespeare. I recommended that he should read the history plays, which underlined the importance of political stability. He nodded with interest.

Not everything was harmonious. We had strong disagreements about human rights, and it often fell to me at our regular meetings with the Chinese government to set out our criticisms of China's record. We had agreed with the Chinese that we should have a separate dialogue between experts on human rights, which we supported with programs for training judges, developing democracy at the village level, and funding some civil society NGO activities. The dialogue was courteous enough, but it did not really make much progress, a point we would raise from time to time with our Chinese colleagues. The exchanges could become quite boisterous, especially with any of the Chinese leaders who were prepared to depart from their script. After a meeting in Copenhagen at which the formidably impressive Chinese prime minister Zhu Rongji led the Chinese team, we had a vigorous debate about capital punishment. The premier and I traded the sort of arguments that I have not heard since I used to have to discuss such questions with my constituents in Bath.

I usually got assigned the job—though it was really a matter for each of the member states—to set out the EU's views on the continued relevance of the arms embargo that had been first imposed after the Tiananmen killings in 1989. This did not come up at every meeting, but when it did, the Chinese position was always the same, expressed firmly though not with table-banging passion. It went like this. We had different interpretations of Tiananmen. In any event, things had moved on since then. China had changed: a new generation of leaders was coming to the top. China did not want the embargo relaxed in order to make huge new arms purchases; it wanted this so as to end a humiliating situation in which it was placed in the same category as Burma and Sudan. This was an affront to China's dignity. When I replied, my line was usually to say that we understood the Chinese position; that even if we were to drop the embargo, there was still a code of conduct on arms sales that would restrict them; and that, while we were not suggesting that there was any linkage, it would help us to persuade leaders in Europe to look at this situation again if China were to ratify the UN Covenant on Civil and Political Rights and to take other measures in the human rights field, such as allowing Red Cross visits to China's prisons. Then we would move on. I think I am sufficiently experienced in negotiating with Chinese officials to know the difference between an issue on which they feel strongly and one that will help determine the whole relationship. Arms sales fell into the former category; attitudes to Tibet and Taiwan into the latter. When I opened a strictly commercial office in Taiwan to deal with some of the problems associated with the republic's entry to the WTO, as well as to handle our commercial interests in what was Europe's third-largest Asian market, I took elaborate care to explain this position very carefully to Chinese officials. There was no protest.

The stalemate on arms lasted until the end of 2003 and the beginning of the following year, when the Schröder-Chirac duo sought—initially successfully—to railroad a change in policy through the European Council of Ministers. On a visit to China, during which he was heavily promoting German exports, Chancellor Schröder announced that in his view the arms embargo was out of date and should be dropped. At the European Council meeting of heads of state and government shortly afterward, President Chirac—after trying to get the European Commission's president, Romano Prodi, to raise the issue—did so himself. Since the whole council had voted to impose the embargo, it required a vote of the whole council to drop it. Chirac wanted an early decision that could be announced during President Hu Jintao's state visit to France scheduled for the following month, January 2004. Chirac was unable to get the quick decision he wanted, but other European governments—including the British—seemed prepared to go along with dropping the embargo, provided we could point to a more transparent and effective code of conduct restricting the sale of arms where they might, for instance, be used for internal repression or could contribute to regional instability. But greater transparency about sales did not attract as much enthusiasm from the French as dropping the embargo.

As the months rolled past, as we gave a good working demonstration of how not to conduct a European foreign policy, and as meetings of experts went round and round the same old arguments, it became increasingly clear that, while dropping the embargo might lead to a modest warming of Europe's relationship with China, it was likely to lead to a sharp deterioration in our relationship with America (which was also a much bigger market for European arms sales than China) and in particular our relationship with Congress (where Europe was seen to be living up to its reputation for cynical shopkeeper diplomacy). Particularly tricky, European arms production depends heavily on America as most defense companies are now transnational (and mainly U.S.) conglomerates, and Europe is especially dependent on the import of high-tech components. The flow of those components would be threatened if the United States believed that they would make their way to China.

Of course, America's hands on this whole issue are not entirely clean. According to calculations made by the Friedrich Ebert Foundation, at present 6.7 percent of China's arms imports come from America, compared to only 2.7 percent from Europe. Moreover, American Humvees—

the armored troop carriers so familiar from news footage from Iraq—are actually made in China for the People's Liberation Army. But to be fair to America, the worry was not primarily about such low-technology equipment; Washington was more concerned about the sort of high-technology exports that could be used by China in the digital warfare imagined in the future. Yet, after Russia, the second-largest arms seller to China is Israel, which reverse-engineers technology it gets from America (for example, in fighter planes and helicopters) and sells it to its clients, which also include Cambodia and Burma. When an American surveillance plane was forced down over China in 2001 by F-8 fighters, they were seen in photographs of the incident to be carrying Israeli-built Python 3 missiles under their wings. China itself has a profitable arms trade, selling, for example, missiles and launchers to Iran. America should take a more comprehensive look at the arms sales issue than simply to stamp its feet about Europe. This is a good area for international agreements.

Nevertheless, the European position did appear irresponsible and short-sighted, not only to America but also to other Asian countries, like Japan and Taiwan, especially when China maladroitly passed legislation authorizing the use of force to counter any Taiwanese assertion of independent sovereign statehood. It is America, not Europe, that guarantees stability in Asia, and America therefore deserves to be properly consulted about any policy change. The arguments adduced publicly for the new policy were confused and even absurd. On the one hand, it was claimed that Europe's shift would not lead to an increase in arms sales—it might even lead to a reduction. Yet the French defense minister, Michèle Alliot-Marie, argued that a benefit of Europe selling arms to China would be that China would not manufacture the arms itself. It's an argument that could, I suppose, be used just as easily (or cynically) to justify selling nuclear technology and missiles to North Korea. Europeans also cited the need to respond to China's hurt dignity, but underneath this lay the stronger motive of coaxing China to purchase more European exports in general, starting with the Airbus. There is no evidence that China does business on a basis any different from everyone else; it seeks the best product at the best price. The fact that it goes on hinting that friendship and compliance with Chinese positions can lead to big fat contracts is a tribute to Western (including American) gullibility. We cannot blame the Chinese for this. If we so regularly behave like suckers, why shouldn't they treat us like suckers?

During the course of 2005 the whole wretched arms embargo saga slipped and slithered into European attempts to backtrack to more defensible ground, returning with what self-respect we could muster to our original position, before the Schröder-Chirac initiative: to drop the embargo will require a significant Chinese gesture in the human rights field and agreement on a transparent code of conduct. We returned full circle. In the course of this policy ramble, Europe lost face with America, China, and the rest of Asia. Europe cannot conduct its relationship with China on the basis of ill-judged commercial aspirations. We need to talk to America about China, and to China about America. And we must encourage these great countries to talk to each other. It is important to work at convincing Washington that China should not be regarded as a strategic threat but as a crucial partner. If the arms embargo rumpus has damaged our credibility on China in America, we will have done no one any favors.

Indeed, the greatest peril we face in China is not how we can cope with its continuing success, but what we can and should do if China gets into difficulties. The most troubling prospect is the mismanagement of the political shift that will at some time inevitably follow today's sweeping economic and social changes. Some still argue that it is misguided to think that China can become democratic and pluralist. But history does not suggest that Confucianism is inherently hostile to freedom, any more than it supports the notion that Christianity always favors it. For much of the first half of the last century, following Sun Yat-sen's democratic revolution, China debated and even from time to time practiced democracy—before Mao slammed the door shut on it. And he did this because he was a tyrant, not because he was Confucian. Modern-day Taiwan is Chinese, Confucian, and noisily democratic. An even more pessimistic argument asserts that recent Chinese experience—division, warlordism, civil war—has left the Chinese twisting and turning between the alternatives of stability with servility on the one hand or instability plain and simple on the other. So it is said that China needs an emperor with a strong hand, even if having one makes it more difficult for China to join the modern world. But why should this be the case? Reports of widespread rural and urban protest against social inequity and arbitrary misrule do not lead one to believe that China (under its modern emperor) is very stable. Moreover, while technology was once thought to entrench totalitarian rule, today it liberates the individual. Over 250 million Chinese have mobile phones and more than 70 million are regular Internet users. Even blocking some of the most politically sensitive Web sites cannot give the government the total control over access to information that it once enjoyed. The handling of the SARS epidemic was one indicator of the incapacity of even an authoritarian state to write its own story and to cope with modern menaces without greater transparency. We watch nervously to see how China will deal with the future threat of Avian flu. For its own stability and prosperity, China will increasingly need a democratic movement.

China, like other authoritarian regimes in recent years in Asia, merely demonstrates that it is possible to develop an economy without democracy. But you cannot sustain for long a modern economy without democracy and its principal fixtures and fittings—pluralism and the rule of law. A tightly controlled and inflexible political system does not create an environment conducive to innovation and creativity. It is to our own academic and commercial benefit in the West that so many of China's brightest scientists and entrepreneurs come to America and Europe to study, work, and register companies. For all China's professed interest in creating a legal system that will be regarded as fair and predictable by foreign investors and companies, it is well-nigh impossible to do this so long as the law is still regarded as one of the Communist Party's main instruments of control. The authority of government still depends in part on public anxiety about exactly where the limits of an admittedly enhanced personal freedom lie. How much can the individual write or think or say without overstepping an invisible line? This is the phenomenon described by the American Sinologist Perry Link as "the anaconda in the chandelier."

On a visit to China in 2002, I was invited to speak to the Central Party School. "What would you like me to speak about?" I inquired. The reply came back that the cadres (the then boss of whose school is now the president, Hu Jintao) would like me to give my thoughts on politics in a post-ideological age. This seemed rather a Blairite, New Labour-ish sort of subject, but I nevertheless sought to oblige. I tried to argue, with perhaps an excess of subtlety, that globalization was one of the factors that was breaking down the old divisions between the politics of the individual and the politics of the state, between market choice and command economics, between pluralism and authoritarianism, between Right and Left. But at the same time, as globalization narrowed the ground over which the political battle was customarily waged, it also asserted its own tested orthodoxies about what was most likely to sustain economic development and to guarantee stability. We were slowly but surely—East and West—moving toward similar approaches to good governance. By my own standards, I was cautious and even tortuous in front of this Central Party group, but I think I must have conveyed my meaning because the first question I received from the audience was about how greater government openness could help address corruption and money laundering.

Chinese leaders are wholly correct when they respond to criticism by saying that life has got far better for their citizens and that they enjoy more freedom today. They also point at Western failings and double standards. But none of this remotely justifies the continuing widespread abuse of human rights—the imprisonment of dissidents, the incontinent use of capital punishment, the persecution of religious groups and sects, the treatment of Tibet. The real threat to the regime from Falun Gong was not its beliefs, which appear to embrace traditional Chinese views on breathing exercises and pretty harmless generalizations about the condition of humanity; the threat emerged when China's leaders woke up one morning to find thousands of the sect's followers sitting outside the leadership compound without any prior warning, without any security in place, and without any knowledge about their intentions. Where were the police? How could this sect mushroom and organize without the state's knowledge—and without the state's authority and permission? At a meeting with European leaders, when we quizzed Prime Minister Zhu Rongji about the government's handling of the Falun Gong, he expressed his frustration. He said that he had taken the trouble (the political risk as well, probably, given the story of Zhao Ziyang's visit to the student demonstrators in Tiananmen) to go out and try to talk to some of the crowd. They were not open to reason, he said. But what sort of reason is it that tries to deny individuals the right to believe what they want? And what alternative belief system is offered by the Communist Party in China today? Whatever else it may be, it is not Communism. Its main philosophical refrain is little more profound than the old soldier's ditty, "We're here, because we're here, because we're here, because we're here."

How much do China's leaders understand the need to change? Is change something they can manage smoothly, or will they face—as Tocqueville noted of the ancien régime in France before the revolution— the maximum danger of instability at precisely the moment that they try to loosen the screws? Can they simply manage their way through a continuing period of controlled turbulence, juggling so many awful problems at the same time without anything clattering to the ground, thanks to a continuing growth-induced "feel-good" factor?

There is undoubtedly a good deal of debate in China about how change might be managed, building, for example, on the experiments in democratic village governance and in extending the choice offered among party candidates for official positions. Early hopes, however, that President Hu Jintao might prove a closet reformer have borne no fruit, perhaps not completely surprising given his stint as party secretary in Tibet in the late 1980s, a tenure that concluded with the imposition of martial law in Llasa. He has on the whole been judicious in his decisions on foreign policy and has shown a commendable concern about rural poverty and the environment. But he has also cracked down on the media, religion, the Internet, and all forms of dissent. The view of party leaders appears at best to assume that China can change the way the system works without changing the system itself. This is almost certainly impossible. Until attempts are made to change not only the way the system works but the system itself, there is a continuing and growing danger that when change inevitably comes it will be massively disruptive. America, the United Kingdom, and Europe cannot wait until that moment and then pick up the pieces. Instead, we must welcome our newest economic competitor into the marketplace and urge our newest potential political partner to share in managing and solving the problems faced by the international community.

With China teetering on the brink of fundamental change, India can too often be overlooked by America, the United Kingdom, and Europe, overlooked by both businessmen and politicians. We worry about the outsourcing of jobs; we cluck anxiously around India's dispute with Pakistan; and we (it's a particularly British attitude for understandable reasons) try to disentangle our romantic recollections of the Raj from our relationship today with a vast and growing modern economy and society. Whatever else happens there, India, already the world's largest democracy and in some respects its greatest one, will not be faced with the sort of seismic shift that threatens China. India is poorer than China— enjoying only half that of China's national income per capita—and its growth rate is lower. India's population, on the other hand, is growing faster than China's, and the country will outstrip China in people during the course of this century. India's economic performance, which has been called the sluggish Hindu rate of growth, is sometimes deemed to be a consequence of its pluralism; it is said to be the price that India pays for its majestic democracy.

That assessment underrates the achievements of Indian democracy. Since the bloody days of the transition to independence, India's political progress has been remarkable. Democracy has helped to ensure that ethnic and religious tensions have not blown the country apart. Moreover, as the economist Amartya Sen has observed, it has helped to preserve India from calamity. There has been no man-made famine such as killed tens of millions in China. There has been no cultural revolution. There has been no bamboo gulag. There has been no Mao (though there are a lot of Indian Communists who, unlike their Chinese cousins, appear still to believe in Communism). The problem in India has come not principally from pluralism and participative government, though admittedly the Indian political system sometimes has difficulty forging decisions out of the debates that lie at the heart of any democratic society. The real brake on India's progress has been the dogged pursuit of socialist rather than capitalist economic policies in obedience to the very preamble of the country's constitution, written in 1950.

Change began slowly under Rajiv Gandhi in the 1980s and then moved ahead more rapidly in response to a foreign exchange crisis in the 1990s. With Manmohan Singh as finance minister (he became, thanks to Sonia Gandhi's statesmanship, prime minister in the 2000s), India took the first steps to abandon what was called the "license raj," scrapping overregulation and controls and opening up the economy. This liberalization has further to go and India still suffers from too many of the relics of a centralized socialist economy. There is still insufficient investment in infrastructure and in telecommunications and the manufacturing sector remains too weak. But growth has picked up; real per capita incomes rose by about 50 percent in the 1990s; there was a fall in the number of the very poor; and the middle class—described as the "consuming class" by Indian statisticians and numbered at about 150 million—is growing fast. India is moving from the bullock cart to the motorbike to the car.

Thus far the Indian economy has not been held back by its vibrant democracy but by fiscal mismanagement, corruption, and a history of overprotection. Where India has been able to get over these impediments, for example, in information technology, software, and services, it is doing extremely well. Bangalore is home to over 300 software companies and 150 "high-tech" multinationals. One hundred and thirty of the Fortune 500 companies have offices in the state of Karnataka, India's science capital. Yet India remains worried about China's relatively better performance, measured for example by the amount of foreign investment both countries attract. It is true that many Western businessmen overfly India on their way to invest in China, but the figures that suggest a twelvefold Chinese advantage exaggerate the position, largely by ignoring investments in India by its diaspora and by including "round-tripping" through Hong Kong by Chinese investors. India has not, however, yet triggered anything like the enthusiastic interest engendered by China's performance. Greater economic liberalization should in time focus more international attention on the advantages of investing money in a democracy under the rule of law where there are institutional safety valves to cope with crises and where that famous playing field really is flat. One of the most important advantages of supporting India's emergence is the reminder to China of our beliefs in the relationship between political and economic values.

While India may already be our peer in bolstering democracy, it is not without its political hot spots—both the usual suspect of Pakistan and its nervousness about strategic competition with China. The Indian defense minister, George Fernandes, suggested in 1998 that his country's development of nuclear weapons was not prompted by worries about Pakistan, with the Kashmir dispute still proving a drain on both country's resources, but by concern about China. India has certainly had a difficult relationship with China, with a sharp military defeat in the border dispute more than forty years ago, and with the worry today that India is being encircled by Chinese influence in Bangladesh, Pakistan, Nepal, Burma, and even Sri Lanka. For everyone else's peace of mind, and in their own political and economic interest, it is important that India and China establish a harmonious relationship. America, Britain, and Europe must help them both become sustainable dynamo economies and major players in regional and global governance in the twenty-first century.

India and China are inevitably much cited in the debate about the relationship between political and economic freedom and how best the countries that have established both within their borders can foster these freedoms around the globe. I recall the wise remark of Margaret Thatcher when she was once asked during a visit to China which came first, political liberty or economic freedom. She replied that it did not necessarily matter which one you started with, since you would inescapably finish up with both. As with most such aphorisms, there is, however, an exception. One Chinese community combines a free economy and indeed a slightly broader liberty that goes beyond the ability to make money without actual democracy. That community is Hong Kong, the only place I have ever been able to identify that is liberal but not (alas) democratic.

Some modest democratic progress was made, albeit far too late in the day, as a component of the promises to Hong Kong's citizens in the Joint Declaration, signed by Britain and China to guarantee the city's future after the handover in 1997. Sadly, those agreements have been partly and predictably rolled back. Apart from that, a continuing adamantine refusal to countenance greater democracy, and one or two cack-handed interventions in the legal and political affairs of the community, China does appear to have resisted the temptation to meddle constantly in Hong Kong's affairs—at least until recently. Hong Kong has not been politically lobotomized; its high degree of autonomy has been clipped but not suppressed. Hong Kong remains one of the freest cities in Asia, with a resilient economy that has survived and recovered from the Asian crash, and an equally resilient citizenry.

Nearly a decade after the handover, no one can dispute that Hong Kong retains its sense of citizenship; it is the only Chinese city to have one, sustained by a vigorous civil society, strong professions, and clean and efficient public services. Yet Chinese leaders seem reluctant to relax about this and to recognize that they have nothing to fear from Hong Kong's moderate political ambitions. If China's leaders were to learn to trust Hong Kong, it would be an important step on the road toward managing—with wisdom, sophistication, and the prospect of a successful outcome—the political transition that China itself will one day surely have to make. We all have a stake in the smooth attainment of that venture. We will all benefit from a China that succeeds and be damaged by a China that fails, and there is no neutral ground in between.

11

AN EDUCATION TO THE WORLD

International law? I better call my lawyer. . . . I don't know what
you're talking about by international law.

—President George W. Bush, December 11, 2003

Back to the beginning.

At school with the Benedictines in leafy suburban London, most of
the clever boys were pushed into the classics stream: Latin, Greek, and
Ancient History, at least until our first major public Ordinary Level
examinations at the age of fifteen. We were taught the history of the classical world by a Cambridge graduate with a West Country burr, a pen-
chant for turning every subject into a tripartite list (pretexts, causes,
results), and a passion for Thucydides. So we, of course, had to read his
great history of the thirty-year Peloponnesian War, the fracticidal
struggle between Greek city-states that began with the Athenian empire
ruling the seas and ended with its terrible defeat by grim Sparta.

The war exemplified what Thucydides at the time, and Plato and
Aristotle in the long, sad aftermath regarded as the central evil of
politics—namely the abuse of public power. A key and disastrous event
on Athens' road to defeat was the sack of Melos. The Athenians
attempted to bully the Melians into switching sides from Sparta to them;
the Melians declined to do so; they were besieged and captured, the men
slaughtered, the women and children sold into slavery. Thucydides
records in detail the dialogue that took place before the atrocity between

the Athenian envoys and the Melians. The representatives of mighty Athens, flexing their muscles, tell those of weak Melos to recognize reality. They must understand a dictate of nature:

> Our opinion of the gods and our knowledge of men lead us to conclude that it is a general and necessary law of nature to rule whatever one can. This is not a law that we made ourselves, nor were we the first to act upon it when it was made. We found it already in existence, and we shall leave it to exist forever among those who come after us. We are merely acting in accordance with it, and we know that you or anybody else with the same power as ours would be acting in precisely the same way.

Then the Athenians give the Melians a sharp lesson in the meaning of justice, telling them, "You know as well as we do that, when these matters are discussed by practical people, the standard of justice depends on the equality of power to compel and that in fact the strong do what they have the power to do and the weak accept what they have to accept."

Until recently, America has not acted like the Athenians. Indeed, American global authority for almost a century has been rooted in an understanding of the lessons of that dialogue and of its consequences for the Athenians, which explains why the rest of the world has on the whole accepted that in the American age there is a difference between ascendancy and intimidation. In the past, America has not stamped its foot and expected the rest of the world to tremble. The ideas of President Woodrow Wilson, and the actions of Presidents Franklin Roosevelt, Harry S. Truman, and their successors, have shaped an international order largely in America's image. It has been marked by three developments. There has been first the end of colonial empires and the triumph of self-determination. At the peace conference in 1919, a young Vietnamese kitchen worker at the Paris Ritz sent a petition to Wilson asking for self-determination for his country. Half a century later, having defeated the French colonial power and the American superpower, Ho Chi Minh got what he wanted, though he interpreted the "self" in self-determination rather literally for democratic tastes. Overall, however, the world did witness—as the second decisive theme of the century—the progress on every continent of democracy and a greater respect for human rights. "The world," Wilson said, "must be made safe for democracy," to which G. K. Chesterton responded, "The world cannot be made safe for democracy, it is a dangerous trade." So it has proved, in Congo, for example, and in Chile; yet the advance of democracy has by and large brought the benefits of better government, greater prosperity, and more stability to most countries. And America has intervened directly again and again to promote democratic progress. Just over the past two decades, the United States has played a big part in bringing democracy to Taiwan, South Korea, and the countries of Central and Eastern Europe as well as of the Balkans; exerted economic and diplomatic pressures on repressive regimes like South Africa; and in the 1980s alone stopped military coups in Bolivia, Peru, El Salvador, Honduras, and the Philippines. From the end of the Second World War, America tried to alchemize its own sense of constitutionalism, due process, and civil liberties into a rulebook for the whole world. The dead president's widow, Eleanor Roosevelt, led the efforts to found the 1948 Universal Declaration of Human Rights, which promoted the values enshrined in the U.S. Constitution. "We wanted as many nations as possible," she said, "to accept the fact that men, for one reason or another, were born free and equal in dignity and rights, that they were endowed with reason and conscience and should act toward one another in a spirit of Brotherhood." Finally, the last half-century saw the victory of capitalism and the opening of national markets under rules that most obeyed. So the twentieth century ended as it had begun, with surging trade—albeit with too many unfair restrictions on the economic activities of today's Melians, the poorer, weaker countries.

Over the decades, U.S. military power has been deployed to secure freedom and, in much of the world, stability. In Western Europe, American missiles and soldiers guarded democracies against Soviet advance. In East Asia, where the absence of a reconciliation between Japan and China on par with the one that Europe witnessed between Germany and France denied the continent an equivalent geopolitical stability, the American fleet helped to keep the peace. But just as important for the superpower has been the sense in other parts of the world that its awesome might was a force for good. Resentment, envy, and anger at what America represents and what it does have usually been overwhelmed by a stronger sense that, for all its mistakes and imperfections, America really is "the city on a hill," to whose standards most aspire and whose values most admire. This is at the heart of what is called soft power, America's weapon of mass attraction.

Soft power has many components—economic, cultural, political, military, and educational. The last of these is hugely influential and (if public spending priorities are any guide) greatly underrated in Europe. America is not only the city on a hill, it has most of the campuses on the hill. Look at any league table of the world's greatest research universities and it is dominated by America, with Europe a poor second threatened with being overtaken by Asia and Australia in the next couple of decades. This is largely a matter of money. America spends twice as much on research and development as Europe, both on campuses and through industrial laboratories. American universities have far higher private endowments than European ones (only two European universities— Oxford and Cambridge—would make it onto a list of the top 150 American universities in terms of private benefactions), and the American taxpayer has also been more generous to research and universities than his or her European equivalent. One result is that American universities act like a magnet to many of the brightest and best students around the world. This should give the United States a great opportunity to inculcate its values in the next generation of academics, business leaders, and politicians, except to the extent that so many foreign-born graduates stay in America when they have finished their courses, adding to America's economic, educational, scientific, and cultural wealth.

Much of this can be welcomed by Europeans. Scholarship knows no boundaries, and universities from Harvard to Stanford probably have a much more benign effect on all our futures than the Pentagon (though it does admittedly pour dollars generously into many of their research programs). European concern should not be about what Americans do well, but about what Europeans are now doing so badly. What does our underfunding of universities and research tell us about ourselves—we Europeans with all our pretensions to sit around and safeguard the cradle of Western civilization? We lose some of our best minds at the moment in their academic lives when they are likely to embark on the sort of research that wins accolades like the Nobel Prize. Ten years ago, half the

European students on doctoral programs in the United States returned home after completing them; today the figure is one-quarter. Europeans beat our chests about our aspirations to have a more competitive economy, drawing its strength from pushing the frontiers of knowledge, but the European budget favors yesterday over tomorrow, subsidizing farmers who contribute 2 percent of our GDP rather than investing in scholarship and technology. Above all, what does Europe's collective meanness about research and universities say about our position on the world stage? Self-confident societies invest in their futures and leave an intellectual legacy to future generations. It is possible to dig up passable excuses for the extent to which America outspends us on armaments and military power, but what possible excuse is there for the huge discrepancy in our investment in knowledge? In these days when it is getting harder and harder for immigrants to come to the United States for education, perhaps Europe can offer the alternative.

A central feature of American soft power used to be that the United States usually accepted that its hard power—its ability to get its own way if it wanted by virtue of its size and strength—should be constrained by a network of rules and agreements. The rules that it wished others to follow, it would follow, too. Naturally, if it wanted it could ride roughshod over the rest of us. But that is not the path America has customarily chosen. It has followed the advice of Thomas Jefferson in the Declaration of Independence and shown "a decent respect to the opinions of mankind." Doing that, it has respected its own better self, and secured its own better interests, another example of where doing right is also to do the right thing.

It should not come as a surprise that globalization—of economic activities, of the prospects for betterment, and of the threats of calamity—has led to a broadening and deepening of the structure of agreements that America helped to assemble after World War II. The environment, the theft of other people's bright ideas, the security of investment, the opening of markets, the proliferation of weapons, the laundering of illegally acquired money—all these issues and many more have brought a growing web of rules and agreements. It is called the international rule of law. It is what protects us from the other sort of law that would otherwise fill the growing space that globalization creates, the law of the jungle. It protects the weak, the Melians, and allows the strong, the Athenians, to hold on to their power without being hated for having it. It does not threaten the identity of the nation-state; instead it allows nation-states to deal with one another in a more harmonious and civilized way. Like domestic law, international law conserves order. Big, strong conservatives should be its greatest admirers and advocates.

Some Americans suggest that there is no need to sign up to a nebulous international rule of law to show their better face to the world; their crusading commitment to democracy should suffice to achieve this goal. But the point about the rule of law is that it applies everywhere; the fight for democracy tends, for old-fashioned reasons of realpolitik, to vary in enthusiasm and consistency from region to region and country to country. The cause itself can therefore be discredited by the perception that it is only being pursued selectively.

No one doubts that Washington today wishes to see democracy unroll across that part of western Asia we call the Middle East. But what happens when we reach the Silk Route countries to the north of Afghanistan—Tamburlaine's stamping grounds—or to Pakistan to the south? Pakistan provides a high-octane example of double standards. Democracy has had a hard time of it there. Government has tended to move, turn, and turnabout, from Punjabi soldiers to often corrupt but elected Sindi landowners, both ruling castes dependent on usually excellent civil servants. General Pervez Musharraf represents the latest military turn of the wheel. The streets of his capital, Islamabad, bear the names of all the appurtenances of a pluralist constitution, but the real constitution is down the road at the military cantonment in Rawalpindi. Musharraf is an impressive soldier—courteous, bright, voluble (not least when telling you things you know are not true about weapons proliferation or terrorist attacks on Kashmir). One can quite see why the American administration and many in Europe regard him as a reliable buttress against the dangers of Islamic extremism in his country. *Après lui, le déluge*. He has supported efforts to weed out the Taliban and Al Qaeda in Afghanistan, and while we cannot overlook the fact that Pakistani military security helped to plant them there in the first place, we can perhaps allow them the excuse that at least initially they were acting as surrogates in America's efforts to tie down the Soviet Union in Afghanistan and then expel it from the country. When great powers sow bramble patches, they do not always remember that plants grow.

But whatever you say about General Musharraf, he is not a democrat. He installed himself in a military coup; under his leadership the military has infiltrated swathes of commercial life and civil society; he has flirted with elections but the nearest he has come to the real thing is to rig a referendum in his own interests. There may well be arguments for turning a blind eye to all this, to the continuing disgraceful treatment of women and the inadequate efforts to replace the schools run by Islamic extremists with state-managed or -controlled institutions (the latter two areas where private citizens can apply pressure in lieu of their governments). But Musharraf will not last forever. A strongman will not save Pakistan from extremism, unless he is encouraged to develop strong institutions to underpin his rule. It would be better to talk to President Musharraf about participative democracy rather than sell him American F-16 fighter jets. The F-16s are not going to safeguard Pakistan, however attractive the roar of their engines in the officers' mess in Rawalpindi.

Travel north and double standards become more blatant still. The Central Asian republics are not an alarming accident waiting to happen but an accident well under way. They have remembered more than they have forgotten from their decades as Soviet colonies. Political repression, corruption, and command economies hold them back and gnaw at their foundations. Kazakhstan is probably the most secure thanks to its huge energy resources, and elsewhere smaller oil and gas reserves ensure Chinese and Russian support—but that will not be enough to defy reality. Cotton production has created terrible environmental problems, depleting the Aral Sea; in Turkmenistan, Tajikistan, and Uzbekistan cotton has enriched small cartels of government-favored traders who rely on cheap—including child—labor. Turkmenistan suffers under one of the world's most oppressive regimes, its economy mired in corruption and criminality (with evidence of official involvement in drug trafficking) and its political system in thrall to a president whose stamp on affairs runs as far as banning gold teeth, though not gold statues of himself. Kyrgyzstan has already witnessed the overthrow of one regime, though we await evidence that its successor will be a significant improvement. Impoverished Tajikistan has recovered from its bloody civil war in 1997 but still lives uneasily with the tensions generated by the rivalries of warlords.

Uzbekistan—with a population of 25 million—is cause for the greatest worry. To the romantic names of Tashkent, Samarkand, and Bukhara, we must now add the less well known name of Andijon, the city in the east of the country where in May 2005 up to 750 mostly unarmed Uzbeks, including many children, were gunned down to end what the government mendaciously claimed was a revolt by Islamist extremists. President Islam Karimov is an unreconstructed Soviet toughie. It is quite difficult to pinpoint a redeeming feature. At a two-hour meeting with him in the spring of 2004, he did not give an inch on any of the concerns I raised with him: torture did not happen in his country; his opponents were dangerous jihadists; the economy was doing fine. Uzbekistan is what the World Bank rather coyly calls a "low-income country under stress," which is a diplomatic way of saying that it is a failing state that could implode at any moment. Official figures seek to cover up a miserable economic performance that has seen widespread social discontent and high unemployment among the young. Opponents and critics of the regime are harassed, locked up, and routinely tortured. Karimof's government drives moderate Islamists into the hands of extremists and, sadly, the West—especially America—is seen to support it. These points were all made trenchantly by the last British ambassador in Uzbekistan, Craig Murray, who, whether or not it is connected to his outspokenness, is no longer a member of the diplomatic service. Why do we take such a feeble position regarding a repressive government that plays the role of recruiting sergeant for extremists in such a dangerous part of the world? During a visit to Tashkent in February 2004, Donald Rumsfeld spelled out the reasons, stating, "The U.S.A. recognizes Uzbekistan as a key initiator as regards maintaining peace and stability in central Asia and all the region as a whole. It supports the country's clear-cut efforts in this direction. Relations between the two countries are aimed at achieving exactly these goals." So Uzbekistan can go its own miserable way because it is a useful base for fighting extremism in Afghanistan. In due course, will we be using bases in Afghanistan to fight extremism in Uzbekistan?

A researcher in Bukhara, cited by the International Crisis Group in one of its reports on the country, quoted an Uzbek schoolteacher who told him, "I had heard a lot about American democracy. I thought that the appearance of American troops here would change the situation for the better. Now I see that the regime has only been strengthened, and arrests and abuses only increased." America's $300 million assistance to the Uzbek government in 2002–03 largely supported a security relationship that threatens to produce long-term insecurity. Europe for its part has settled on cooperation agreements and modest assistance programs that achieve very little, though we hold our share of meetings at which we tut-tut about human rights and the lack of economic reform. Surely America and its European partners should look again at their strategy in this region.

America's status as a superpower is not going to be eclipsed by Europe. But Europe should be encouraged to act effectively as a global partner, to adopt the political will necessary to do so, and to invest the money often required to play this role effectively. For then we will be able to help America act as a world leader in ways that enhance a system of global governance that suits market democracies, great and small. We have not got much time if we in Europe want to put our own stamp on this process. I wrote in the last chapter of the reemergence of China and India as substantial economic players in the world; their economic significance will have political consequences beyond the rights of their citizens. China and India will not simply accept the West's agenda in finance, trade, the environment, or security policy. Is Europe's only choice to side with them against America or with America against them? Or should we instead try to persuade both America and Asia, but most important at first our Atlantic partners, to develop a truly multilateral system and a compelling rule of law that will enable these reemerging older powers to live peacefully and prosperously side by side with the more recently established powers of the West?

In most of the key areas that will determine our future safety, prosperity, and well-being, China is crucial, beginning with the environment. China's economic growth has been one of the reasons for the recent rise in oil and other commodity prices, forced up by escalating demand. Today, China uses over 8 percent of the world's oil—replacing Japan as the world's second largest consumer—and has been responsible for two-fifths of the increase in global consumption since 2000. Its oil demand has doubled in the past decade, and energy (as well as the need for other natural resources) has started to shape China's foreign and security policies. China deployed 4,000 troops in Sudan to protect an oil pipeline that it had helped to build there, and was notably reluctant to support UN sanctions against that country proposed because of the Darfur atrocities. China's basic manufacturing industries guzzle energy, burning today 40 percent of all coal burned in the world. What does all this economic development and energy use mean for the environment? At the beginning of the century, China was the second-biggest emitter of carbon (according to the Pew Research Center), responsible for 14.8 percent of emissions compared to 20.6 percent for America, 14 percent for Europe, and 5.5 percent for India. Emissions will grow, and simple extrapolation can easily cause nightmares, even perhaps for a Texan oilman like President Bush.

Take car ownership. At the moment only one Chinese citizen in every seventy has a car, compared to one in two in America. What happens as this gap is closed? How many Chinese Sports Utility Vehicles would we be happy to see on East Asia's roads? Together, China and India have a combined population of over 2.25 billion. As their economies surge ahead, they burn ever more fossil fuel. If we want them to do something to ensure that their *future* growth is more environmentally friendly than was the developed world's *past* growth, how can we persuade them to act differently? Is the best way of doing this for America, the world's greatest emitter of damaging gases, to tell them, "Don't do as we do, but do as we say"? Or does Washington continue to contend that the problem does not really exist or that it is exaggerated? Is the American administration really in denial? America is by a very long way the biggest emitter of greenhouse gases per capita of population, as well as in absolute terms. The average American produces each year about 12,000 pounds of CO_2 emissions. These American emissions contribute mightily to what the United Kingdom's chief scientific adviser, Sir David King, has called a bigger threat to the world than terrorism. While a tiny minority of scientists deny the evidence, there is an overwhelming consensus—backed by a number of the main private energy companies—that the phenomenon of heat being trapped by gases close to the earth has grown steadily with industrialization since it was first observed in the early nineteenth century, and that it is changing our climate and threatening the survival of some communities. In 1988, the UN Environment Program and the World Meteorological Organization established the Intergovernmental Panel on Climate Change to assess the evidence. Their work led directly to the convention on climate change that was adopted at the world's Earth Summit in Rio de Janeiro in 1992 and signed by the first President Bush. That agreement led in turn to the negotiation of the 1997 Kyoto Protocol that committed developed countries, which have, after all, created most of the problems, to limit or reduce greenhouse gas emissions to at least 5 percent below 1990 levels in the period from 2008 to 2012. During this period, developing countries would not be forced to make cuts in carbon emissions, but in later stages (that still have to be negotiated) they will have to play a part in combating this global threat.

And the threat is real and immediate. In my own city, London, the evidence grows each year. Before 1990, the barrier across the Thames at Greenwich, which prevents serious flooding of the city, used to be raised once or twice a year. The average has now risen to four times a year and is predicted to rise to thirty times a year by 2030. Indeed, it is predicted that later in the century the barrier will fail altogether. This would put Westminster under six feet of water. We are not unaccustomed to rain in London, but freak weather conditions (as predicted by the European intergovernmental panel) brought storms in 2004 that caused flooding and killed thousands of fish as 600,000 tons of raw sewage were discharged into the city's river. So even in my own country, global warming has started to exact a toll, with more flooding and coastal erosion forecast by the government's experts. The problems in poorer, developing countries are far greater, with threats to health, economic development, and the survival of species.

President Bush's unilateral broadside in 2001 against the Kyoto Protocol appeared to be based on three arguments. First, America faced an energy crisis. But what crisis? Presumably the president was not referring to the badly botched deregulation of the power industry in California. If there actually is a crisis, or the makings of one, it is surely America's incontinent consumption of oil. Yet it is still cheaper to fill up the tank in America than anywhere else; bottled water costs more than cans of petrol. America is a vast country; many Americans live in suburbs; public transport is bad; the car is king. So no American politician wants to make an enemy of motorists. But should not leadership consist in trying, even at the margins, to get people to be more responsible about their use of energy? And if as a conservative you believe in markets, is there any better way of doing this than through more realistic pricing, thus reducing the demand for a product that more than ever America has to import? Is it now impossible for any American politician to get elected on a policy that would serve his or her country's strategic, economic, and environmental interests?

Second, President Bush argued that if America was to reduce its emissions too sharply, U.S. growth would be cut back and the whole world would suffer. The immediate impact of Kyoto compliance on economic growth is exaggerated, but most of the rest of us have in any case started to discuss growth in terms of its sustainability. It may be that a greater present-day threat to sustainable growth in America is the heavy dependence of its economy on the savings of Chinese peasants, but a longer-term, growing, and grave threat is surely excessive dependence on fossil fuels.

Third, like other American politicians—and indeed like the government in Australia, a country which is itself a big and irresponsible energy guzzler—President Bush declined to sign on to an agreement that for the time being let developing countries off the hook. This is both curious and worrying. The notion of common but differentiated responsibilities was enshrined in the 1992 Rio treaty and passed unanimously by the U.S. Senate. It is that principle Kyoto repeats. We face a common threat; the developed countries have done the most to create it; the rich should bear initially the largest share of responsibility for tackling it. In time, we shall need developing countries to join the effort. That will require persuasion. How do rich countries persuade poor ones to act, if the richest country of all refuses to budge?

At this point relative politeness is strained beyond the breaking point. U.S. policy is not only selfish but foolish and self-destructive. Higher energy taxes would reduce dependency on the Middle East; encourage people to start insulating their houses and businesses; promote more exploration; and help to fill the alarming revenue gap that has opened up since the Clinton era. American industry claims that there would be dire economic and employment consequences, but that has not been the European experience (though we have made a good job of driving up unemployment and depressing our economies in many other ways— notably through labor market inflexibilities).

And once again we find ourselves gaping at the change in America's approach to these problems. The irony is that in the past we have successfully negotiated deals on the environment between developed and developing countries that have recognized the differences in their responsibilities. With America's forceful and conservative leadership in the 1970s and '80s, America was active and creative in multilateral environmental diplomacy. President Nixon supported the creation of an environment program in the United Nations, and himself proposed the World Heritage Convention to protect areas of unique worldwide worth. In succeeding years, America was active in negotiating agreements on oceans, fisheries, and endangered species. I was able to witness the most successful example of America's work for the environment when in 1990 I chaired the London Conference that extended the provisions of the 1987 Montreal Protocol to impose constraints on the production and use of ozone-depleting substances such as hairspray propellants and the chemicals in refrigerators. America had pressed for action and, despite skepticism and foot-dragging by several European countries, a series of tough and effective measures were demanded and taken. The Reagan administration got Europeans to accept the so-called precautionary principle—action to prevent what could be serious threats, in this case hazardous rays piercing the thinned ozone layer—even when the science was not totally proven. There was, however, a problem. It was very expensive for developing countries to comply with the terms of the protocol. They needed to invest in new technologies and to buy new products. They thought it unfair that they would be penalized economically for a problem that richer developed countries had been primarily responsible for creating. The Indian and Chinese ministers at our conference in London made it clear that, while the threat we were discussing had global causes and global effects, they had no mandate to assume new burdens that would, for instance, make it more expensive for their citizens to own a refrigerator—something most citizens of developed countries would consider a necessity. With America using charm, creativity, money, and muscle, we drafted new rules giving India and China a grace period of ten years to meet the targets for banning the production and use of the restricted chlorofluorocarbons and halons. We supported India and China with technology transfer and with financial assistance to enable them to comply with the protocol. It was a model of how sensible persuasion and generosity could broker a global agreement. No one—for example, no Australian minister over whose country the most prominent hole in the ozone layer loomed—grumbled that the Indians and Chinese were being allowed to postpone their commitments. No American official suggested that others should combine to save the ozone layer but not the United States since the relative cost to the world's strongest economy might trigger a global slowdown. No one argued that the world could meet its obligations through voluntary action. No one argued that the "precautionary principle" was too expensive, and that we should await a few hundred thousand more cases of skin cancer before we could be sure of the case for acting. What has happened to persuade America that this approach to environmental hazard is wrong?

Several American states are trying to take action on greenhouse gas emissions themselves. There are also bipartisan efforts, for example, by Senators Joe Lieberman and John McCain, to build a coalition for a much stronger policy. Senator Lieberman clearly hopes that evangelical Christians may be encouraged to pray for a presidential conversion on this question. He notes wryly that "the earth is, after all, a faith-based initiative." We all need a Bush conversion to succeed on the road to Delhi and Beijing. Unless America is prepared to accept its environmental responsibilities for the future, it is difficult to see how we will ever get India and China to do so.

Further, the energy demand of India and China raises political as well as environmental issues. When I visited Kazakhstan in 2004 all the talk was about Chinese enthusiasm for building oil and gas pipelines eastward from Central Asia. The year before, in our gloomy hotel in Tehran, there were groups of visitors from India and China who were there to talk about oil and gas. Both countries have invested heavily in Iranian energy production, with the main Chinese oil and gas company—Sinopec—

particularly prominent. Whether we like it or not, China, and increasingly India, will be competing for political favor in this hot zone.

So far as we know neither country has been sharing its military secrets with potential nuclear powers, though the Americans are suspicious about the activities of some of Sinopec's subsidiaries in the field of weapons proliferation. But there has been no suggestion of the existence of a Chinese or Indian illicit network to rival that of the Pakistani nuclear scientist A. Q. Khan.

Khan's activities demonstrate one of the most pressing threats facing the world, a threat that requires greater and tighter international cooperation among the countries of the West and China and India. In the past fifty years, we have been reasonably successful in controlling the spread of nuclear weapons. But now it is possible, as the head of the International Atomic Energy Agency (IAEA), Mohamed El Baradei, has argued, to design nuclear components in one country, manufacture them in a second, ship them through a third, and assemble them in a fourth, with the prospect of eventual turnkey use in a fifth. Such an assembly line could irrevocably destabilize the globe. There are three dangers ahead. First, a terrorist organization might get hold of a nuclear weapon; second, other countries likely will develop the capacity to enrich uranium or reproduce plutonium so that they can move quickly, if they wish, to become military nuclear powers; and third, preventing any more countries from taking this route and joining the nuclear club of eight countries—America, Britain, France, Russia, China, Pakistan, India, and Israel—will be difficult and essential. China and India will be crucial to the accomplishment of these aims not least because of the relationship they both have with Iran, and the fraught relationship that China has with North Korea, which claims that it already has nuclear weapons and could probably set itself up quite quickly as a weapon production line for others.

For thirty years the main instrument for dealing with this problem has been the Nuclear Non-Proliferation Treaty (NPT, 1968–70), which provides the global framework for preventing the spread of nuclear weapons, for stopping the development of nuclear energy for the purpose of producing weapons, and for nuclear disarmament. The treaty, along with the strategic standoff between the West and the Soviet

Union, helped to keep the worst predictions about proliferation from coming true. For example, President Kennedy feared that by 1975 there could be fifteen to twenty-five countries with nuclear weapons. We stopped that from happening and, indeed, when some countries tried in the 1980s and '90s to develop weapons in secret, intelligence, verification, and diplomacy exposed their activities, and in the case of Libya and Iraq halted them in their tracks. Libya abandoned its efforts voluntarily and Iraq's program was in effect dismantled by the IAEA in the 1990s (as their inspectors would probably have been able to confirm if given a little more time before the invasion of the country in 2003). That leaves the main threats of Iran and North Korea, but about another forty countries also possess the intellectual and technical capacity to produce nuclear weapons. We depend heavily on their goodwill not to do so.

The seriousness of this issue is beyond dispute. It recalls Albert Einstein's observation, "Since the advent of the Nuclear Age, everything has changed save our modes of thinking and we thus drift towards unparalleled catastrophe." To avoid that, we need tougher international rules with more effective political backup and sanctions. It is not obvious that there is any better way of doing this than through the United Nations—and principally the UN Security Council—and its specialized nuclear-watch arm, the IAEA. We need a system that makes verification tough and mandatory, to prevent clandestine activity, for every country that signs the NPT, with a strict policy of sanctions against noncompliance or withdrawal from the treaty. We require tighter controls over the export of sensitive material and technology. There should be limits on the production of new nuclear material through reprocessing and enrichment. We have to agree on how we can share the international responsibility for the management and disposal of spent nuclear fuel. We must get rid of the weapons-usable nuclear material that is already in existence, and we must help countries to halt the use of weapons-usable material in their civilian nuclear programs.

Strengthening the NPT in this way would make the world a lot safer, but it also represents what much of the world regards as an unfair bargain. So long as there are as many nuclear weapons in store as there are, threats to our safety clearly remain. Moreover, the non-nuclear countries question a bargain that is framed, so far as they are concerned, almost entirely in the interests of the existing nuclear club, the N8. Why should others—Brazil, South Africa, not to mention Iran—sign on to a treaty in which all the "give" is on their side of the table, and all the "take" on the other? They refuse to accept that it is morally acceptable for some countries to have nuclear weapons, while others are regarded as outlaws if they wish to retain the capacity to join that club. Realistically, this standoff will not be solved by pressing for a ban on all nuclear weapons and the destruction of all stockpiles; that will simply not happen before the dawning of that, alas, improbable day when we reconfigure the world's security structure around our shared humanity. But the existing nuclear powers, led by America, must make *some* gestures to the others. They must be more open about the weapons they already have. They must get rid of many of them. They must verify and bring into force the Comprehensive Test Ban Treaty. And they—principally the United States, in this case—must abandon any further research and development to produce yet more advanced nuclear weapons. If we are going to draw the line more firmly and clearly around the existing possession of nuclear weapons, then the line cannot wobble and wiggle when it comes to the obligations of the N8. Britain and France, as one-quarter of the nuclear eight, can help to lead the way, but America must join. Only when the other nations of the world believe that the terms of negotiation are transparent and reasonable will we be in a better position to secure our safety.

This is particularly true as other countries begin to rival the United States. American interest in the rise of India and China will continue to grow exponentially as their weight of numbers and economic muscle constrain America's ability as the only superpower to do what it wants, when it wants, simply by an exercise of will. There are other and better ways of asserting the primacy of the values in which America has always believed than ultimate dependence on American exceptionalism and the corresponding stance that America can get away with it. International agreements and the rule of law offer more effective ways of guiding the international community and protecting America's interests. This is presumably what Mr. Rumsfeld meant—at least in part—when he hoped and prayed that "China enters the civilized world," a slightly odd turn of phrase given China's history over the last three thousand or so years. A full millennium before the Periclean Golden Age that preceded Athens' fall in the Peloponnesian War, the Chinese were casting in bronze and weaving silk. I have a beautiful figure of a small sleeping dog of about that period, carved out of jade. Most of us would think that a country that could produce such things was an impressive civilization. We must assume that the American defense secretary had other things in mind when he made his statement: the transformation of the last huge totalitarian state into a pluralist democracy, one that obeys the norms of what we associate with civilized behavior at home and acts responsibly within an infrastructure of global rules and institutions abroad. How do we best secure such a transformation?

Here we have the worrying consequence of current American behavior. Around the world, America is seen more and more to contravene the principles that it enjoins others to follow. It appears too often to obdure its own ethos, to repudiate its own history. Time was when piazzas and parks, boulevards and buildings around the world were named after American presidents and public officials. Looking through the London street map, the *A to Z Gazetteer*, I can see a Roosevelt Way in Dagenham, a Truman Close in Edgware, an Eisenhower Drive in the East End, and Kennedy Courts, Closes, Gardens, and Houses all over the city. The same is true in other cities and other lands. It seems unlikely if not impossible that we will one day name our squares and streets after Bush, Cheney, Rumsfeld, and Rice.

America was founded on the rule of law; the heart of Britain's first Atlantic empire, it broke loose from the shackles of a dynastic state partly because of what it deemed to be the illegal actions of King George III and his ministers. America's Constitution and Bill of Rights removed from the new nation state's government those features of the Old World that were deemed to be unjustifiable in the New. In more recent years, America has been a pioneer of international agreements and the rule of law. America pressed, for example, for the establishment of war crimes tribunals in Nuremburg and Tokyo, and then supported the establishment of the tribunals to deal with the atrocities committed in Yugoslavia and Rwanda. In the countries of the former Yugoslavia, America linked the provision of assistance to explicit compliance with The Hague tribunal, and regularly pressed myself and others to take an equally firm line as far as Europe was concerned. Why then has America now become so hostile and obstructive toward the creation of the International Criminal Court, an institution almost fifty years in the making?

American negotiators participated in the drafting of the statute that would establish a court to deal with war crimes, genocide, crimes against humanity, and gross violations of human rights. The final outcome met some, though not all, of America's concerns. The International Court will only act if national authorities have failed to do so themselves, and there are safeguards to prevent rogue prosecutions. But America did not secure the right of permanent members of the UN Security Council to veto investigations. This was a curious aim for America to assert, given that it has always criticized the potential within the court for politicizing international justice (a point that also sits oddly with the politicization of judicial appointments in America). The Bush administration has not only refused to have anything to do with the court, but has campaigned actively to obstruct its establishment and undermine its ability to operate. In particular, the United States has pressed other countries to sign what amount to bilateral immunity agreements, under which these countries undertake not to surrender any American national to the court without American approval. Many of those who decline to endorse such agreements lose military aid as a result.

This issue triggered some of the most heated arguments between America and Europe during my years at the European Commission. In the summer of 2002, one of the German commissioners, Gunther Verheugen (responsible for our enlargement negotiations), and I heard that Washington was putting great pressure on 2004 candidate countries, including Poland and the Baltic States, as well as putative candidates in the Balkans to sign immunity agreements. This was unacceptable. The European Union had been a strong supporter of the establishment of the International Criminal Court; we had worked to achieve its creation for years; we helped to fund organizations that themselves acted as advocates for the court. Europe had adopted a common and united position, and countries that wanted to join the European Union and thus benefit politically and economically from EU membership should not have been (and should not be) bullied into taking a hostile line. Romania—a candidate for EU membership in 2007—had buckled to American pressure by the time we heard what was going on. But we set out the EU position clearly for the other countries and provided detailed legal advice on the sort of deals they could negotiate with America without, in the EU's view, breaching the agreement they had signed to set up the court and prescribe its jurisdiction. We just managed to hold the line, but not without some bruising telephone conversations with normally more affable colleagues in the U.S. State Department, who must have been under strong pressure from elsewhere in Washington. I recall setting off on holiday in July and getting three calls on this subject within the space of the two-hour drive (at least with my chauffeur!) from Brussels to Charles de Gaulle airport in Paris. It was one of many occasions when I have cursed the existence of mobile phones.

Of course, it is legitimate for the world's superpower, so often called on to stand in the front line to keep the peace, to prevent vexatious legal actions launched for political reasons against its soldiers, diplomats, and leaders. The statute that establishes the court appears to others to provide such guarantees. They are sufficient to satisfy Britain and France, for example. The court does not have jurisdiction over wars of aggression, which is an issue left to be decided to the day, probably just this side of the Greek Kalends, when a common definition of *aggression* can be agreed. There is also more than a hint of double standards—indeed, they parade in dress uniform, bands playing and flags flying—about pressing international jurisdiction on Serbs and Croats but denying its legitimacy, even theoretically, for Americans.

This really is all about America being able to get away with it. To most of the world it does not look as though America exercises this power because it is different from and better than others, but because it is all too similar to the rest of fallen humanity. That is the heavy price that America pays for Guantánamo Bay, Abu Ghraib, equivocation over torture, and exporting suspects in secret so that others can torture them. There was a time when America might have been excused for saying, "We won't sign up to all these international norms because we don't need to; the rest of you do, so sign on the dotted line." No longer. It is not that America behaves worse than others in similar circumstances. Look at the record of Britain and France as colonial powers. Recent allegations of British abuse of human rights in colonial, pre-independence

Kenya during the Mau Mau emergency remind us that our own colonial record has a seamy, unsavory side. Torture and murder during the last years of French colonial rule in Algeria divided France then and still do today; the violence, the murder, and the abuse of human rights extended to the streets of Paris, with for instance the savage repression of demonstrators there in 1961–62. So we in Europe even in the postwar years could ourselves say with Thomas Jefferson, "I tremble for my country when I reflect that God is just." But the public discovery that this scorching piece of self-criticism has recently been so relevant to America's behavior, too, does not buttress the case that America should be above the international rule of law.

What have we witnessed? There was the deliberate creation of a legal black hole down which 650 terrorist suspects were dropped in Guantánamo Bay. For how long will this legal outrage continue and how will it be ended? There were the awful degrading pictures from Abu Ghraib revealing porno-sadistic practices for which no one could be held responsible above the lowest ranks of the lumpen military. There was the logic-chopping, morality-mincing debate about what constitutes torture and how America could evade the explicit provisions of the Geneva Conventions. Was it really torture to keep a suspect's head under water or to slip needles beneath his nails? Could hooding, the denial of painkillers to the injured, beatings, and sleep deprivation not be justified? Was not the president in his role as commander in chief of America's military entitled to place himself above the quaint prohibitions of international law? Surely if an interrogator's primary purpose was trying to obtain information not to cause pain, he could apply the pincers wherever he wanted? For me, it was this cool, bureaucratic argument about an issue that has been at the heart of almost every human rights agreement that caused most offense and, to be frank, surprise. I simply did not believe that America could behave like this—the America to whose lawyers, human rights organizations, and politicians I tried to justify the investigative methods, transparency, and conclusions of my police inquiry in Northern Ireland. We fought terrorism in the United Kingdom. Spain fought terrorism in Madrid and Bilbao. We knew that our democracies had to fight terrorism with one hand tied behind our backs, because that was the only way in the long run we would win, because to act otherwise was to obliterate the moral gap between the state and the terrorists, because to behave like the terrorists was to deny all that we thought we were and wished to be. And who stood for that most resolutely, proudly, persuasively, openly in the world? America. But perhaps that was then.

America surely wants to help create a world again where its embassies do not all have to be replicas of Fort Apache. It must want to shrink the distance between the etchings on the Statue of Liberty and how it behaves around the world. It should want the whole world as its friend and not much of it as a sullen vassal. It should be reminded to put its faith again in the sort of global order that it created over fifty years ago and will only abandon to its lasting cost—and to our cost as well, in Europe as in other continents. Because it remains the case, in the words of General John Shakishavili, the former chairman of the Joint Chiefs of Staff, that without American leadership, "things still don't get put together right." If Europe can only forget its prejudices and introverted preoccupations, it should see the importance of working to help America put things together in the right way. That sort of partnership should help restore American faith in its better self, in international cooperation, and in the rule of law for all of us.

In 1994, the Bodleian Library in Oxford published a pamphlet first issued by the United States War Department in 1942. It had been prepared for the American servicemen who were going to Britain to prepare for the invasion of occupied Europe. As the librarian of Rhodes House (where the original copy is held) has written, it is a "'snapshot' of wartime Britain, as seen by a sympathetic outsider." I was particularly struck by the good sense of some of the important dos and don'ts that the pamphlet lists: "Be friendly—but don't intrude anywhere it seems you are not wanted. . . . Don't show off or brag or bluster—'swank' as the British say. If somebody looks in your direction and says, 'He's chucking his weight about,' you can be pretty sure you're off base. That's the time to pull in your ears. . . . By your conduct you have great power to bring about a better understanding between the two countries."

It puts me in mind of the history book with which I began this chapter. Some time before Thucydides records the debate between the overbearing Athenian envoys and the Melians, he reports the famous funeral oration that Pericles gave at the end of the first year in that long war that was to destroy the supremacy both of Athens and of those virtues with which Pericles was identified. The speech probably reflects what Thucydides thought Pericles should have said and would have meant rather than what he actually declaimed. It is trenchant, powerful, eloquent, and relevant—to Athens then and to today's great power. Once the bones of the Athenian dead had been laid in their burial place, on the most beautiful approach to the walls of the city, Pericles mounted a high platform and addressed the mourners proclaiming the virtues of his city, a democracy in which he argued that everyone was equal before the law. Athens was a model for others to follow, he claimed. "I declare that our city is an education to Greece."

For so much of my lifetime America has been an education to the world—to every nation, every continent, and every civilization. It has been a living lesson, a paradigm to which others could aspire, an example for others to follow. I hope that Europe can help America to be that again. When it is, it will not be America that triumphs, but the ideas that America has traditionally represented. So the century ahead will not be America's, as was the last one. It will belong to mankind. It will be a century dominated by the values that American history enshrines and that American leadership at its best embodies and defends without bragging or blustering: democracy, pluralism, enterprise, and the rule of law.

ACKNOWLEDGMENTS

I had a first-class team of officials in my private office—or *cabinet* in Brussels-speak—when I was a European Commissioner from 1999 to 2004. For the first three years, it was led by Anthony Cary, for the last two by Patrick Child. They were, respectively, the best that Britain's Foreign Office and Treasury could have provided. The whole team contributed to my education and therefore to this book, and Anthony Teasdale who works in the European Parliament helped me to understand its beguiling mysteries. They were all friends and, with my wife Lavender and my daughters, kept me sane and (usually) quite cheerful. The book represents my own prejudices as refined and occasionally recast by this amiable and accomplished life-support unit, for whom I was not perhaps quite the Commissioner expected. I hope it does not blight any careers.

Once again, I owe a huge debt of gratitude to my agent, Michael Sissons, and to my editors, Stuart Proffitt and Robin Dennis. I hope that this book will not be as exciting an adventure for Stuart and me as the last one turned out to be. Robin has worked with great skill and commitment to make this Englishman's English comprehensible on both sides of the Atlantic.

I can only type with one finger and my writing is tiny and wickedly crabbed. The book would not exist without patient deciphering by my wife, my daughters, Alice and Laura, Dame Shirley Oxenbury, and Penny Rankin. Their reward will come in heaven. My eldest daughter, Kate Meikle, should be grateful that she was in Rome while the runes were being read.

Universal Declaration of Human Rights, 1948, 273
universities, funding, 274–75
Uzbekistan, 277–79

values, 17–20, 196–97
Verheugen, Gunther, 289
Vidal, Gore, 35
Vietnam
  Graham Greene on, 4–5; international criticism of war in, 25; lessons of, 227; postwar British-American relations, 113–14; resisting Americanization, 3

Waldegrave, William, 53–54
Walker-Smith, Sir Derek, 42–43, 56, 85
Wall Street Journal, 131, 225, 246
Wall Street Journal, Asia edition, 251
Wal-Mart, 153, 250
War and the American Presidency (Schlesinger), 239
War Crimes Tribunal, 184
war on terrorism, 198
Washington Post, 24, 222–23, 231
Watts riots, 34
Waugh, Evelyn, 113
Weight, Richard, 116
Weisglass, Dov, 212–13
West Bank, 212–13
West Point Military Academy, 104
West, Mae, 152
Westminster, 42
What Went Wrong? (Bernard Lewis), 195
Who Wants to Be a Millionaire?, 196
Will, George F., 222
Wilson, Harold
  Britain in European Union (EU), 59; disappointment in, 33; on European issue, 41, 77; Vietnam war, 114

Wilson, Woodrow, 52–53, 272–73
Winand, Pascaline, 110
Windsor family, 61
Winthrop, John, 10
Wodehouse, P. G., 72
Wolfe, Tom, 14
Wolfowitz, Paul, 162–63, 224–26
Woodward, Bob, 28
Wooldridge, Adrian, 19, 96
World Bank, 109, 182, 278
World Heritage Convention, 283
World Meteorological Organization, 281
World Trade Organization (WTO)
  China, 250, 257, 259; Russia, 215–16, 218
World Transformed, A (Bush and Scowcroft), 118
World Values Survey, 13
World War I, 3, 52, 226
World War II
  America entering, 3–4, 64, 108–9; Britain, impact on, 61–64; causes, 63; Cold War following, 192; democracy following, 273; French resistance during, 64; reconstruction following, 52, 151–52, 226–28
Wynn, Terry, 148

Xian, 248–49

Yeltsin, Boris, 216–17, 218
Young, Hugo, 91
Yugoslavia, 168–70, 185–86, 288
Yukos affair, 215, 218

Zagreb, 187
Zakaria, Fareed, 26
Zhu Rongji, 261, 265–66
Zia-ul-Haq, General Muhammad, 178
Zogby International survey, 196–97

ABOUT THE AUTHOR

CHRIS PATTEN, chancellor of Oxford and Newcastle universities, was from 1999 until 2004 European Commissioner for External Relations. He was previously the member of Parliament for Bath, chairman of the Conservative Party, and the last British governor of Hong Kong. He is the author of *East and West: China, Power, and the Future of Asia*. He lives in London.